IN-LAWS AND OUTLAWS:
Kinship and Marriage in England

IN~LAWS
— and —
OUTLAWS

Kinship and Marriage in England

SYBIL WOLFRAM

CROOM HELM
London & Sydney

© 1987 Sybil Wolfram
Croom Helm Ltd, Provident House, Burrell Row,
Beckenham, Kent BR3 1AT

Croom Helm Australia Pty Ltd, Suite 4, 6th Floor,
64–76 Kippax Street, Surry Hills, NSW 2010 Australia

British Library Cataloguing in Publication Data
Wolfram, Sybil
   In-laws and outlaws: kinship and
   marriage in England.
   1. Marriage—England—History
   2. Kinship—England—History
   I. Title
   306.8'1'0942   HQ615

ISBN 0–7099–2796–7

Typeset by Florencetype Ltd, Bristol
Printed and bound in Great Britain by
Biddles Ltd, Guildford and King's Lynn

Contents

Acknowledgements

Introduction   1

Part 1

1. Basic Ideas   11
   1. Equivalence and Similarity
   2. The Unity of Husband and Wife
2. The Prohibited Degrees of Marriage and Incest   21
   1. Reformation Changes
   2. The Deceased Wife's Sister Controversy
   3. Twentieth-century Changes
3. Degree Reckoning in Mourning   52
4. Kinship Terminology and Marriage Preferences   64
   1. Kinship Terms
   2. Marrying Up or Down
5. Divorce   77
   1. Early History
   2. The Matrimonial Causes Act of 1857
   Appendices
6. The Marriage Bond   107
   1. Property
   2. Sex
   Appendix

Part 2

7. Popular Explanations   137
   1. Incest and In-breeding
   2. Divorce and the Emancipation of Women
8. Experts Past and Present   161
   1. Early Theories of 'Incest'
   2. Anthropologists and 'Exogamy'

Contents

9. Fact and Theory   186
10. Indigenous Structuring   197
11. The Future   207

Bibliography   219
Appendix: Chronological Table   231
Index   235

Acknowledgements

I should like to thank a large number of professional associates for assistance with one or another aspect of this book, whether by discussion, helpful suggestions on written drafts etc. I must particularly mention Dr A. Ashworth (Oxford), Professor P.S. Atiyah (Oxford), Professor T.E. Downing (Arizona), Professor L. Dumont (Paris), Dr N. Felix (UCL), Dr R. Finnegan (Open University), Mrs P.R. Foot (UCLA), Dr K. Forsyth, Dr B.M. Levick (Oxford), Professor C. Lévi-Strauss (Paris), Dr G. Lienhardt (Oxford), Dr N. Mackie (Aberdeen), Professor H. Oberdiek (Swarthmore), Dr J. Overing (LSE), Professor D. Pocock (Sussex), Professor D. Schneider (Chicago), Mrs L. Sciama (Oxford), Mr Charles Stewart (Oxford), Professor Sir Peter Strawson (Oxford), Mrs G. Taylor (Oxford), Mr and Mrs Tomiak (Oxford), Professor Alan Watson (University of Pennsylvania).

L'Homme 1, 1961 published my first researches into the controversy over marriage with a deceased wife's sister, *The Listener* 1966 an early draft of work on the decline of English mourning, the *Criminal Law Review* 1983 some of my researches on the 1908 Punishment of Incest Act, and the *Oxford Journal of Legal Studies* 1985 a more extended version of my findings on the history of English divorce 1700−1857 than is given here in Chapter 5. A more elaborate study of surrogacy (Chapter 11) was presented to the Society for Applied Anthropology at its annual meeting at Reno, USA 1986 (in press). I am grateful to the Board of Literae Humaniores of Oxford University for a grant assisting me to attend this meeting, as well as for a grant in 1983 for research assistance in perusing *The Times* on nineteenth-century divorces.

Sybil Wolfram
Oxford, 1986

To Louis Dumont

Introduction

I have two principal objects in this book. The first is to increase understanding of the style of kinship found in the Western world, by presenting one example, England in the nineteenth and twentieth centuries.[1] In reading or talking about features of English (and Western) kinship, one meets explanations, often common to the society and long-lived, which do not fit the facts. A second aim is to examine this theorising, a phenomenon of some interest, and where possible to dispose of false theories in favour of more promising methods.

Background

Kinship has been a major branch of social anthropology since McLennan's *Primitive Marriage* (1865). Theoretical discussion has led to much expertise, theoretical apparatus, and sophistication. Fieldwork monographs supply a vast body of empirical knowledge about the way in which kinship is organised and thought about in other societies. Such works as Malinowski's famous study of the Trobriand islanders *The Sexual Life of Savages* (1929) made a wide Western public acquainted with a society whose kinship customs and beliefs differed greatly from their own, a society in which, for example, the suggestion that a man plays a part in the procreation of his wife's children is greeted with incredulity and counter-argument. Lévi-Strauss's *Les Structures élémentaires de la Parenté* (1949), translated into English in 1969 as *The Elementary Structures of Kinship*, displayed, perhaps more clearly than ever before, the immense variety of kinship systems existing in different parts of the world.

Western social anthropologists have not studied the kinship of their own society or societies with the same intensity that they have accorded to others. For this the emphasis on fieldwork may be partly responsible. To acquire its language and live in a society as much as possible like a native is the method *par excellence*, often the only one, of finding out about a society which is not the ethnographer's. But it is not necessarily so rewarding when the

1

society under investigation is his own, and clearly incomplete if it is highly literate.

There has been another source of malaise among anthropologists. This is the belief that kinship is not, or is no longer, an important aspect of life in Western societies and does not throw up material of similar interest nor yield to the kind of systematisation which has proved successful in the study of the kinship of other societies. This impression seemed confirmed by the problems of fitting the Western 'cognatic' system into existing theoretical frameworks, expatiated on, for example, in Fox's classic textbook *Kinship and Marriage. An Anthropological Perspective* (1967) and by the 'modest results' attained by anthropologists like Maranda who in his book *French Kinship: Structure and History* (1974) could find almost nothing of interest to say.[2]

In the last few years the situation has begun to change. Historians have turned their attention to the history of the family and of sex and marriage in England, and several substantial works have appeared, notably Stone's *The Family, Sex and Marriage in England 1500– 1800* (1977).[3] Another work, this time of anthropological origin, Goody's *The Development of the Family and Marriage in Europe* (1983), attempted a more global treatment, ranging over much of early Europe.

Field

In this study I concentrate on England in the present and recent past. The Christian, or ex-Christian, world shares an ancient and distinctive kinship system, sufficiently unusual in the world at large to baffle social anthropologists, whose work has lain elsewhere. But within a broadly uniform pattern, it has many local and temporal variants.

England, for instance, unlike Russia, recognises no relationship between the kin of two spouses. Mourning at the death of relatives, still found in France, has long vanished from English life. The United States is more favourably inclined to commercial 'surrogate' motherhood than England.[4] England differs in detail even from Scotland, with which it was united in 1707. For example, in Scotland divorce was permitted for adultery or desertion by either spouse from 1560 onwards. It was nearly four centuries (1937) before this was so in England. In Scotland incest has been a crime since 1567. It became so in England only in 1908, and then between a far narrower range of relatives than in Scotland. Initially separate studies are clearly indicated.

Several aspects of English kinship have changed during the nineteenth and twentieth centuries. The rate of divorce has increased 1,000-fold since 1858. Prohibitions on sexual unions between relatives by marriage have been progressively whittled away, and some of the remnants are currently under discussion. 'Incest' has narrowed in scope. Formalised mourning, a conspicuous feature of mid-nineteenth-century England, began to decline at the end of the century and is now scarcely in living memory. The nature of the marriage tie, apart from greater ease in dissolving it, has altered. So has the standing of extra-marital unions, and the position of wives. The part played by the Church and religious belief has greatly diminished.

Some changes occurred almost imperceptibly. Others, such as the transformation of divorce into a judicial procedure in 1857, alterations in the property relations of husband and wife in the 1870s and 1880s, or that 'eternal blister', legalising marriage with a deceased wife's sister, provoked controversy, in the last case for more than 60 years.

Over the centuries English lawyers and theologians[5] have given systematic accounts of many aspects of kinship. Parliamentary debates on legislative changes are recorded verbatim in *Hansard*. Often these are preceded by official fact-finding Commissions, and accompanied by vociferous unofficial argument in books, pamphlets, journals, newspapers. Before 1857, when divorces were effected by private Act of Parliament, proceedings and Acts of every divorce are preserved. Court and public mourning was regulated by orders published in the *London Gazette*. Documentation is extensive, so extensive that in this study I can make no pretensions to completeness.

Many facets of English kinship are governed by custom rather than law, and here I have employed, among other sources, fiction of the day. The novel, particularly in the nineteenth century, supplies a wealth of information about social beliefs and conventions. It helps us to trace changes in, for example, the custom of mourning or the attitude to extra-marital sexual unions, or to reconstruct past conventions. It is also one of the sources that assist us in seeing that, amid all the change, many aspects of

English kinship have undergone no alteration, or so little as to appear negligible by the side of other societies. The vocabulary, known among social anthropologists as 'kinship terminology', is virtually identical. Servants have vanished, but the proper composition of the household is otherwise little changed. The ideals of marriage remain in many respects the same. So do the principal concepts by which English kinship is organised.

Organisation

The pattern of the ethnographic part of this book (Part 1), where I present facts about English kinship, is largely modelled on the anthropological field-work monograph, to a lesser extent on legal writing about what is now known as 'Family Law'.[6] Separate chapters or sections are devoted to aspects of kinship conventionally studied in the field, such as prohibitions of sexual unions between relatives, mourning for the dead, kinship terminology, preferences in the choice of a spouse, the nature of the marriage tie and (less usual in anthropological studies) divorce. In the final chapter I turn to a recently born subject: the effects on kinship of new techniques affecting the production of babies. Emphasis throughout is on the relationship between the aspects of kinship described, which I claim fit together in a systematic fashion.

Development over time is more extensively included than would be usual in either anthropological or legal works but the whole is not presented in the manner most common in historical works. Apart from the fact that I concentrate on areas which have interested social anthropologists (as well as indigenous lawyers or novelists), I do not divide the time into periods and I follow a chronology only where it is relevant for my purposes.[7] There is less description of the personnel involved in particular activities or disputes than is favoured by many historians. On the other hand I attend more to laws, customs, beliefs known to every native, and taken for granted in England. I avoid technical anthropological vocabulary (except for the occasional use of such rudimentary terms as 'unilinear', 'patrilineal', 'matrilineal' and 'cognatic'),[8] but I aim to supply material comparable to that available on the kinship systems of other societies.

English life has of course changed in many ways since the early nineteenth century: in transport, modes of communication, production of goods, distribution of wealth, the structure of social classes. Or one might cite, during the period, the introduction of universal education, the rise of science and technology, the growth of the media, the decline of the Church, the loss of an empire. The list is almost endless. That there have been such changes in England is common knowledge to most English people, and those of related societies, even if dates and details are by now often shrouded in obscurity. Most have been extensively written about. Information on such points is included in the text only where it is necessary, for example to understanding an argument or evaluating an explanation. Sometimes it is relegated to notes.

Justification

Members of a society will commonly try to justify their customs if they are called in question or alternatively attempt to supply good reasons for making some change. The justifications considered appropriate clearly differ from society to society, over periods of time, sometimes from one setting to another. For example, to claim that something accorded with the Scriptures, or God's Word, used to be an accepted way of justifying it in England. In the course of the nineteenth century it was gradually replaced by citing the findings of experts, notably scientists.[9] Certain specific arguments make good platforms. In Parliament, that something is not really a change, that it brings England into line with Scotland or opens to the poor what is open to the rich assists the passage of a new law. Conversely, the claim that it is a change, will necessitate some other change, etc., is an argument against a measure. Some popular justifications, for example, the English belief that the laws against incest are designed to prevent idiot children, may persist, sometimes even conjoined with inconsistent beliefs. The style and content of justification in a society are of evident sociological interest.

In the course of this book, I cast doubt on the validity of some English justifications as explanations of English laws and customs or changes in them. In Part 2 I turn to the problems of explaining features of English kinship in more detail.

Explanation

Some aspects of English kinship have received little theoretical attention. In other cases explanations have been attempted. Sometimes, as with 'incest prohibitions', explanations have been extensively debated. But the theories which have been put forward rarely appear well founded. When examined they commonly turn out to be seriously defective. Counter-evidence does not generally dislodge them: it is resisted, evaded or ignored. The scientific attitudes supposed to operate in the society do not appear to function well in this area.

If, as I try to show by example, extant explanations of, let us say, why incest is forbidden in England, why mourning has vanished or the divorce rate risen, are not correct, the obvious next step is to look for better explanations. It proves very difficult to find them. The enterprise is much more complex than is often appreciated, and generally fails, especially if customs are taken in isolation from each other and we limit ourselves to the usual types of explanation.

It is noticeable that in England a law or custom which appears desirable (like the prohibition of incest) is generally assigned a useful purpose. Less attractive or apparently undesirable developments like the increase in extra-marital unions or the growth of divorce will more often be attributed to a cause, such as improved contraception or the emancipation of women. The common failure of causal and purposive explanations makes it necessary to consider whether a different type of explanation may not be more apposite.

Rationality

In Western society, a considerable premium is placed on rationality both of action and belief. At one time primitive societies, and their customs and beliefs, were regarded as irrational, with a 'pre-logical mentality'. Later, arguments were adduced either to separate off areas in which irrationality might be expected to occur or to prove the universality of rational action and belief. Thus Malinowski suggested that rationality does not prevail, whether in savage or civilised societies, in what he called 'the realm of belief': 'beliefs quite contradictory to each other . . .

may co-exist' he wrote.[10] Quine and other philosophers have held
that inconsistent beliefs are impossible and any appearances to
the contrary misleading.[11]

It is a theme of this book that there are customs and beliefs
which are neither strictly speaking rational nor properly called
'irrational'. Among them are many of our beliefs about kinship,
and, as I shall claim, consequent assertions, actions, customs, and
laws.

Notes

1. 'England' refers to England and Wales throughout. It does not include
Scotland or Ireland.
2. Maranda complained of his 'modest results', p. 11. He used almost no
primary sources. See S. Wolfram Review of P. Maranda *French Kinship: Structure and History* (The Hague and Paris 1974) in *Man. Journal of the Royal
Anthropological Institute* vol 10, London 1975, pp. 158–9 for further comments
on his *modus operandi*.
3. E. Shorter *The making of the Modern Family* London 1976 uses pre-
dominantly eighteenth-century sources on France 'with parts of Germany and
Scandinavia thrown in from time to time' (p. 14). He believes them to be 'typical
of the West as a whole', if admitting the conclusion to be 'precipitous' (p. 15).
4. 'Surrogate' mother is the term used for a woman who bears a child for
another woman, from her own ovum or the commissioning mother's. See below
Chapter 11.
5. The importance of ecclesiastical law in matters of kinship, which will
become apparent, means that much theological writing can also be regarded as
legal writing.
6. Earlier more commonly as e.g. 'The Marriage Law of England'.
7. Appendix A pp. 231–3 contains a chronological summary.
8. These terms may qualify e.g. inheritance, or we may speak e.g. of a name
descending 'patrilineally' or of 'patrilineal' groups (composed of patrilineal relatives, i.e. those patrilineally related). 'Patrilineal' means 'through males only',
'matrilineal' 'through females only', 'unilinear means 'patrilineal or matrilineal'
i.e. in one line only, 'cognatic' means 'through either sex'. The terms are often
extended to whole kinship systems or even societies. The terms 'exogamy' and
'endogamy' have entered legal and other non-anthropological writing. Like 'incest
prohibition', they lack clear meaning. Their history and ambiguities are discussed
at length in Chapter 8 Section 2.
9. It is instructive to note that while 'evenings of biblical criticism' occurred in
Parliament throughout the deceased wife's sister controversy (1842–1907), the
Church of England turned to Malinowski in 1940 and to other anthropologists in
1984 for expert advice on permitting marriage with hitherto forbidden relatives-in-
law. (See Church of England *Report of the Commission on Kindred and Affinity
as Impediments to Marriage* 1940, Appendix 3; Church of England *No Just Cause*
1984, Appendix VI.) The medical bias in the 1980s, for instance in discussions of
'surrogacy' etc. 1984–5 is also noteworthy. Scientific authority generally ousted
religious authority some decades before 1907.
10. B. Malinowski 'Baloma; the Spirits of the Dead in the Trobriand Islands'

Journal of the Royal Anthropological Institute London 1916, reprinted in B. Malinowski *Magic, Science and Religion and other Essays* Illinois 1948, pp. 194, 210.
    11. W.V. Quine *Word and Object* MIT 1960, Section 13, and in many other works. See S. Wolfram 'Facts and Theories: Saying and Believing' in J.Overing (ed.) *Reason and Morality* ASA monograph 24 London 1985a, pp. 71–84 for details and discussion.

Part 1

1 Basic Ideas

English kinship is very much more systematic than is often appreciated, whether in everyday life or by modern historians, lawyers, sociologists and social anthropologists. The indigenous tendency to explain individual practices in terms of their supposed functions and causes has probably helped to obscure the existence of pervasive principles of thought uniting one practice with another. It would be a mistake to claim that English laws and customs are entirely consistent or that changes never owe anything to relatively fortuitous circumstances.[1] Nevertheless, as I hope to show, when we understand the concepts in terms of which English people think about kinship, we can discern order, even in change.

1. Equivalence and Similarity

The idea that things are grouped into kinds, not by God or nature, but by man has a long history in English philosophical thinking. It was already a major theme of Locke's *An Essay Concerning Human Understanding* (1690) that 'it is men who . . . range [particular things] into sorts, in order to their naming', 'the boundaries . . . whereby men sort them, are made by men', the 'sorting of things is the workmanship of men'.[2] In the nineteenth and twentieth centuries social anthropologists became increasingly aware of the corollary that in different societies, men may sort many things, including kinship ties, in radically different ways.

By the late nineteenth century it was well known that the linguistic grouping of relatives could take many forms, cousins perhaps being assimilated to brothers and sisters or different cousins distinguished, and that 'blood' relationship is frequently traced not as in England through both parents, but 'unilinearly', that is, only in the male line ('patrilineally') or only in the female line ('matrilineally'). At first, differences from England and other civilised nations were generally regarded as somewhat strange and exotic, and often as indicating the infantile or barbarous state of the societies in question.

During the twentieth century the climate changed. Such seemingly basic facts as that someone's mother or father is a direct 'blood' relation came to be seen not as facts but as matters of local classification. Malinowski was still perplexed when he found the 'father' treated as a relation by marriage among the Trobriand Islanders, in many respects as rational as any civilised society, and toyed with hypotheses of ignorance of physical paternity or Freudian style repression.[3] In the 1950s, Dumont was able show beyond reasonable doubt that even someone's mother may be considered as a relation by marriage, and such inferences drawn as that her brother is related to him not as his uncle, as he would be in Europe, but as his father's brother-in-law, a relation by marriage, resembling his own brother-in-law.[4] By this time, anthropologists were acutely aware of the pitfalls of 'enthnocentricity', and no longer regarded concepts of their own society as closer to reality or superior to those of others. Indeed, at present it is more often English or Western kinship than that of other societies which they find problematic.[5] To English people not acquainted with the different ways in which relatives can be classified, on the other hand, English classifications have appeared, and still do appear, not as one mode of grouping among many but as if they represented facts of nature, so obvious as not normally to demand mention. They require description.

In England 'relatives' are distinguished from non-relatives. In English legal writing and in common thought, relatives are divided into two kinds. On the one hand there are blood relations. On the other there are relatives by marriage, known as 'relations-in-law' and 'step-relations'. In legal parlance these are distinguished as 'consanguineous' and 'affinal' relations. Two people are consanguineous, or 'blood', relations when one is a direct descendant of the other, i.e. is his or her child, child's child etc. or when both are descended from some common ancestor. 'Affinity' or relationship by marriage is the relation between a person and his or her spouse's blood relations and blood relations' spouses.

Anthropologists often still employ these categories of consanguinity, or descent, and affinity in order to describe kinship systems in other societies. But they normally also emphasise that the existence of two (or more) such categories of kin does not entail similarity either in the attributes of each or in the relatives that are assigned to them. Societies clearly differ greatly in their view of 'descent' or 'affinity' as well as in their divisions of relations between them.

The English term for one category of kinship, viz. 'blood relation' probably derives from a particular theory of heredity which was prevalent in England until about 1900. This is that characteristics pass from parent to child through blood. According to Dobzhansky:

> The parental 'bloods' were supposed to mix in the progeny so that the heredity of the child was a solution, or an alloy, of equal parts of parental heredities. The heredity of a person was thought to be an alloy in which the heredity of each of its four grandparents were represented by one-quarter, of each of eight great-grandparents by one-eighth, etc. (1955)[6]

It is consistent with this theory, and with the genetic or Mendelian theory of heredity which replaced it,[7] that in England a person is considered to be related in the same way to both parents and to the kin of each.

Several distinctions are drawn between blood relations. In some contexts, for instance, the 'direct line' from parent to child is contrasted to 'collateral' relationship, where two people are both descended from a common ancestor. Within the 'direct line', ascendants (parents, parents' parents, and so on) are distinguished from descendants (children, children's children, and their children etc.). Again, there is 'half-blood' as well as full blood: children with both parents in common are 'full blood'; those who share only one parent are 'half-blood'. Relationship may be 'legitimate' or 'illegitimate'. Someone is 'illegitimate' if his parents are not married. If he is illegitimate, then he is not a legitimate relative of his 'natural' parents and their relatives, but only an illegitimate one.

Relationship is also distinguished by distance. Some relatives are considered 'closer' than others. The idea of distance of relationship is formalised. It is computed in 'degrees', a relative in the first degree being closer than one in the second, and so on. The formalisation requires more detailed description. There have been two methods of reckoning degrees in England. One prevailed before the Reformation. The other replaced it.

Figure 1.1   The canon law reckoning of degrees (Numbers indicate the degree from Ego)

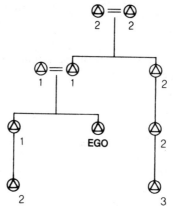

⊘   indicates men or women
△   indicates men
○   indicates women

Figure 1.2   The civil law reckoning of degrees (Numbers indicate the degree from Ego)

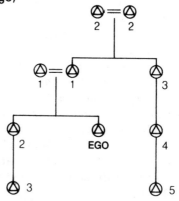

The first, of Germanic origin, was the 'canon law' reckoning of degrees, which was employed by the Roman Catholic Church. On this computation, the degree of relationship between two people depended on the number of generations one of them was distant from their common ancestors. If they were of different generations, the number of generations of the person more distant from the common ancestors determined the degree of relationship. Thus parents and children and brothers and sisters, were in the first degree, while first cousins, uncles and nieces, and aunts and nephews were in the second degree of consanguinity.

The second mode of computing degrees derived from Roman law,[8] and was known as the 'civil law' reckoning. On this reckoning each step up and down from common ancestors counted as a degree.

By the civil law reckoning of degrees, only parents and children are in the first degree. Brothers and sisters join grandparents and grandchildren as in the second degree. Uncle/aunt and niece/nephew are in the third degree, first cousins in the fourth degree. Common thinking in England follows the same pattern. Parents and children are considered to be more closely related than brothers and sisters or than grandparents and grandchildren. Uncles and aunts and nephews and nieces (who are in the third degree) are thought of as more distantly related, and cousins more distantly still.[9]

Clearly, relatives do not have to be classed as nearer or more remote by either of the principles employed in England. And other methods have featured in literature about kinship, sometimes perhaps somewhat misleadingly. For example, in his 'analysis' of French kinship in 1974, P. Maranda treated husband and wife, parents and children and siblings as all in the 'first order', their first order relatives as 'second order', et seq.[10] He gave no reasons for this ordering and made no mention of French computations, which do not in fact follow this pattern. Again, the English Criminal Law Revision Committee in 1980 and 1984 referred to 'parties to an incestuous union . . . related in the first degree (father and daughter, brother and sister)', without justifying the divergence from the usual English treatment of siblings as second degree relatives, popularly considered less closely related than parents and children.[11] There is no technically correct way of computing distance of relationship. Like kind of relationship, it is a matter of local classification.

When particular things are grouped together, they may be spoken of as 'equivalent', 'the same', 'alike'. We shall encounter many kinship practices and many arguments about them in which relatives are 'the same' or 'equivalent', or alternatively 'different'. So it is important to note that such concepts are incomplete in themselves. Things are not 'equivalent' as such but only in some way or for some purpose such as exchange or the fulfilling of some function. Nor are they simply 'like' one another. They are alike in particular respects: shape, colour, size, origin, breeding, style, monetary value, kind or distance of relationship. However it is commonly the case in societies that things or persons are grouped together and thought of as alike or equivalent to each other or to some other sort of thing without specification of the nature of the resemblance. So, for example, relatives grouped together as blood relations or as relatives in the first degree, or e.g. as 'sisters', will often be treated or spoken of as 'the same'.

It is important to notice that it is not only things grouped together which may be thought of as alike in a society. What is regarded as one kind of thing may also be considered to resemble something of another kind. In England, for instance, certain animals in certain circumstances are 'pets'. Animals are sharply distinguished from people, but pets are thought of as rather like people and are supposed to be treated accordingly. They should have names, ought to be looked after, must not be killed if possible, and, if killed, not eaten.[12] Similarly, while affinal relationship is certainly different in kind from blood relationship, it also used to resemble it closely.[13] This view of affinity derived from the English concept of marriage.

2. The Unity of Husband and Wife

According to English thought, husband and wife are not relatives. Instead, they occupy the position of being 'as one', or as it used to be expressed 'of one flesh'. This view of marriage is often spoken of as the Christian concept of marriage, and it is probably unique to the Western world.

It is notorious in anthropological literature that in many societies a marriage creates, not as in England a union of two persons in which they become as one, but an alliance between two groups of blood relations. So much have anthropologists been impressed by this type of view that Leach, who once studied such a society, at one time *defined* marriage as an 'alliance between two groups',[14] apparently oblivious of the quite different concept of marriage in his own society, England. In England a marriage creates no relationship (or alliance) between the kin of the spouses. The blood relations of a husband and wife are in no way related. Relationship exists only between the married couple and the kin on each side.

The unity of husband and wife, which might well be regarded as the centrepiece of the English kinship system, had a vast variety of aspects and implications. Some but not all remain.

Among them was, and is, that at marriage a husband and wife take on each other's relationships. Each becomes the 'in-law' relation of the other's blood relations, and the pattern of in-law relationship follows that of blood relationship in every detail. Thus, the terms used for blood relations ('parent', 'child', 'sister' etc.) apply equally to the blood relations of spouses and the spouses of blood relations. The distinction in kind of relationship is marked by the addition of 'in-law' (or in certain circumstances 'step-').[15] So, for instance, a spouse's parent is a 'parent-in-law', a husband's or wife's brother a 'brother-in-law', and so on. A daughter's husband is a 'son-in-law', a brother's wife a 'sister-in-law', and similarly for the rest.[16] A person is related in the same way and in the same degree to his or her spouse's relations as to his own, with only the difference that the relationship is one of 'affinity' or 'by marriage', instead of one of consanguinity. Consanguineous and affinal relations were never exactly the same. For example succession and inheritance pertained only to consanguineous relatives. However in the past, there were other purposes for which consanguineous and affinal relatives were assimilated. Mourning for the dead supplies one example. Legal restrictions on marriage and sexual intercourse another.

The importance once attached to the assimilation of affinity to consanguinity can be seen in the strength and nature of the opposition to the attempt to legalise marriage with one of the forbidden affinal relations, the deceased wife's sister. This was the most difficult of all the changes in English kinship in the nineteenth and twentieth centuries to effect. The controversy is discussed in detail in the next chapter.[17]

When two people married they became 'as one' in many respects other than taking on each other's relatives. No one of course supposed that a husband and wife were literally one person or of 'one flesh'. But numerous laws and customs distinguished a married couple from any other pair of people and treated them as nearly as possible as if they were one person.

Husband and wife had the same surname. Their property was held in common. Neither could give evidence at law against the other, nor could they form a conspiracy. They had the same domicile whether living together or not. They enjoyed the same rank and status. Sexual intercourse was supposed to be confined to husband and wife. The union was to all intents and purposes for life.

Some aspects of the unity of husband and wife was brought about by the wife becoming, as it used to be expressed, 'part' of the husband, 'bone of his bone'. At marriage the woman took her husband's name, rank and status. Her domicile was wherever he was living. Property and custody over children were vested in him. So was liability for debts. The requirement of sexual fidelity applied more stringently to the wife than to her husband.

In the course of the nineteenth century, the doctrine of the unity of husband and wife altered and became eroded. In some cases, this occurred by legislation, and the changes were then debated in Parliament. It is interesting to note that the unity of husband and wife was never attacked as such. Overt criticism was directed only at one of its aspects, viz. the incorporation of the wife in the husband. It was commonly agreed that Christianity had put men and women on an equal footing, and the argument that a wife should not have rights inferior to those of her husband nor be treated as 'part' of her husband in a way that he was not treated as 'part' of her, was of common occurrence in trying to effect changes and on occasion also in the course of opposition to changes.

At one time it was fashionable among anthropologists to build models of kinship organisation and to claim that this or that model represented what occurred in this or that society, irrespective of its own ideas. The ideas I have outlined are not of this kind. The basic ideas by which I suggest that English kinship is governed can be seen in many laws and customs. In everyday life, and other connections, they are for the most part taken for granted. On occasion, especially when controversies arise, they are explicitly stated and it seems a fair inference that principles stated in one connection may also be operating in another, even if not then stated as explicitly or sometimes not at all.

In considering controversies, for example about changes in the laws governing restrictions on sexual unions between relatives, divorce and married women's property, I shall often be drawing attention to arguments employed or desisted from for political purposes. The nature of 'good platforms' in a society is a study in itself. But my concern with this feature of controversies is initially to locate them. The justification for regarding certain arguments, such as that a measure will open to the poor what is open to the rich or make England more like Scotland, as 'platforms' is that they recur in widely discrepant contexts whenever they can be made to appear plausible. But unlike the ideas that I am suggesting are basic to English kinship (such as that husband and wife are as one) or individual theories about individual aspects of kinship in England (like the view that incest is forbidden to prevent idiot children), they appear largely in political settings, that is, where the object is to effect or to prevent some change.

Notes

1. A.Watson *Society and Legal Change* Edinburgh 1977, p. 38ff, cites the Emperor Claudius' marriage to his brother's daughter Agrippina (p. 38ff) which, in spite of being foul incest in Roman eyes, resulted in marriage with a brother's daughter remaining legal for nearly 300 years, while marriage with a sister's daughter was forbidden, as one of many instances in which laws do not 'fit' societies. Explanations of the failure of laws to fit societies include such factors as tenacity of existing law, influence of legal writers, poor procedure for effecting alterations, and 'legal transplants' i.e. where laws pass from one society to another for such reasons as where lawyers study, a potent reason for the difference between Scottish and English law (A. Watson *Legal Transplants. An Approach to Comparative Law* Edinburgh 1974, e.g. Chapter 7), or which book happens to be printed (Watson ibid. 1974, pp. 93−4).

2. J. Locke *An Essay Concerning Human Understanding* 1690, Book 3 Chapter 6 Sections 36−7. Revised editions 1694, 1695, 1700 and 5th edition published posthumously 1706. Currently preferred edition P.H. Nidditch (ed.) Oxford 1975, based on the 4th edition. Like many philosophical points this is contentious. Not everyone agrees with my reading of Locke nor with the general point that all classifications are made by men. For example, it is sometimes maintained that species of living things, elements and chemical compounds are 'natural kinds', if with some obscurity about exactly what constitutes a 'natural kind'.

3. B. Malinowski 'Baloma; the Spirits of the Dead in the Trobriand Islands' *Journal of the Royal Anthropological Institute* 1916, reprinted in B. Malinowski *Magic, Science and Religion and Other Essays* Illinois 1948; *The Sexual Life of Savages in North-Western Melanesia. An Ethnographic Account of Courtship, Marriage, and Family Life among the Natives of the Trobriand Islands, British New Guinea* London 1929, especially Chapter 7, and many other works.

4. L. Dumont 'Hierarchy and Marriage Alliance in South Indian Kinship' Occasional papers *Journal of the Royal Anthropological Institute* 1957; L. Dumont *Une Sous-Caste de l'Inde du Sud. Organisation Sociale et Religion des Pramalai Kallar* Paris 1957, Part 2.

5. See above Introduction and below Chapter 9 for some examples.

6. T. Dobzhansky *Evolution, Genetics and Man* New York 1955, pp. 24–5.

7. See below Chapter 7, Section 1 and notes 11A and 44 for some details of Mendelian Theory.

8. Justinian *Institutes* AD 533, Book III, Title VI 'De gradibus cognationis' in *Imperatoris Iustiani Institutionem* (J.B. Moyle (ed.), Oxford 1883, 5th edn. 1912) p. 370ff, translated as 'Of the Degrees of Cognation' in *The Institutes of Justinian* (J.B. Moyle (trans.), Oxford 1883, 5th edn. 1913) p. 116ff.

9. See below Chapter 4, Section 1 for details.

10. P. Maranda *French Kinship: Structure and History* 1974, especially pp. 50, 85. Cf S. Wolfram review in *Man. Journal of the Royal Anthropological Institute* 1975, vol 10, pp. 158–9 for criticism of Maranda's procedure. French computations resemble English.

11. Home Office, Criminal Law Revision Committee *Working paper on Sexual Offences* London October 1980, HMSO, p. 41 para 113; Home Office, Criminal Law Revision Committee 15th Report *Sexual Offences* London 1984, HMSO Cmd 9213, p. 65 para 8.9. The 1980 reference was in connection with children of these unions having 'a high risk, nearly one chance in two of being born with serious defects'. In 1984 the risk was said to be less than had been said in 1980, cf Chapter 7, Section 1.

12. Cf S. Wolfram 'Basic Differences of Thought' in R. Horton and R. Finnegan (eds) *Modes of Thought* 1973, pp. 357–74.

13. Figuratively 'affinity' means 'similarity of character suggesting relationship, family likeness' (*The Concise Oxford Dictionary*). See D.M. Schneider 'Kinship, Community, and Locality in American Culture' in J.A. Lichtman and J. Challoner (eds) *Kinship and Community* Washington DC 1979, p. 156ff for discussion of 'blood' and 'in-law' in American contexts.

14. E.R. Leach 'Rethinking Anthropology' in E.R. Leach *Rethinking Anthropology* London 1961, revised edition London 1966, p. 20.

15. See below Chapter 4, Section 1 for a discussion of 'step-' vs 'in-law'.

16. See below Figure 2.1 and Chapter 4, Section 1 for details of English kinship terminology.

17. Chapter 2, Section 2.

2 The Prohibited Degrees of Marriage and Incest

Relationships which bar marriage or sexual intercourse are known as the Prohibited Degrees of Consanguinity and Affinity, the Prohibited Degrees of Marriage, or simply 'The Prohibited Degrees'. These prohibitions and their development are a convenient starting place for a study of English kinship. Prohibitions of marriage and sexual unions between relatives have always attracted interest. For centuries there have been rival theories, both popular and expert, purporting to 'explain' them. From 1865 onwards, following McLennan's *Primitive Marriage*[1] and coining of the word 'exogamy', prohibitions of sexual unions between relatives have formed a staple part of anthropologists' kinship studies, although rarely with any eye to the English style of rules. Current proposals for change give the subject local topicality. Last but not least, some of the points made about English kinship in the last chapter can be seen particularly clearly in this area.

There have been two major changes in the Prohibited Degrees since the thirteenth century. Between 1215 and the sixteenth century marriage prohibitions were very extensive, if mitigated by the possibility of procuring dispensations which allowed the marriages to go forward. The relatives forbidden to marry were those up to and including third cousins by blood or in-law, or in legal terms relatives in or within the fourth degree of consanguinity and affinity by the canon law reckoning of degrees.

The prohibitions, which had been even more extensive before 1215, were drastically curtailed in the sixteenth century. Legislation enacted by Henry VIII and finally accepted by Church and State permitted marriage between first cousins by blood and in-law. Thereafter only relatives closer than these were forbidden to marry. The new prohibitions, shown in Figure 2.3, prevented marriage only between relatives in or within the third degree of consanguinity and affinity by the civil law reckoning of degrees.[1A]

In 1907 a further step was taken: a Statute was passed to allow marriage with a particular affinal relative, the deceased wife's

Figure 2.1 Roman Catholic prohibitions of marriage in or within the fourth degree of consanguinity

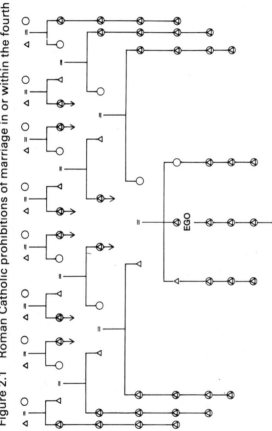

Ego is forbidden to marry any of the persons shown i.e. any descendant of four or fewer generations from any ancestor four or fewer generations from himself. The same relatives of a spouse (i.e. in or within the fourth degree of affinity), also forbidden, are omitted for reasons of space.

For reasons of space some of the relatives are shown:

These arrows indicate lines through male and female descendants of three further generations.

sister. This was the first stage in removing restrictions on the marriage of affines, a process now nearing completion.

Both the sixteenth-century changes and the legalisation of marriage with a deceased wife's sister were greatly disputed and much thinking about English kinship was made explicit in the ensuing controversies. There was a great deal of discussion surrounding Henry VIII's legislation, which has been described in detail by Scarisbrick.[2] I shall only sketch out what occurred and then turn to more recent changes.

1. Reformation Changes

The method by which the sixteenth-century reduction in restrictions on marriage between relatives came about was complex. Henry VIII passed four Statutes about prohibited marriages. The first pair (1533 and 1536)[3] specified relatives who could not be married. These are most easily seen in diagrammatic form. They consisted of the relatives mentioned in the Old Testament Book of Leviticus Chapters 18 and 20, with the one addition of the wife's sister.

The second pair of Henry VIII's Statutes, 1536 and 1540,[4] did not specify prohibited relatives. They simply stated that all marriage not forbidden by divine law was to be valid. Thus in 1536 (28 H 8 c 16 sec 2): marriages 'not prohibited by God's laws, limited and declared in the act made in this present parliament . . . or otherwise by Holy Scripture, shall be . . . good, lawful and effectual'. And in 1540: 'no reservation or prohibition, Goddes law except, shall trouble or impeche any marriage without the Leviticall degrees.'

Henry VIII's Statutes were repealed by Mary in 1553 and 1554,[5] and only the last two were re-enacted by Elizabeth I in 1558.[6] The law of the land thus rested on 'God's law' and 'the Leviticall degrees'.

The question of which relatives were thereby prohibited was complicated by two factors. One was relatively minor, though it cast important shadows on the future. This was that Henry VIII's Statutes had added the wife's sister to the relatives specified in Leviticus as those whose nakedness might not be uncovered. After repeal and re-enactment, it was not clear whether the reference in the later 1536 Act to the earlier Act of the same year

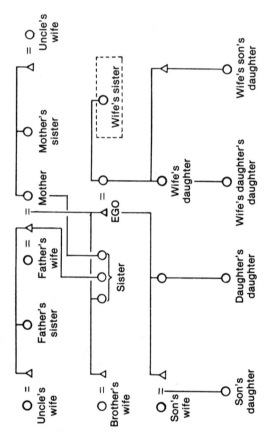

Figure 2.2 Relatives forbidden in Leviticus (Named relatives are forbidden)

Figure 2.3 Relatives forbidden to marry in Archbishop Parker's Table (Named relatives are forbidden)

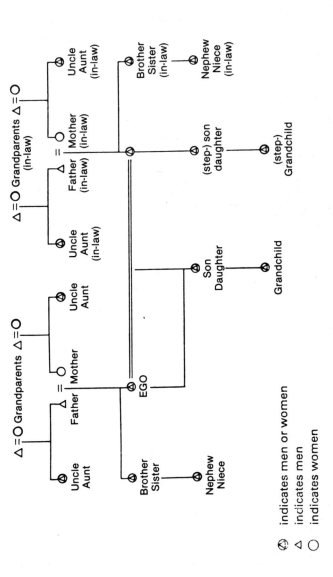

(28 H 8 c 7), not itself re-enacted, meant that the wife's sister was forbidden, or whether the reliance placed on Leviticus itself in the later Acts meant that the deceased wife's sister, who was not mentioned there, was on the contrary supposed to be permitted.

Of more immediate importance was that in 1603 the Church of England adopted a Table of Levitical Degrees proposed by Archbishop Parker in 1563. The Table was printed in *The Book of Common Prayer* of 1662 and hung in every parish church, where it may still be found, entitled 'A Table of Kindred & Affinity, wherein whosoever are related are forbidden in scripture and our laws to marry together'.[7] It rested on an altogether different construction of the 'Leviticall degrees', and it resulted in a far wider set of relatives than those specified in Henry VIII's Statutes being forbidden. These are shown in Figure 2.3.

Parker's Table enumerated forbidden relatives not, as in my Figure 2.3, by common language terms, but more descriptively. A man was said to be forbidden to marry his grandmother, his grandfather's wife . . . etc., a woman her grandfather, her grandmother's husband etc. In earlier versions, such as those of 1594, 1605, 1696, the canon law degree of each relative was given. Later, the list of the 30 blood and in-law relatives forbidden to a man, or the 60 forbidden when those a woman could not marry were set out as well, was printed without such annotation. As was often explained, has already been mentioned and can readily be seen by comparing Figure 1.2 (the depiction of civil law degrees) and Figure 2.3 above, Archbishop Parker's Table forbade marriage between all relations in and within the third degree of consanguinity and affinity.

The rationale for this Table was what was known as the 'Parity of Reason' interpretation of Leviticus. On this interpretation relatives thought of as equivalent to those specified in Leviticus were considered to be implicitly included as forbidden. Two principles were employed. The first was that any relation as close as a relation specified in Leviticus must be forbidden too. ('Closeness' went by the civil law reckoning of degrees.[8]) The second was that consanguineous and affinal relatives being alike, any affinal relative was forbidden if the same consanguineous relative was expressly prohibited in Leviticus. Comparison of Figures 2.2 and 2.3 shows that the prohibitions in Parker's Table follow from the application of these principles to the prohibitions specified in Leviticus.[9] That Parker's Table was much more in line with English kinship concepts than what came to be termed the 'literal' interpretation of Leviticus, probably explains its initial acceptance, as well as its longevity. It organised the Prohibited Degrees in what was, in English eyes, the natural way. The acceptance by the English of particular sorts of categories and relations between them, made the list we find in Leviticus appear illogical, that in Parker's Table logical.

The precise legal position was complicated in a number of ways, particularly by the relations of the ecclesiastical and common law courts.[9A]

Until 1857 the ecclesiastical courts had jurisdiction over matrimonial cases, and they adhered to Archbishop Parker's Table, adopted into the canons of the Church of England in 1603. However, the case of Hill v. Good, reported in 1677,[10] established a position whereby the common law courts could prevent a case of marriage outside the Levitical Degrees from coming before the ecclesiastical judges. In practice the common law courts adhered to the Parity of Reason interpretation of Leviticus and did not prevent 'marriages' forbidden in Archbishop Parker's Table but not in Leviticus from reaching the ecclesiastical courts. However, the position was not considered to be entirely clarified until as late as 1847 when, in two cases concerning marriage with a deceased wife's sister, the common law courts explicitly declared in favour of the Parity of Reason interpretation.[11]

The concepts of consanguinity and affinity were not themselves altered during the Reformation. Consanguinity continued to be, as it had been in Roman Catholic law, a relationship between parents and children or between persons descended from a common ancestor. From the point of view of the prohibited degrees (and of what constituted 'incest'), consanguinity was as strictly as possible a matter of blood, or biological, relationship. There was, and is still, considered to be consanguinity between a man and his illegitimate child. There is no consanguinity between a man and a child conceived by his wife during the marriage if he can be shown not to be the natural father of that child.

Affinity is now created by marriage. It is the relationship between a person and his or her spouse's consanguineous relatives (legitimate and illegitmate). In Henry VIII's Statutes of 1536, however, and in Archbishop Parker's Table (item 3) affinity was created, as in Roman Catholic law, by extra-marital intercourse as well as by a consummated marriage. The precise nature of 'affinity' assumed importance in Henry VIII's affairs on account of the question of whether Katherine of Aragon's marriage with his brother had or had not been consummated, which played a part, well described by Scarisbrick[12] in Henry VIII's arguments with the Pope. And there was in any case a divergence of opinion among the learned as to whether it was sexual intercourse or only marriage which created affinity. From the legal angle, the important point was that 28 H 8 c 27 includes intercourse. It says '. . . it is to be understood that if it chaunce eny man to know carnally eny woman, that then all and singular persons being in any degree of consanguinity, as is above written to any of the persons carnally offending, shall be deemed and ajudged to be within the cases and limits of the said prohibitions'.

This view was reaffirmed in Parker's Table and, although the relevant Statute had been repealed, it continued to be repeated by legal writers until at least the end of the seventeenth century. It bothered Defoe's Moll Flanders in 1722 that she had 'lain with two brothers' by dint of marriage with her seducer's brother.[13] The first divorce secured by a woman, Mrs Addison, in 1801, was for her husband's incestuous adultery with her sister, his sister-in-law; it was granted because any further intercourse with her husband would have been incestuous by the rule that intercourse creates affinity.[14] But in 1861 it was clearly stated that, at least according to common law, extra-marital intercourse did not create affinity. In Wing v. Taylor[15] a man sued for nullity of his marriage on the grounds of previous intercourse with his wife's mother. The case was decided against him on the grounds of the repeal of 28 H 8 c 27, and it was said that no such case had been brought for 300 years.

It is one thing to say that a marriage is 'prohibited', another to explain exactly what this involves. Henry VIII brought about one very important change in this respect. Catholic prohibitions were doubtless very extensive. On the other hand, it was possible in the right circumstances to procure dispensations which allowed the marriage. The right circumstances differed at different periods and the whole matter formed a large part of Henry VIII's problems in dissolving his marriage with Katherine of Aragon.[16] Henry VIII abolished dispensations altogether.

Initially the new, less extensive prohibitions on the marriage of relatives were absolute. But once more custom intervened. The position came to be, and remained until 1835, that a marriage within the prohibited degrees was voidable by the ecclesiastical courts. If it was declared by them to be void, it was void from the beginning and all the children of the marriage were illegitimate. Through the intervention of the common law courts in the case of Harris v. Hicks 1692,[17] the practice soon grew up that such marriages could be declared void only during the lifetime of both partners. Cases had to be brought by interested parties (e.g. for the purposes of inheritance) and it was possible to keep friendly suits going until one partner died, so that the marriage was preserved.

Canon 99 of the Church of England 1603 declared that all marriages within the degrees prohibited by Parker's Table were to be 'ajudged incestuous and unlawful'. The 'unlawful' part was comprised under the fact that such marriages were voidable. The 'incestuous' aspect was separate. Incest was subject to penalties of excommunication or public penance by the ecclesiastical courts, and a case for incest could be brought against one party even after the death of the other.[18]

In the light of more recent thinking it is worth stressing that consanguinity and affinity were on precisely the same footing with regard not only to the voidability of marriage but also to incest. Thus as late as the nineteenth century there were four cases reported between 1810 and 1816 in which there was declared to be incest; with a brother's widow, a deceased wife's sister, a mother's brother's widow and a wife's daughter. In the last, the only one in which the incest, as opposed to the validity of the marriage, was in question, the 'usual' penalty of public penance was inflicted.[19] *Hamlet* (1602) bears witness to the earlier incestuous nature of marriage with a husband's brother.[20] *Moll Flanders* (1722) says of her erstwhile seducer, her husband's brother, that she 'committed adultery and incest with him every day in my desires'.[21] Divorce Acts before 1835 specifically forbade (i.e. declared void) marriage between divorcee and paramour when these were within the Prohibited Degrees: Edward Addison and his wife's sister 1801, the Countess of Rosebery and her deceased sister's husband, Sir John Mildmay, in 1815, Mr Turton and his wife's sister 1830.[22]

The possibility of 'incestuous marriages' came to an end in 1835, when previously voidable marriages became void,[23] or at latest 1861, when the courts refused to make an exception of 'marriages' contracted abroad.[24] There was also a period when no court had jurisdiction over incest and there was no penalty: 1857–1908. But unlawful marriages and incestuous intercourse continued united, appertaining to the relations of in-laws as well as blood relatives, until well into the twentieth century, under the notion of 'incestuous adultery'. 'Incestuous adultery' was one of the few grounds for which a woman could divorce her husband by the Matrimonial Causes Act of 1857. It was there defined as: 'Adultery committed by a husband with a woman with whom if his wife were dead he could not lawfully contract marriage by reason of her being within the prohibited degrees of consanguinity or affinity'.[25]

Between the Reformation and the nineteenth century, English law was simple in its prohibitions, apart from the complication about voidable marriages. No one could marry or have intercourse in or within the third degree of consanguinity or affinity by the civil law reckoning of degrees. In the nineteenth century a further seeming simplification was made. In 1835 there was an Act of Parliament, known as Lord Lyndhurst's Act. According to a persistent rumour, this Act was instigated by the Duke of Beaufort who had contracted a marriage with his deceased wife's half-sister which he wished to safeguard. The Statute differed greatly from the original Bill, intended to abbreviate the time during which voidable mariages could be made void. It had two parts. One rendered legal all marriages between affines already contracted at that time. The other simplified the law, or so it seemed. It made all future marriages within the prohibited degrees void *ab initio*, that is, they were not marriages at all.[26] It was almost certainly this tightening up of the law which ushered in the new phase: a determined attempt once more to reduce the extent of marriage prohibitions.

2. The Deceased Wife's Sister Controversy

In 1907 a Statute was passed allowing a man to marry his deceased wife's sister. The Deceased Wife's Sister's Marriage Act[27] was the outcome of one of the most protracted struggles in British Parliamentary history. It took 65 years, 46 sessions of debate, 18 successful second readings in the House of Commons[28] to effect this piece of legislation, and in the meantime there had been annual leaders in *The Times* on the subject, pamphlets in their hundreds, a Marriage Law Defence Association and a Marriage Law Defence Union.

There was an initial attempt to legalise marriage between a man and the niece as well as sister of his deceased wife. Bills including both were introduced in Parliament between 1842 and 1849.[29] In 1848 a Royal Commission reported in favour of legalising marriage with a deceased wife's sister.[30] It maintained that Lord Lyndhurst's Act of 1835 had proved ineffective in preventing marriage within the Prohibited Degrees. A survey in selected districts had (it was claimed) revealed 1,364 such marriages since the Act, and 'of these', it said, 'upwards of nine-tenths have been contracted with a deceased wife's sister'.[31] Only 88 couples had been deterred from an intended marriage by the Act, and 32 of them were said to be living in open cohabitation. 'We are constrained . . . to express our doubt,' the Commissioners said '. . . whether any measure of a prohibitory nature would be effectual.'[32] Soon thereafter reformers concentrated their efforts on legalising marriage with a deceased wife's sister, and there was continual controversy until they were finally successful in 1907. As one legal writer put it in 1887, 'the subject . . . has been more frequently and earnestly debated and disputed than any other point connected with our marriage laws'.[33]

The arguments employed remained uniform throughout the large number of Parliamentary Debates and in the accompanying plethora of pamphlet literature.[34] Apart from discussion about the relation of civil and church marriage,[35] about whether the Deceased Wife's Sister's Bill should extend to Scotland, and whether or not public opinion was in favour of it, the arguments were divided by contemporaries into two main categories: social and Biblical. The latter were sometimes sub-divided into purely Biblical and those based on the 'principles' of English marriage prohibitions, and opponents of the Bill considered them the more important.

The social arguments about legalising marriage with a deceased wife's sister centred on three issues: the effect on the possibility of their maternal aunt caring for a widower's children, the effect on the relations between sisters, and the effect on the relation between man and his sister-in-law.

Both sides were agreed that a married woman's sister should be her most intimate companion and that it was indispensable, especially among the poor, that if a man's wife died, it should be possible for her sister to care for his children. They also agreed that extra-marital sexual relations were extremely undesirable.

One of the arguments against the Bill was that if a man could marry his wife's sister, she would be unable to live in his home after her sister's death, or even during her lifetime since 'it was a rule of society, that parties of different sexes capable of being united in marriage, should not live together without that union'.[36]

There were two standard counter-arguments. One was to cite the findings of the 1848 Commission, and to maintain that extra-marital unions between a man and his deceased wife's sister were not only common but also 'uncondemned by the conscience of the parties, and untouched by the extreme censures of society'.[37] Consequently, an unmarried girl could not in fact properly live in her sister's husband's household. 'I ask [you]' it was urged 'whether you would allow any daughter of yours, even in the present state of the law, to reside alone in the house of a young brother-in-law?'[38] The alternative argument was to maintain that if a man and his wife's sister could marry, this would not prevent her from living in his household even if they did not do so.[39] In the New England States, where such marriages were legal, there was no problem 'provided the gentleman were sufficiently respectable'.[40] Indeed, there might be less scandal than now, since if they did not marry, it would be assumed that they had formed no attachment.[41]

It was not difficult to reply to these arguments. Opponents of the proposed legislation questioned the frequency of 'marriages' with a deceased wife's sister. They 'could not consent, in order to prevent unlawful concubinage of an incestuous character, to legalise marriages of a nature equally incestuous'.[42] A maternal aunt might prove no kinder than any other step-mother:

> Once let her become a mother herself, and there will arise in the mother's heart the fierce selfishness of the mother's love and the mother's jealousy; and from that moment she is a step-mother to her sister's children, her maternity has destroyed in her all the tenderness of an aunt.[43]

Further, convention forbad a man to re-marry at once. He was supposed to wait two years.[44] A widower would therefore be deprived of his sister-in-law's help when he most needed it —

unless indeed 'the coffin of the wife [was] to be the altar before which the marriage of the sister was to be contracted'.[45]

Arguments and counter-arguments continued throughout the debates. The other 'social' arguments were equally commonly put forward and equally indecisive.

Against allowing a man to marry his deceased wife's sister, it was urged that it 'would lead every wife to look upon her sister as her prospective rival, and every unmarried sister to regard with fear and trembling the innocent attentions of her brother-in-law'.[46] As Gladstone expressed it:

> . . . the purity of sisterly love itself, which afforded, perhaps, the most beautiful picture, when it was manifest in its perfection, which it was given to human eyes to witness on earth, and was redolent of heaven more than any other object with which we could be conversant, was threatened to be tainted by the invasion of possible jealousies.[47]

Harrowing pictures were drawn of 'the sufferings of the woman who has been deprived by sickness of the charms which formerly attracted her husband, and who has to endure the mental torture of seeing his affections transferred to her sister . . .'.[48] 'Even the most faithfully loved might in an evil hour of feminine weakness, joined to a momentary or unguarded indiscretion of her husband's, catch a spark of that fatal flame of jealousy, which should render her weary of her life . . .'.[49]

Supporters of the Bill retorted that the suggestion that as soon as a man could marry his wife's sister after his wife's death he would give cause for jealousy during her lifetime was 'based on a view of the domestic morality of Englishmen and Englishwomen that was perfectly monstrous':[50] 'Men do not speculate in that way on their wife's death.'[51] And 'the picture of a dying wife, made happy in her last moments by the grim thought that, come what may, her sister, at all events, cannot succeed to her husband's affections' was 'grotesque, and ridiculous in the last degree'.[52] On the contrary. Often, 'nothing would more soothe her dying hour than the hope that . . . [her children] would fall into the hands of one already bound to them by a tie almost as strong as that of the mother herself'.[53]

The opponents of the Bill also 'pleaded for sisters-in-law as they were. The relations of sister-in-law and brother-in-law was one of the most beautiful and endearing of all family relationships. There was a sweet tenderness and a depth of affection in it . . .'[54] The existing relationship of a man and his wife's sister was contrasted with that which would result from legalisation of marriage between them. Now the relationship had,

> With the frankness, the cheerfulness of affection, that exists naturally between a brother and a sister . . . a freshness, united with a certain degree of tacit respect . . . which . . . detracts nothing from the playful confidence or the ingenuous warmth which distinguishes it. In no situation, perhaps, is a female seen to greater advantage . . . she is never so much at her ease, never so agreeable or attractive, never apparently less selfish, or more amiable . . .[55]

But if the restriction were removed:

> Restraint must take place of affectionate familiarity; the tie of relationship is severed, each is to the other what strangers are; the wary and modest female will assume the armour of womanly reserve, womanly prudence and caution, and substitute mistrust for confidence; while the husband, no longer daring openly and freely to evince his regard for the sister . . . must confine himself within the bounds of polite friendliness . . .[56]

Reformers drew on foreign examples to show that where marriage between a man and his wife's sister was legal, sisters-in-law 'are the same valuable, the same admirable, and the same lovable persons in a family that they are found to be in so many families in this country'.[57] They claimed that the relation of a man and his sister-in-law had been no different in England before 1835, when the vast majority of marriages between a man and his wife's sister had been allowed to stand. Alternatively, they used to declare that 'no man feels that a sister-in-law is in reality any sister of his'.[58] In this connection it was often pointed out that the law of inheritance did not treat a wife's sister 'like a sister'. His wife's sister did not inherit from a man who died intestate, and if a woman were left a legacy by her sister's husband, she paid the death duties customary for unrelated people because she was a 'stranger in blood'. Cousins who were considered sufficiently distantly related to marry paid at a reduced rate.[59]

The question of the relation between a man and his sister-in-law was held by opponents of change to be part of a question about all affinal relatives. The idea that a sister-in-law was 'a sister in some sense' was part of the idea that husband and wife took on each other's relationships, and this in turn derived from the view that husband and wife are as one or 'one flesh'. Opposition to removing the prohibition on marriage with a deceased wife's sister insisted on the secondary, and inconclusive, nature of social arguments. The prohibition was part of a *system* of Prohibited Degrees, itself ordained by God.

Biblical argument was at least as prominent in the deceased wife's sister controversy as social argument. It centred on the two interpretations of Leviticus we have alredy encountered,[60] both sides agreeing that the Levitical prohibitions were binding.

Advocates of removing the prohibition on marriage with a deceased wife's sister generally adhered to the 'literal' interpretation. The prohibitions stated in Leviticus were exhaustive: a man was forbidden by God to marry the relatives specified and no more. The deceased wife's sister was not mentioned, and was indeed permitted by implication, since Leviticus xviii, 18 forbids a man to take his wife's sister *during his wife's lifetime*.[61]

Defenders of the *status quo* adhered to the Parity of Reason interpretation of Leviticus, on which English law was based.[62] They claimed that the relatives mentioned were intended as examples, and that God forbade man to marry not only these, but also any analogous to them. In their view, verse 18: 'Neither shalt thou take a wife to her sister during her lifetime to vex her . . .', was correctly rendered 'Neither shalt thou take one wife to another . . .'. It was not a prohibition of marriage with the wife's sister, but a prohibition of polygamy.[63] Marriage with a deceased wife's sister was forbidden by implication since Leviticus xviii, 16 expressly forbids a man to marry his brother's widow, who is exactly analogous. They used to point out that Leviticus did not specifically forbid marriage with a grandmother, niece or daughter and predicted that if marriage with a deceased wife's sister was legalised, the legalisation of marriage between a man and his niece would follow,[64] or, in their lighter moments, demanded of anyone accepting the literal interpretation of Leviticus that he 'marry his grandmother like a man'.[65]

The Parity of Reason interpretation of Leviticus rested on the view that relatives analogous to those mentioned were intended to be forbidden. Leviticus was addressed to men but intended to apply to both sexes, so that if a man were forbidden to marry his brother's widow, a woman could not marry her sister's widower. According to Genesis ii, 24 and the New Testament,[66] husband and wife are 'one flesh', and this entailed that if someone was forbidden to marry a relative of his own he was forbidden to marry a similar relative of his spouse.

Opponents of the Bill regarded it as a general attack on this latter principle. It was often predicted that the legalisation of marriage with a deceased wife's sister would lead to legalisation of marriage between all affines, even those expressly forbidden in Leviticus, and that relations not only with a sister-in-law but with all affinal relations would be destroyed. Contemporary comment was pungent. 'The Bill rests on no principle whatever. The present law does rest upon principle, but when we depart from it, we can have no principle whatever except that of sweeping away all the prohibitions of affinity'.[66A] 'If you are not to go by this rule, you must either allow all persons in affinity to marry as they please, or, if you still forbid some, you must do it on *no principle at all*.'[66B] 'The lawfulness of marriage with a wife's sister can be maintained only on the much more sweeping and altogether untenable ground that the death of either spouse in a marriage makes an end to the whole affinity which came by it with the kindred of the other.'[66C] It would then no longer be the case that 'when a man marries a woman, her mother becomes his mother, her aunt his aunt, her sister his sister'.[67] Since the text that husband and wife are 'one flesh' was also a prohibition of divorce, polygamy, and adultery, it was prophesied that a relaxation of the divorce laws, an increase in conjugal unfaithfulness, and even the legalisation of polygamy would follow.[68]

Promoters of the Deceased Wife's Sister's Marriage Bill resisted the suggestion that they intended to sweep away all restrictions on marriage between affines, and scarcely ever proposed consanguinity as the rational basis for prohibiting marriage.[69] They tried to confine the issue to the deceased wife's sister, by the claim that this marriage was not generally regarded as incestuous, by using the social arguments described above, and by declaring that logic was a poor weapon against practical exigencies and public demand. Sometimes they attempted to weaken their opponents' position by pointing out inconsistencies in it, and the ensuing discussions contained sharp exchanges on the nature of the English treatment of affinity.

There were three common attacks on the view of affinity propounded by defenders of the existing English Prohibited Degrees.

The most frequent was that the prohibition on marriage between affinal relatives should entail that the consanguineous relatives of one spouse could not marry the consanguineous relatives of the other.[70] If it were maintained that the siblings of one spouse became the siblings of the other, then, it was argued, it should equally be maintained that the siblings of one spouse became the siblings of the other's siblings. And yet it was not proposed that two brothers should be forbidden to marry two sisters. The usual reply was simply to reiterate that a marriage created affinity between one spouse and the kin of the other but did not create affinity between the kin of one spouse and the kin of the other.[71] Sometimes it was pointed out that although one party to a marriage became a member of the other's family, there was no fusion between the two families.[72] One writer expressed this by suggesting that just as the consanguinity of siblings depended on their common parentage, so did the affinal sibling relationship depend on the fact that a person became a child of his spouse's parents. He did not become a child of his siblings' spouse's parents, and therefore did not become a sibling of his siblings' spouse's siblings.[73]

A second attack was that not only was it the 'very extravagance of analogy'[74] to deduce from the text that husband and wife are one flesh that the affinity between a person and his spouse's kin endured even after the death of his spouse, but also the doctrine was not consistently adhered to. The immortal bond between husband and wife was not held to prevent a person from remarrying after the death of his spouse.[75] The answer to this was generally simply that affinity endures beyond the death of either spouse but does not exclude the formation of new affinal ties.[76] Once or twice it was pointed out that in fact the social relationship between a person and his spouse's kin did outlast the death of the spouse.[77] And several writers added that to suggest that the death of one spouse ended the affinity between his kin and the surviving spouse was like suggesting that the death of their parents brought the consanguinity of siblings to an end: just as consanguinity was traced through parents, so was affinity traced through husband or wife.[78]

The third, and probably least common, attack was on the analogy between the husband's brother and the wife's sister on which opponents of the Deceased Wife's Sister's Marriage Bill used to insist, and which they based on the idea that husband and wife were equal and a woman's relations to her husband's kin exactly the same as those between a man and his wife's kin. Advocates of the Bill would point out that Jewish law had not put husband and wife on the same footing.[79] Polygamy, but not polyandry, had been allowed. Adultery had been punishable in a woman but not in a man. A woman was incorporated into her husband's kin, but a man did not become part of his wife's kin. 'It *may* be, therefore', it was said, 'that even in the Law of Leviticus, *that* is permitted to a man which was forbidden in a woman',[80] namely, that a man might marry his deceased wife's sister although a woman was forbidden to marry her husband's brother. When their opponents replied that Christianity had made husband and wife equal,[81] they pointed out existing differences in the relations of husband and wife to each other. A woman took her husband's name. A wife's adultery was sufficient grounds for her husband to divorce her, a husband's adultery not (alone) sufficient for her to divorce him.[82] One or two people even maintained that the 'latest discoveries of physiology' had revealed that a woman became part of her husband in a way in which a man did not become part of his wife.[83] Consequently it was quite logical to legalise marriage with the deceased wife's sister without at the same time legalising it with the brother's widow. The reply was generally a repetition of the view that Christianity 'reestablished the proper dignity of women' and that a wife's kin became the husband's just as the husband's kin became the wife's. One writer added that it was not a question of names or property, but of 'intercourses and sympathies and attachments'. 'In Christian England,' he continued, 'the kindly intimacy between a man and the natural kindred of his wife is . . . on the whole as great as that between a woman and the natural kindred of her husband.'[84]

There is no need to dwell further on views of affinity, its resemblance to consanguinity and relation to the doctrine of the unity of husband and wife. But it is worth mentioning another point which emerges from all these arguments. This is the close tie conceived to exist between being related to someone and being forbidden to marry them, as if by allowing marriage between two people, it followed, *ipso facto*, that they would no longer really be relations. The same thought can sometimes be found in fiction of the period in connection with cousins, who occupied the ambiguous status of being related and yet being marriageable. 'Coosins!' says Andy Gowran in Trollope's *The Eustace Diamonds* (1876), after observing Lizzie, then a young widow, in the embrace of her cousin Frank. ' "Coosins!" he said yet again.'[85]

Several other apparently more momentous changes in kinship than allowing marriage with a deceased wife's sister (or other affines) took place in the nineteenth century without the same difficulty, and there is therefore a problem about why it took so long to effect this particular alteration, as well as why it was so continually promoted and ultimately accepted.

One probable reason for lack of success lay in the reformers' lack of a good platform. In trying to make divorce a judicial procedure in the 1850s, or to give all married women the right to own property a little later in the century, it was possible to put forward such arguments as that it was not really a change at all, or followed from earlier changes, that the rich already enjoyed the position now sought for all, that it would help to bring English law into line with Scottish or equalise the sexes. No such arguments could be used to assist legalisation of marriage with a deceased wife's sister. It was forbidden in Scotland as in England. It was not, and never had been, a prerogative of the wealthy. It was not proposed to revert to the position before 1835, when marriages in the prohibited degrees had been voidable, but to remove some Prohibited Degrees altogether. Far from equalising the sexes, it would introduce a new disparity, viz. that a husband could marry his wife's sister while a woman could not marry her husband's brother. Arguments for confining the issue to the deceased wife's sister were implausible. Suggesting that all those related only by affinity should be allowed to marry was evidently too radical to do anything but lose support for any change.

The defenders of the status quo were in the happier position of having a clear and straightforward principle to defend, as Winston Churchill expressed it in 1903, 'the principle, . . . that when a man and a woman were married they became as one, and . . . any person the man could not marry by reason of consanguinity to himself he could also not marry if similarly related to his wife'.[86] Bereft of a principle of their own which they could air, promoters of legalisation of marriage with a deceased wife's sister could do no better than try to weaken their opponents' position by arguing, not very effectively, that they too were inconsistent.

The fact that marriage with a deceased wife's sister (and subsequently other in-laws) was finally legalised in the early twentieth century probably owed something to coincidental factors. By then it was allowed in colonial countries,[87] and the House of Lords, a bastion of opposition to the Deceased Wife's Sister's Marriage Bill, having rejected it 18 times when the House of Commons had passed it, was in an increasingly weak position under the threat of the reform which overtook it in 1911.[88] But it seems very likely that the passage of the Bill, and the consequent legalisation of marriage with other affinal relatives also owed much to the changes which had been taking place while it was under discussion, especially to the reduced implications of the view that husband and wife were 'as one' and to the already dwindling consequences of relationship in general.

3. Twentieth-century Changes

With hindsight, it seems evident that opponents of the Deceased Wife's Sister's Marriage Bill were right in considering it to be a more general attack on the Prohibited Degrees of Affinity than its promoters were prepared to admit. Legalisation of marriage with a deceased wife's sister in 1907 was followed comparatively swiftly and easily by further reductions in restrictions on the marriage of in-laws.

Predictably the next relative to go was the other sister-in-law, a brother's widow. In 1921, the Deceased Wife's Sister's Marriage Act was amended to 'remove the anomaly in the present law which prohibits marriage with a deceased brother's widow although marriage with a deceased wife's sister is legal'.[89] There was little opposition. Many were unaware of the change. In 1956 E.M. Forster could still believe that it had not taken place.[90] The Deceased Brother's Widow's Marriage Act of 1921 was followed four years later by the annual introduction of further amending Bills, which issued in 1931 in the Marriage (Prohibited Degrees of Relationship) Act.[91] This Act legalised marriage between a man and his deceased wife's aunts and nieces and his nephews' and uncles' widows.

After an extensive Commission appointed in 1937 and reporting three years later, the Church of England, which until then continued to forbid marriage between any affinal relatives,[92] came into line with the then Statute law in the first year of World War II, in 1940.[93] The Commission was assisted by such eminent figures as Haldane and Malinowski. The latter advised that changes in the composition of the English household, which now included fewer relatives, had helped to remove the need for the prohibitions.[94] In 1960 an Act of Parliament allowed all the corresponding relatives of a divorced person to marry.[95] The Church of England disliked marriage between any divorced persons and would not consider it until 1983, and even then it met opposition so that in 1985 the question was still being debated.[96]

At present the only remaining restrictions on marriages between affinal relatives are between those in the so-called direct line, that is, with the direct ascendants and descendants of dead and divorced husbands and wives, and these are in the process of disappearing.

In 1978 and 1979 Bills to legalise these marriages too were proposed. By this time the Baroness Wootton of Abinger could argue this did not 'herald moral or social revolution . . . [but] attempts only to bring to its logical conclusion a development which has been going on throughout the greater part of this century'.[97] The Bills failed.[98] However, individuals succeeded in obtaining private Acts of Parliament to permit them to marry. In 1980 a personal Bill to enable one Mr Berry to marry his step-daughter, Mrs Ward, his deceased wife's daughter, was accepted by the House of Lords. Its passage was untroublesome, if sufficiently noteworthy for some front page reports in *The Times* and mentions on the television news.[99] Similar Bills went through in 1982 without publicity, one allowing a marriage with a deceased wife's daughter, the other a marriage with a father's widow (= deceased husband's son).[100] In the meantime, in 1981 a modified version of the 1979 General Marriage (Enabling) Bill was rejected, and in 1982 another, this time to affect only step-parents and step-children, was withdrawn in favour of an Enquiry.[101] In the same year (1982) the Archbishop of Canterbury appointed a Group on Affinity to consider the legalisation of marriage between 'step-relations', that is, betweeen a person and his or her parent's spouse/spouse's child. By the time it reported, in June 1984, it also considered the other remaining affinal relatives, a descendant's spouse and spouse's ascendant, who rate as in-laws, not step-relations. It recommended by a small majority that they should all be permitted to marry, except that step-parents and step-children should not be allowed to do so until the younger was 18 years of age, or 21 years if they had lived in the same household.[102] A Minority Report recommended that step-parents and step-children who had never 'lived together such that one was a child in the family of the other'[103] should be allowed to marry if both were over 18 years of age. Similarly what they called grandstep-parents and grandstep-children. It favoured removing the restriction between grandparents-in-law and grand-children-in-law but not between parents-in-law and children-in-law (i.e. spouse's parent and child's spouse) nor between step-parents and step-children (i.e. parent's spouse and spouse's child) if one had ever been a part of the other's family.[104] A month later, in July 1984, *The Times* bore a headline 'Man's wish to marry his ex-mother-in-law to be considered by Parliament.'[105] It appears that legalising marriage between the remaining affines is only a matter of time.

In 1908, the year after the notorious deceased wife's sister issue was settled, Parliament passed an Act that it had rejected a few years earlier, in 1903. It attracted little opposition or attention at the time. This was the Punishment of Incest Act of 1908, which made incest a criminal offence for the first time, subject to 3–7 years penal servitude or 2 years imprisonment.[106]

Incest, for centuries an ecclesiastical offence for which ex-communication or public penance (later commutable into 6 months imprisonment)[107] could be exacted, had by then been unpunishable for half a century. The Matrimonial Causes Act of 1857 transferred jurisdiction over matrimonial cases to other courts, but failed to make any provision for the punishment of incest. This may have been sheer inadvertence. But there were also persons at the time with a strong interest in going free if they committed incest. The marriages that had been rendered void by the 1835 Act continued to take place, especially abroad. The 1848 Commission on marriage between affinal relatives had reported them to be quite common,[108] and marriages within the Prohibited Degrees contracted in countries where the marriages in question were legal were still of uncertain status in 1857. In 1861, in the case of Brook v. Brook (House of Lords),[109] which concerned a man's marriage to his deceased wife's sister in Denmark, it was decided that such marriages too were void unless the parties were domiciled abroad. By all accounts concubinage 'of an incestuous nature' continued to take place nevertheless, in some cases under the aegis of marriage ceremonies in distant parishes.

In any case, whether accidentally or not, no one could be in trouble for incest between 1857 and 1908. The 1908 Act was ostensibly designed to fill a rather obvious gap. It applied its penalties to intercourse with specified relatives which took place with knowledge of relationship.

The Punishment of Incest Act was of more moment than it may seem at first sight. The reason for this is not the point which was mainly discussed, the introduction of a new sexual offence or making incest a crime. It was, after all, scarcely a serious departure to have a penalty for it. What was novel, indeed almost revolutionary, was the narrow range of relatives included: mother, sister, half-sister, daughter and granddaughter, that is, blood relatives only, and (since grandmothers are apt to be omitted) in effect blood relatives in the second degree. Intercourse between third degree blood relatives who still cannot be married is not now incest, nor is intercourse between affinal relatives in the direct line who are forbidden to marry.[110]

The 1907 Deceased Wife's Sister's Marriage Act specifically declared that adultery between a man and his living wife's sister was to continue to rate as incestuous adultery and thus to furnish grounds on which his wife could divorce him. The Deceased Brother's Widow's Marriage Act of 1921 made a similar provision about adultery with a brother's wife.[111] The category of incestuous adultery disappeared from English law in 1923 when a woman could divorce her husband for any sort of adultery.[112]

The importance of the new narrower application of 'incest' lay originally in the fact that it rapidly promoted a different concept of incest, which became highly influential among the new experts in the field, sociologists and social anthropologists, many of them English or resident in England. The extensive literature produced shows little sign of recognising that in England intercourse between affinal relations was for many centuries on a footing with and as much incest as intercourse between close blood relations.

The 'Incest Taboo' which achieved prominence in many well-known English, as well as other, anthropologists' works was the limited prohibition introduced by the 1908 Incest Act.

It is probable that the Act will also prove to have been of practical significance to the marriage law. In the progressive erosion of the Prohibited Degrees, there are some natural stages. Nearly thirty years separate the legalisation of marriage with the relatives of a deceased spouse in 1931 from legalisation of marriage with the same relatives of a divorced spouse (1960). Another twenty years elapsed before any inroads were made in the next area, that of affinal relatives in the direct line. So far no attempt has been made to reduce the Prohibited Degrees among blood relatives. But if this comes to be mooted, which seems not unlikely, the most obvious first move would be the removal of restrictions on marriage between relations in the third degree, intercourse between whom has specifically not been incest for nearly three-quarters of a century.

By 1980, the Punishment of Incest Act was under review. The Criminal Law Revision Commmittee was discussing reductions of penalty and range of relatives and even considering the elimination of the category of 'incest' altogether.[113] 'The name "incest" was thought by some . . . to be undesirably emotive . . .', and they proposed the substitution of 'unlawful familial intercourse' as 'less likely to arouse strong feelings'. This did not find favour with the majority which preferred 'the continued use of the term "incest", considering that it will serve to mark the strong disapproval of such conduct generally felt in the community'.[114] In its final Report in 1984, the Committee confirmed that 'the name "incest" should be retained to describe the offence between blood relatives'[115] and with an adopted child, and recommended the creation of an analogous, if separate, offence of 'unlawful sexual intercourse' with a step-child under 21. It did not suggest reducing the penalty for incest, but it did propose that children and grandchildren under 21 should be exempted from convictions, and that sexual relations between brothers and sisters should 'cease to be an offence where they have both reached the age of 21'.[116]

Notes

1. J.F. McLennan *Primitive Marriage. An Inquiry into the Origin of the Form of Capture in Marriage Ceremonies* Edinburgh 1865.

1A. See above Figure 1.2.

2. J.J. Scarisbrick *Henry VIII* 1968, Penguin edn. 1971.

3. An Act concerning the King's Succession 1533, 25 H 8 c 22 sec 3 and An Act concerning Succession of the Crown 1536, 28 H 8 c 7 sec 11.

4. A Provision for Dispensations &c 1536, 28 H 8 c 16 sec 2 and Concerning Precontracting & Degrees of Consanguinity 1540, 32 H 8 c 38.

5. An Act Declaring the Queen's Highness to have been born in most Just and Holy Matrimony 1553, 1 Mary 2 c 1 sec 8, repealed the first pair of Statutes; An Act repealing all Articles and provisions made against the See Apostolick of Rome since the 20th year of King Henry VIII 1554, 1 & 2 P & M c 8 sec 16 repealed the second pair.

6. The Act of Supremacy 1558, 1 Eliz I c 1 secs 10 and 11.

7. Published in 1563. It was adopted into the canons of the Church of England (canon 99), given royal assent in 1603, and required to be in every Church publicly set up and fixed at the charge of the Parish.

8. See above Figure 1.2.

9. See Chapter 4, Section 2 for a slightly different mode of deriving it.

9A. See Chapter 6, note 11A for description of the common law courts (and Equity). The ecclesiastical courts consisted of local Bishops' courts with appeal to the courts of the Archbishops of Canterbury and York, and thence, after 1832, to the Privy Council. They exercised jurisdiction over clergy, and until 1857 over matrimonial cases and wills bequeathing property.

10. E. Vaughan *Report & Arguments of that Learned Judge Sir John Vaughan Kt . . .* London 1677, pp. 302−29.

11. R. v. Chadwick and R. v. St. Giles-in-the-Field reported in J.L. Adolphus and T.F. Ellis *Queen's Bench Reports* (new series) London 18 vols 1843−56, vol 11 (1850) pp. 205−44 and pp. 173−247.

12. Scarisbrick *Henry VIII*, p. 249ff.

13. D. Defoe *The Fortunes and Misfortunes of the famous Moll Flanders &c* 1722, Rinehart edn. 1949 (printed from the third edn.) pp. 20−55.

14. An Act to dissolve the marriage of *Jane Campbell* with *Edward Addison*, her now husband on Account of Incestuous Adultery with the Sister of the said Jane Campbell, 1801 41 Geo 3 *c 102*.

15. In M.C.M. Swabey and T.H. Tristram *Reports of Cases decided in the Court of Probate & in the Court of Divorce and Matrimonial Cases*, London 4 vols 1860−71, vol 2 pp. 278−99.

16. Scarisbrick *Henry VIII*, Chapter 7.

17. W. Salkeld *Reports of Cases Adjudged in the Court of the King's Bench* London 3 vols 1795, ii p. 548.

18. R. v. Sherwood & Ray 1837 in W.C. Curteis *Reports of Cases Argued and Determined in the Ecclesiastical Courts at Doctor's Commons* London 3 vols (1840−4) vol i, 1840 n.b. p. 202ff.

19. J. Phillimore *Reports of Cases Argued and Determined in the Ecclesiastical Courts at Doctor's Commons; & in the High Court of Delegates* London 3 vols 1818−27: Aughtie v. Aughtie 1810, i, pp. 201−3, Faremouth & others v. Watson 1811, i, pp. 355−7, Elliot & Sudjeon v. Gurr 1812, ii, pp. 16−22, Blackmore & Thorpe v. Brider 1816, ii, pp. 359−63.

20. W. Shakespeare *Hamlet* 1602:

Act 1 sc. ii: Hamlet (of his mother):
  married with my uncle,
  My father's brother . . . within a month . . .
  She married. O, most wicked speed to post
  With such dexterity to incestuous sheets . . .

Act 1 sc. v: Ghost (Hamlet's father about his own brother who murdered
him):
  Ay that incestuous, that adulterate beast
  . . . won to his shameful lust
  The will of my most seeming virtuous queen
  . . . damned incest . . .

Act 3 sc. iii:
  . . . the incestuous pleasure of his bed.

Act 5 sc. ii:
  He that hath killed my king, and whored my mother . . .

21. Defoe *Moll Flanders*, p. 55.

22. (Mrs) Addison 1801, 41 Geo 3 *c 102*; (Earl of) Rosebery 1815, 55 Geo 3
c 104; (Mrs Turton), 1 & 2 W 4 *c 35*. When the divorce was procured by women
as with Mrs Addison and Mrs Turton, the acts referred to the 'incestuous
adultery' of the husband. Women unlike men were not able to get divorces for
adultery simpliciter. See Chapter 5. Heathcote's divorce Act of 1851, 14 & 15 Vic
c 24, where the wife's adultery was with her full brother was unusual for the
period in bastardising issue of the adulterous union but did not mention incest
nor forbid the parties to it to marry. The incest was irrelevant, adultery being
sufficient for the divorce of a wife and marriages within the prohibited degrees
were by then in any case void.

23. With Lord Lyndhurst's Act 5 & 6 Wm 4 c 54 (1835).

24. Brook v. Brook, House of Lords 1861, ruled that such marriages were
void even when celebrated abroad unless the parties were domiciled abroad. See
Chapter 2, Section 3.

25. The Matrimonial Causes Act 1857 20 & 21 Vic c 85 sec 27.

26. The Marriage Act 1835 5 & 6 Wm 4 c 54 (known as Lord Lyndhurst's
Act). The Act was much criticised for its inconsistent treatment of affinity, and
Lord Lyndhurst was still explaining 'the Bill which passes under my name' in
Parliament in 1858. It was an 'Act to limit the time for commencing suits . . . so
far as they may affect the children of parents married within the prohibited
degrees'. The circumstance leading to the introduction of the Bill 'was the
marriage a noble Lord of high rank in this House': the result was 'as happens in
many other cases, that a particular instance of hardship led to a general allevia-
tion in the state of the law'. Lord Lyndhurst explained how the 'whole character
of the Bill was entirely changed in committee . . . The history of the measure is
quite curious' *Hansard* 3rd series vol 151, 1974−6 (et seq) (Lords 1858).

27. The Deceased Wife's Sister's Marriage Act 1907 Edw 7 c 47.

28. The second reading is usually the critical stage in the passage of a Bill.
There are three readings in each House i.e. the Bill is discussed three times. It
proceeds further only if it receives a majority vote. It is also sent to Committee
(i.e. a subsection of the House) usually after the second reading. Many are
radically altered, or lost, at that stage. After passing through Parliament, it must
receive Royal assent. Then it is an 'Act' i.e. law.

29. 1842, 1845, 1849, also 1851 and 1855. The Bill of 1850 and all Bills after

1858 included the wife's sister only. Before the late 1860s Bills usually had titles like Marriages Bill, Marriage Law Amendment Bill, Marriages of Affinity Bill. For simplicity I use the title of the later Bills 'The Marriage with a Deceased Wife's Sister Bill' to refer to all Bills attempting to legalise marriage with a deceased wife's sister.

30. *First Report of the Commissioners Appointed to Inquire into the State and Operation of the law of Marriage as Relating to the Prohibited Degrees of Affinity, and to Marriages Solemnised Abroad or in the British Colonies* London 1848, Cmd 973, reprinted *British Parliamentary Papers* vol 1, Dublin 1969.

31. Ibid. 1848, p. viii.

32. Ibid. 1848, p. xii.

33. J.T. Hammick *The Marriage Law of England* second revision and enlarged edition 1887, pp. 33−4.

34. A bibliography of 1887 by A. Huth in *The Marriage of Near Kin considered with respect to the laws of nations, the results of experience, and the teachings of biology*, second revision and enlarged edition 1887, lists about 250 pamphlets between 1840 and 1887. I have found at least 50 more between those dates, as well as later ones. Quotations and references from this literature are intended as examples only. The same points can be found in almost any debate or pamphlet on the subject. Tracts of the Marriage Law Defence Union were published in two volumes in 1889 as well as separately at earlier dates. They are referred to by number (without author or original date). Details may be found in the Bibliography.

35. From 1836 onwards marriage could take place in a Registry Office, instead of as before only in a Church, or certain other accredited places of worship. See Chapter 5 and Chapter 6, Section 2. The Church could, and still can, refuse to allow a couple permitted by law to marry from celebrating their marriage in a church.

36. *Hansard* 3rd series vol 56, 703 (House of Commons 1842). See also e.g. *Hansard* 3rd series vol 114, 983 (Lords 1851); 4th series vol 92, 1206 (Lords 1896); vol 102, 479 (Commons 1902); anonymous [1850] *An Earnest Address on the proposed Alteration in the Law of Marriage*, p. 7; W.P. Wood *A Vindication of the Law prohibiting Marriage with a Deceased Wife's Sister?*, 1861 p. 20; H.W. Simpson 'An Argument to Prove that Marriage with a Deceased Wife's Sister is forbidden by Scripture' 1860 in C.W. Holgate *A Memorial of H.W. Simpson* 1902, pp. 130−5, Marriage Law Defence Union no 30, p. 17.

37. Anonymous [H.R. Reynolds] (A Barrister of the Middle Temple) *Considerations on the State of the Law regarding Marriage with a Deceased Wife's Sister* 1840, p. 7. See also e.g. R. Bickersteth etc. *Marriage with a Deceased Wife's Sister* 1851, pp. 8−12; *Hansard* 3rd series vol 163, 302 (Commons 1866); *Hansard* 3rd series vol 200, 1941 (Commons 1870).

38. *Hansard* 3rd series vol 270, 777 (Lords 1882). See also e.g. T.C. Foster *A Review of the Law relating to Marriages within the Prohibited Degrees of Affinity and the Canons and Social Considerations by which the law is supposed to be justified* 1847, pp. 129−31; anonymous [H.F. Bacon] Συγγένεια *A dispassionate Appeal to the Judgment of the Church of England on a Proposed Alteration of the Law of Marriage* 1849, pp. 39−42; *Hansard* 3rd series vol 138, 268 (Commons 1855); anonymous (One who does not want to) *Should Englishmen be Permitted to Marry their Deceased Wives' Sisters?* 1883, p. 7ff; *Hansard* 3rd series vol 305, 1797 (Lords 1886); *Hansard* 4th series vol 92, 1190−1 (Commons 1901).

39. See e.g. *Hansard* 3rd series vol 350, 416 (Commons 1891) and anonymous [Reynolds] *Considerations* 1840, pp. 54−6.

40. *Hansard* 3rd series vol 201, 902 (Lords 1872).

41. See e.g. *Hansard* 3rd series vol 205, 646 (Lords 1871); vol 270, 777−8

(Lords 1882); 4th series vol 42, 1208 (Lords 1896).

42. *Hansard* 3rd series vol 104, 1169 (Commons 1849).

43. *Hansard* 3rd series vol 209, 806 (Commons 1872).

44. See Chapter 3 for mourning conventions.

45. *Hansard* 3rd series vol 106, 612 (Commons 1849). See also e.g. *Hansard* 3rd series vol 270, 798–9 (Lords 1882).

46. Beresford Hope in the Commons, probably 1859, quoted in anonymous (B.A.W.) *The Woman's Question and the Man's Answer; or, Reflections on the Social Consequences of Legalizing Marriage with a Deceased Wife's sister* 1859, p. 15.

47. *Hansard* 3rd series vol 106, 630 (Commons 1849).

48. *Hansard* 3rd series vol 205, 650 (Lords 1871).

49. Anonymous (A Member of the University of Oxford) *Marriage with a Deceased Wife's Sister in a Social Point of View Inexpedient and Unnatural* 1858, pp. 13–14. See also e.g. Marriage Law Defence Union no 15, p. 4; H.N. Oxenham *The Deceased Wife's Sister Bill considered in its Social and Religious Aspects* 1885, p. 20.

50. *Hansard* 3rd series vol 104, 1102 (Commons 1849). See also e.g. *Hansard* 3rd series vol 183, 302–3 (Commons 1866).

51. *Hansard* 3rd series vol 205, 646 (Lords 1871).

52. *Hansard* 3rd series vol 270, 781 (Lords 1882).

53. *Hansard* 3rd series vol 150, 126 (Commons 1858). See also e.g. *Hansard* 3rd series vol 205, 653 (Lords 1871); vol 270, 780–1, 794 (Lords 1882).

54. *Hansard* 3rd series vol 270, 800 (Lords 1882).

55. Marriage Law Defence Association (A Sister and a Widow) no 5 *An Englishwoman's Letter to the Right Honourable Sir Robert Harry Inglis, bart. M.P. on the proposed Alteration of the Marriage Law* 1849, p. 3.

56. Ibid. 1849. See also e.g. *Hansard* 3rd series vol 104, 1237 (Commons 1849); Marriage Law Defence Union no 26, p. 9; C. Wordsworth *An Address on Marriage with a Deceased Wife's Sister*, pp. 9–10.

57. *Hansard* 3rd series vol 195, 1317 (Commons 1869). See also e.g. *Hansard* 3rd series vol 205, 645 (Lords 1871); *Hansard* 3rd series vol 270, 795 (Lords 1882).

58. J.F. Denham *Marriage with a Deceased Wife's Sister not Forbidden by the law of Nature, not Dissuaded by Expediency, not Prohibited by the Scriptures* 1847, p. 7.

59. See e.g. *Hansard* 3rd series vol 205, 648 (Lords 1871); *Hansard* 3rd series vol 335, 1485 (Lords 1889); anonymous *The Reply to Mr Commissioner Kerr's 'Question in Common Law'* 1864, p. 12; anonymous (A Solicitor) *Observations on the Deceased Wife's Sister Question* 1872, pp. 21–2.

60. See Chapter 2, Section 1.

61. See e.g. *Hansard* 3rd series vol 104, 1198 (Commons 1849); anonymous [Reynolds] *Considerations* 1840, p. 21ff; anonymous (A Graduate in Classical and Mathematical Honours, Cambridge, of BD Standing) *The Present State and the Proposed State of the Marriage Law, Theologically, Morally, Socially and Legally Considered* 1864a, pp. 9–15.

62. See Chapter 2, Section 1.

63. See e.g. *Hansard* 3rd series vol 104, 1212–15 (Commons 1849); Marriage Law Defence Union nos 22 and 45; Marriage Law Defence Association no 8 *Remarks on Dr. McCaul's Plea from Lev. xviii, 18, for Marrying a Deceased Wife's Sister*.

64. See e.g. *Hansard* 3rd series vol 150, 119ff (Commons 1848); Marriage Law Defence Union no 39, p. 37.

65. See e.g. *Hansard* 3rd series vol 137, 513 (Commons 1855). It was often

quoted, e.g. *Hansard* 3rd series vol 138, 256 (Commons 1855); Marriage Law Defence Union no 43, p. 9.

66. Matthew xix, 6; Mark x, 8; Ephesians v, 31.

66A. *Hansard* 3rd series 201, 948 (Lords, 1870).

66B. Marriage Law Defence Union no 4, p. 3.

66C. Marriage Law Defence Union no. 8, p. 17.

67. F.A. Dawson *May a Man marry his Deceased Wife's Sister?* 1859, pp. 4–5. See also e.g. anonymous (An Anxious Observer) *Marriage with a Deceased Wife's Sister Forbidden by the Word of God* 1869, pp. 3–4; Wood *A Vindication* 1861, p. 17. Philadelphus [F. Pott] *Marriage with a Deceased Wife's Sister* 1885, pp. 29–32.

68. See e.g. F. Hockin *Marriage with a Deceased Wife's Sister Forbidden by the Law of God* [1881] pp. 16ff; J. Le Mesurier *A few Words on the Real Bearings of the Proposed Change in the Marriage Law from a Clergyman to his Parishioners* 1883, pp. 15–17; C. Wordsworth *An Address* 1883, pp. 11–12; Marriage Law Defence Union no 12, p. 5; no 30, p. 17; no 34, pp. 3–4; *Hansard* 4th series vol 42, 1198 (Lords 1896).

69. I have found no more than eight instances in the whole course of the debates in 1851, 1855, 1869, 1870, 1873, 1875, 1882, 1902 (references in Chapter 7, Section 1). Lord John Russell also made a reluctant statement to the effect that he felt that the prohibition of marriage with the wife's sister must be removed, and that he could see no other principle, except that of consanguinity, on which the marriage law could then be based (*Hansard* 3rd series vol 152, 455 (Commons 1859)). The statement was quoted against him for years after: see e.g. Marriage Law Defence Union no 43, p. 9.

70. See e.g. anonymous [Reynolds] *Considerations* 1840, pp. 41–2; anonymous [Bacon] Συγγένεια 1849, pp. 10–12; anonymous (One who does not want to) *Should Englishmen* 1883, p. 3; M. Mensor *The Question Solved: or, Inquiry into the law of Marriage with a Deceased Wife's Sister* [c. 1885], p. 21; *Hansard* 3rd series vol 109, 84 (Commons 1849); *Hansard* 3rd series vol 205, 648 (Lords 1871); *Hansard* 3rd series vol 280, 170 (Lords 1883); *Hansard* 3rd series vol 305, 1811 (Lords 1886); *Hansard* 4th series, vol 932 (Commons, 1905).

71. See e.g. J. Macrae *The Scriptural Law of Marriage with reference to the Prohibited Degrees* 1861, p. 10; anonymous (An Anxious Observer) *Marriage . . . Forbidden* 1869, pp. 11–14; Philadelphus [F.Pott] *Marriage with* 1885, p. 30; *Hansard* 3rd series vol 138, 245 (Commons 1855).

72. See e.g. Marriage Law Defence Union no 39, pp. 9–10.

73. J.F. Phelps *The Divine Authority of the 'Table of Prohibited Degrees'* 1883, pp. 32–3.

74. *Hansard* 3rd series vol 201, 896–7 (Lords 1870). See also e.g. J.F. Denham *Marriage . . . not Forbidden* 1847, p. 9; anonymous (A Graduate in Classical and Mathematical Honours) *The Present State* 1864a, p. 28.

75. Mensor *The Question Solved* [c. 1885], p. 23.

76. See e.g. H.H. Duke *The Question of Incest relatively to the Marriage of Sisters in Succession* 1882, p. 55ff; Macrae *The Scriptural Law of Marriage* 1861, p. 10.

77. See e.g. G.C.M. Douglas *The law of the Bible as to Prohibited Degrees of Marriage* 1858, p. 14ff; Marriage Law Defence Union no 53, p. 6.

78. See e.g. P. Hale *Marriage with a Deceased Wife's Sister repugnant to Christian Feeling and contrary to Christian Practice* 1848, pp. 11–12; Douglas *The Law of the Bible* 1858, p. 16; anonymous *Marriage with a Deceased Wife's Sister forbidden to Christians* 1886.

79. See e.g. T. Binney *The Men of Glasgow and the Women of Scotland* [n.d. probably c. 1878] pp. 40–2; anonymous (A Graduate in Classical and

Mathematical Honours) *The Present State* 1864a, Chapter 3; anonymous (A Philosophical Inquirer) *The present state of the Marriage Law proved unscriptural and the proposed illogical* 1860, pp. 6—10 [internal evidence suggests that this is by the same author as anonymous (A Graduate in Classical and Mathematical Honours) 1864a (see above)]; anonymous *The Reply* 1864, p. 13ff; R.C. Jenkins *The Repeal of the prohibitions of marriage with a deceased wife's sister advocated, Doctrinally; Historically; Socially* 1883, p. 12; A. McCaul *The Ancient Interpretation of Leviticus xviii, 18, as received in the Church for more than 1500 years, a sufficient apology for holding that, according to the Word of God, marriage with a deceased wife's sister is lawful* 1859, p. 36ff; Mensor *The Question Solved* [c. 1885], pp. 25—6.

80. Binney *The Men of Glasgow* [n.d.], p. 42. Italics in the original.

81. See e.g. J.F. Thrupp *The Christian inference from Leviticus xviii, 16, sufficient ground for holding that according to the Word of God Marriage with the Deceased wife's sister is unlawful. A letter to the Rev Dr. McCaul* 1859, p. 7ff; Marriage Law Defence Union no 39, pp. 7—8.

82. See e.g. Mensor *The Question Solved* [c. 1885], p. 24ff.

83. This latest discovery was that 'a female who has had children by one father generally imparts some of his characteristics (which means his flesh according to all modern science) to all future children by another father; but nothing of the kind takes place between successive mothers and the same father' *Hansard* 3rd series vol 335, 1514 (Lords 1889). See also e.g. anonymous (A Graduate in Classical and Mathematical Honours) *The Present State* 1864a, pp. 17—18.

84. Thrupp *The Christian inference* 1859, pp. 14—15.

85. A. Trollope *The Eustace Diamonds* London 1876, Chapter 26.

86. *Hansard* 4th series vol 121, 1111 (Commons 1903).

87. It was allowed in New Zealand in 1880 (A. Watson *Legal Transplants. An Approach to Comparative Law* Edinburgh 1974, p. 71), soon before or after in South Australia, and then other parts of Australia, Canada, South Africa, Channel Islands (1899), etc. (*Encyclopaedia Britannica* 14th edn. 1929 vol 14, p. 953).

88. The Parliament Act of 1911, 1 and 2 Geo 5 c 13, removed the power of the House of Lords over Money Bills and to do more than delay other Bills. If a Bill was passed in three successive sessions by the House of Commons within two years, rejections by the House of Lords could not henceforth prevent it becoming law.

89. Deceased Brother's Widow's Marriage Act 1921 11 and 12 Geo 5 c 24.

90. E.M. Forster *Marianne Thornton* 1956, p. 198: 'A man is permitted to marry his deceased wife's sister today. A woman is still impeded in marrying her deceased husband's brother'.

91. The Marriage (Prohibited Degrees of Relationship) Act 1931 21 and 22 Geo 5 c 31.

92. No clergyman was relieved of ecclesiastical censure if he performed such a marriage.

93. Church of England Commission *Kindred and Affinity as Impediments to Marriage*, 1940.

94. B. Malinowski in 'A sociological analysis of the rationale of the Prohibited Degrees of Marriage' Appendix 3 in Church of England Commission *Kindred and Affinity*.

95. Marriage Enabling Act 8 and 9 Eliz 2 c 29.

96. See e.g. *The Times*, 15 July 1983, p. 1 col 3: 'Remarriage in church approved', *The Times* 1 February 1985, p. 3 cols 1—3: 'Bishops leave clergymen to decide on marrying divorced people in church'.

97. *Hansard* 5th series vol 398, 1107 (Lords [13 February] 1979) quoted by

B.M. Hoggett and D.S. Pearl *The Family, Law and Society* London 1983, p. 22.

98. Both Bills were introduced in the House of Lords as Marriage (Enabling) Bill. The first was overtaken by a General Election. The same Bill, re-introduced, was defeated on second reading in June 1979 [14 June].

99. Edward Berry and Doris Eilleen Ward (Marriage Enabling) Act 1980 (*c 1*). See S. Wolfram 'Drawing the marriage Lines' *The Guardian*, 24 June 1980, for some comments on this private Act.

100. John Francis Dare and Gillian Lodel Dare (Marriage Enabling Act) 1982 (*c 1*) and Hugh Small and Norma Small (Marriage Enabling Act) 1982 (*c 2*).

101. For details see Church of England, Archbishop of Canterbury's Group *No Just Cause. The Law of Affinity in England & Wales: Some suggestions for change* London 1984, Appendix II, pp. 114−19.

102. Church of England, Archbishop of Canterbury's Group *No Just Cause. The Law of Affinity in England & Wales: Some suggestions for change* 1984, Chapter 12, pp. 91−5. See also below Chapter 7, note 29.

103. Ibid. p. 109.

104. Ibid. Chapter 13, pp. 96-110. The House of Bishops of the Church of England favoured the Minority Report recommendations [Letter of January 1985].

105. *The Times* 5 July 1984, p. 3 cols 1−3.

106. The Deceased Wife's Sister's Marriage Act 1907, 8 Edw 7 c 45. The Act has since been extensively discussed inter alia in V. Bailey and S. Blackburn 'The Punishment of Incest Act 1908. A case study in law creation' [1979] *Criminal Law Review* p. 708ff and, in reply, S. Wolfram 'Eugenics and the Punishment of Incest Act 1908' [1983] *Criminal Law Review* p. 308ff. See also below Chapter 7, Section 1.

107. Ecclesiastical Courts Act 1813 53 Geo 3 c 127.

108. See Chapter 2, Section 2.

109. Brook v. Brook House of Lords 1861.

110. The Criminal Law Revision Committee 15th Report *Sexual Offences* London 1984 HMSO Cmd 9213 proposed that sexual relations with step-children under 21 should become an offence 'analogous to incest' but called 'unlawful sexual intercourse' p. 70, para 8.31, p. 73, 8.44 (6). See also Chapter 7, Section 1, notes 29 and 30.

111. The Deceased Brother's Widow's Marriage Act 1921 11 and 12 Geo 5 c 24 sec 2.

112. Matrimonial Causes Act 13 and 14 Geo 5 c 19.

113. Home Office, Criminal Law Revision Committee, *Working Paper on Sexual Offences*, October 1980, HMSO paras 108−29.

114. Ibid. para 129.

115. Criminal Law Revision Committee *Sexual Offences* 1984, p. 72, 8.39.

116. Ibid. p. 73, 8.44. See Chapter 7, Section 1.

3   Degree Reckoning in Mourning

By no means all matters concerning kinship are subject to legislation.

An obvious exception in England is the treatment of extra-marital intercourse. Adultery on the part of a woman was and is grounds for divorce, but, apart from a brief period under Oliver Cromwell, it was never punished at law, even when it was considered an act of extreme turpitude, except in the case of the Consort to the Sovereign where the penalty is death. The penalties, as we know from fiction of the period and other sources, were standardised but a matter of informal social action: various degrees of social ostracism. Thus in Jane Austen's *Mansfield Park* (1814) Maria Rushworth is instantly divorced by her husband after her adulterous union with Henry Crawford and has to live in total seclusion. She is thought to have shamed her family, who would never again receive her, and the inference is drawn that she lacked moral principle or she could not so have given way to her passions as to elope.[1]

In real life at the same time (1814–1815) the more attractive young Countess of Rosebery, mother of four children, suffered a similar fate. Her secret adultery with Sir John Mildmay, her dead sister's husband, was discovered in late 1814 and the guilty couple fled abroad. A particularly notorious divorce case followed. *The Times*'s reports and discussions suggest that there was some sympathy for her, even for her paramour, because of their future sufferings, but none for the offence, which was one not only against her husband but against public morality.[2] A previously 'amiable and beloved wife', she was likely to be 'secluded for the rest of her days away from her country, with the man who had reduced her to this hopeless situation, with no associates but the acquaintance of men as profligate as herself'.[3]

Even the taint of an accusation of adultery brought some degree of ostracism. In *The Claverings*, which Trollope published in 1867, a widowed countess, Lady Ongar, had been falsely accused of adultery by her profligate husband. People do not call, even the housekeeper on her inherited estate will engage in only the most formal conversation and she lives in a state of almost complete isolation. 'She was alone, and all the world was turning its back on her'.[4]

Pre-marital intercourse by a woman was somewhat less culpable. It brought shame to herself and her family and was likely to stand in the way of another marriage, but, especially if patched up by marriage to the seducer, was just tolerable. In Jane Austen's *Pride and Prejudice* (1813) Lydia Bennet elopes with the attractive and wicked Wickham. He is persuaded to marry her, she is received by her family, if only after protest by her father that it is an insult to the neighbourhood, and suffers no further penalties, although care is taken that she should live at a distance.[5] In *The Mill on the Floss* (1860), Maggie Tulliver who spends an innocent night away with a man she refuses to marry is ostracised, although George Eliot makes it clear that had a marriage ensued, she would have been not merely received but fawned on.[6]

Examples could readily be multiplied from fiction or fact to illustrate the point that there were conventional social penalties for different sorts of illicit union. It would be interesting to trace their development, perhaps along with the sanctions society continued to use against divorce even after it had been what was known as 'legalised' in 1857.

I want, however, to turn to a different area to demonstrate the point that there may be rigid kinship customs which are a matter of convention and not of law. I have other objects in choosing the custom in question, that of mourning. One is to show that the degree reckoning employed in the Prohibited Degrees was equally in use, virtually unconsciously, in other areas of kinship where lawyers played no part and those articulating the custom might be quite ignorant of legal computations of kinship. Another is to suggest that here as elsewhere there is evidence of the decline in what relationship involved by the late nineteenth century.

According to the Oxford English Dictionary, the word 'mourning' has two meanings. In one sense, which it has had since about the ninth century, to 'mourn' is to grieve. In the other, which it acquired around the sixteenth century, 'mourning' refers to something customarily done at death: in England, until fairly recently, wearing black, withdrawing from society and so on. What was customarily done at death was thought of as an expression of grief. The linguistic union goes along with a connection of thought. Gorer, in *Death, Grief and Mourning* (1965),[6A] was misled into supposing that the 'function' of mourning in the conventional sense was to allow people time for their mourning (= grieving). He believed that English society was at fault in depriving the bereaved of this support by letting the custom lapse.

A study of what actually occurred suggests that as so often the 'function' attributed to a custom in this way is a rationalisation within the society which in no way explains the custom. The idea that going into mourning assists the bereaved is on a par with the common idea that marriage and incest prohibitions rest on the desire to prevent the genetic ill-effects of in-breeding. It is often put forward, but cannot survive even minimal inspection as a mode of explanation: as I hope to show, custom and 'function' are blatantly at variance.[6B] The idea that what was done at death was an expression of grief was however important. In other societies there are other ideas, that the relatives of the dead are polluted for example and must be kept apart to avoid spreading the pollution. Again, the seclusion from society associated with mourning was different from that associated with 'fallen' women. Among other things, women in mourning were 'bereaved', objects of sympathy for the loss they had sustained, not 'guilty' objects of opprobrium for ill conduct.

Whereas marriage prohibitions have been continually discussed by experts, and during the deceased wife's sister controversy by the not so expert, few had much to say about mourning, even in the period of its disappearance from among English customs. To discover what happened or how it was seen by those engaging in it, we have to turn to such relatively slight sources as books of etiquette, memoirs, works of fiction, and some data are difficult to check. For instance, it was often said that mourning was on the decline at dates when there is no evidence of this, and it is almost impossible to ascertain whether this thought is on a par with such beliefs as that morals are not what they were, held at many periods of English history, or whether it was more accurate. In any case, there is clear evidence that in mid-nineteenth-century England the periods of mourning were static, highly conventionalised and, in the case of relations, followed the degree reckoning exactly. The correct periods of mourning were two years or indefinitely for a husband or wife, a year at the death of a parent or child (i.e first degree relatives), six months for brothers and sisters and grandparents/grandchildren (in the second degree) and so on, halving the period for each degree of relationship, down to three weeks for a second cousin.[7]

Curtailment of these periods was permitted only in very special circumstances, in particular when the deceased was peculiarly unworthy, and not because grief had ceased or never begun. It was recognised that there were some relatives whose death caused only the most moderate or no sorrow but it would have been highly improper, indeed almost inconceivable, for someone therefore not to go into mourning or to come out of it on the grounds that he had overcome his grief. If someone could quench his sorrow in less than the appropriate time, he should, as Trollope put it in 1861, 'at any rate not show his power'.[8] The prescribed periods were also not properly exceeded, unless the circumstances were unusual.

Mourning consisted of the wearing of special clothes, coupled with a carefully defined withdrawal from society. The seclusion of the bereaved differed from that of the shamed, among other things in that they lived in the bosom of their families and had the company of their intimate friends. It was worldly gaieties they were supposed to eschew. Although the prescribed periods were identical for men and women, there were far more complex and demanding rules for women than for men, and it is in the rules for women that we can most easily see, and trace the decline of, the custom.

For most of the nineteenth century a man had to wear a black crêpe hatband which was wider the closer his relationship to the deceased. A woman's mourning was divided into depths or stages in which she wore different clothes and jewellery. Mourning began with a depth appropriate to the relationship to the deceased and was gradually lightened until the end of the total period for that relative was reached. In the 1870s for instance 'deep' mourning clothes had to be made of black stuff and crêpe. This was modified to black trimmed with crêpe in 'second' or ordinary mourning, and to black and white without crêpe when 'half' mourning was reached. Most of the clothes were considered rather unbecoming. To make them attractive was not quite in the spirit of the thing.[9]

A man was not supposed to go to balls or other large social gatherings, nor should he go hunting or shooting, or make proposals of marriage in the early stages of mourning for a close relative. A woman was secluded from society for very much longer. In Trollope's *The Duke's Children* (1880), young Lord Silverbridge displays no impropriety when he goes to a 'great garden party' where he means to make a proposal of marriage, whereas 'Lady Mary, his sister, could not even be asked, because her mother was hardly more than three months dead but it is understood in the world that women mourn longer than men'.[10] A woman could return to small dinners fairly soon but not to parties or balls, at least during the period when she was wearing crêpe.

Marriage was not supposed to take place during mourning.[10A] In *The Eustace Diamonds* (1876), Trollope depicts Lizzie Greystock, intent on marriage with the dying Sir Florian Eustace, as obliged to hesitate before agreeing to marry just on a year after her father's death, when her mourning was barely up:

> But still the cup might slip from her lips. Her father was now dead but ten months, and what answer could she make, when the common pressing petition for an early marriage was poured into her ear? This was July, and it would never do that he should be left, unmarried, to the rigour of another winter. She looked into his face and knew she had cause for fear . . . Of course she married him in September.[11]

Mourning, like unmarriageability, was not confined to blood relationship. People went into mourning for precisely the same periods for a relative by marriage as for a blood relative of the same degree. Mourning for a mother-in-law was identical to that for a mother. No one supposed fondness or grief to be the same. But, as we have already seen, the relationship was considered for many purposes identical.

It is an important fact that mourning was not confined to relatives. People also went into mourning at the death of certain superiors and their relatives. Servants, for instance, went into mourning at the death of the head of the household and of his relations. The court, armed forces and general public went into mourning at the death of the Sovereign or a close relative of the Sovereign, and the court also went into mourning at the death of important foreign royalty and heads of important states. In these cases, unlike that of relatives, there was no pretence that mourning was voluntary. Servants were put into mourning by the head of the household. The court, armed forces and general public had to follow orders published in the *London Gazette*. Public mourning, that is, when everyone in the country was 'requested to put themselves into decent mourning' did not generally occur more than about once in every five years, and it never exceeded three months at a time.[12] But court mourning was both frequent and long. There was scarcely a year in the nineteenth century when the court did not go into mourning at all, and it might be in mourning or half-mourning for four months of the year, or even the whole year when the Sovereign died. Not surprisingly, a shop, like the once famous Jays of Regent Street, could devote itself entirely to the provision of clothes for mourning.

As there is, and to all intents and purposes has for many years been no formal mourning in England, a question arises as to when the custom died out.

The usual date given for its decline is World War I, when it was indeed particularly rapid. But there is clear evidence that mourning for relatives was growing shorter and less marked by the end of the 1880s, court mourning began to relax from 1904 onwards, and in 1910 the public mourning at the death of Edward VII was shortened from 12 to 8 weeks, allegedly at the request of the drapers who complained that their trade was suffering.[13] 'The war', as a 1927 book of etiquette explained, 'merely crystallised the trend of previous years in regard to mourning. The old and fast laws had been falling into abeyance for a long time'.[14] By 1910 Bernard Shaw could write to the *The Times* of 'people who like myself abhor mourning and have never worn it for their own nearest relatives'.[15]

A custom which is not a matter of law can go gradually. What we find in the case of mourning is that towards the end of the 1880s, the periods of mourning for all but the nearest relatives are regularly given at about two-thirds the periods specified in the 1870s, and mourning for the most distant relatives for whom it had been customary, second cousins, had become optional. There was contemporary comment. Thus in 1888: 'The various periods of mourning have within the last few years been materially shortened.'[16] Or in 1889: 'A great change has passed over society of late years with regard to mourning, which is neither worn so long or so deep as formerly.'[17] At about the same time men began to wear simply a black crêpe armband instead of the various widths of hatband, and soon after the turn of the century a black tie became sufficient mourning for any relative. Changes in women's clothes illustrate the decline more precisely. Thus, the clothes correctly worn in second mourning in the 1870s were adequate for deep mourning in the 1880s: 'the time-honoured custom of wearing crape is gradually waning';[18] half-mourning brightened up to include mauves and greys. By 1902 we are reading that 'the custom of wearing crape may now be said to have gone entirely out of fashion, black being considered adequate mourning, save in the case of widows'.[19] And the restrictions on social activities, which were closely associated with the wearing of crêpe, were gradually relaxed at about the same time.

It has been held, particularly by Gorer, that the disappearance of mourning in England is attributable to a new and unusual attitude to grief. Many societies, indeed most, enjoin special marks and seclusion from society on the bereaved but they may give quite a different explanation from the English, such as that this prevents the pollution of death from spreading. And it is worth reiterating that whatever the explanation of the decline of mourning in England, a changed attitude to grief cannot be the correct one. In the first place, the form the rules took, in the relatives concerned and the nature of what was enjoined at their death, make it plain that conventionalised mourning was not a straightforward 'expression of grief'. In some cases it was governed by explicit orders. The periods in the case of court and public mourning seem too long. There is no likelihood that grief for in-laws would be the same as for blood relatives, or indeed that everyone felt the same sorrow at the death of the 'same' relatives. Secondly, the supposed changes of attitude towards grief is an illusion: attitudes were almost certainly much the same when mourning was an established custom in England as they are now. Attitudes are not easy to pin-point, but, so far as can be told, those towards the bereaved and their grief in the 1860s and 1870s, when mourning still flourished, were much the same, and no more healthy or open, than they were in 1965, the year Gorer wrote. An 1870s book of etiquette, in the course of explaining that women may now attend funerals, adds that they must of course remember that 'private feeling and private grief should not be displayed in public'.[20] In *Framley Parsonage* (1861),

Trollope makes it plain that people in Victorian England were as reticent about speaking to the bereaved of their loss as they were a century later. Lucy Robarts has been living with her brother and very affectionate sister-in-law since her father's death six weeks earlier. She is in deep mourning. Trollope tells us that:

> Nobody had yet spoken to her about her father since she had been at Framley. It had been as though the subject were a forbidden one. And how frequently is this the case! When those we love are dead, our friends dread to mention them, though to us who are bereaved no subject would be so pleasant as their names.

But, Trollope concludes, much like Gorer a century later: 'We rarely understand how to treat our own sorrow or those of others.'[21] So much for the idea that conventional mourning somehow served the bereaved.

The reasons for conforming to the conventional periods (or sometimes, rightly or wrongly, deviating from them) really had nothing to do with grieving. A 1920s book of etiquette says of mourning that 'the idea [was] not . . . to express the wearer's feelings at all, but to conform to the usage which had established a respect for death'.[22] While not altogether clear, this is nearer the truth. The time for which someone properly went into mourning depended on their tie to the deceased, and, in the case of relatives, it was a function, in the sense of 'varying with', the closeness of the relatives, as computed by the civil law reckoning of degrees. The same was true, although the periods of time were briefer, of court and public mourning for relatives of the Sovereign.

Unlike marriage prohibitions, mourning was connected with legitimate relationships. It would have been improper for a mistress or an unrecognised illegitimate son to go into mourning, however great might be their sorrow. It seems probable that this was because conventionalised mourning operated like a public statement of relationship. It was not correctly claimed, and should not be flaunted, by such illicit relations. Becky Sharp, anxious to claim relationship with her husband's family, who did not recognise her, went into ostentatious mourning for her husband's father. We are invited by Thackeray in *Vanity Fair* (1847−8) to see her over-doing it in the circumstances.[23] On the other hand, the heroine of Maria Edgworth's *Helen* rightly claimed what was actually more than the existing relationship when she 'resolved to continue in mourning [for her uncle] for the longest period in which it is worn for a parent, because, in truth, her uncle had been a parent to her'.[24] To go into mourning for less than the correct period, or not at all, was in effect to disclaim relationship. The black arm-band which Vyvyan Holland put on for his father, Oscar Wilde, at his death in 1900 was, as he puts it, 'ripped away' by his mother's family for just this reason: Oscar Wilde had disgraced them and they wished to disown all kinship.[25]

Such a disclaiming of relationship was justified if and only if the deceased was properly regarded as no loss, one for whom one should not grieve. It went, like mourning itself, by degree. In George Eliot's *Middlemarch* (1871−2) people try to shorten Dorothea's mourning for her husband Casaubon, who had treated her ill.[26] In Trollope's *The Prime Minister* (1875) Emily Lopez' rigorous mourning at the death of her utterly worthless husband is the despair of her family.[27] Amelia in *Vanity Fair* (1847−8) is depicted as misled about her husband when she mourns endlessly for him.[28] On the other hand, anyone who went into mourning for less than the appropriate time for a good husband or father or other relative displayed a lack of respect which reflected badly on themselves. The assumption was that they were worldly or frivolous. Thus, in *The Eustace Diamonds* (1876), Lizzie Eustace's curtailments of her mourning first for her father and next for her husband, Sir Florian, are used by Trollope to show her up. Similarly, although to display a very different personality, we have in another Trollope novel *Can You Forgive Her?* (1864) a wealthy, vulgar, merry widow, Aunt Greenow, who emerges too rapidly from her mourning clothes, pretending cheerfully that her husband's death lay ever further back. She has the charm 'that she was not in the least ashamed of anything she did'.[29]

Widowhood drew much comment, and I cannot resist two more quotations from Trollope, that great expert on the nuances of mourning. Of the heartless Lizzie Eustace, whose husband had done her nothing but good, he says:

> During the first year of her widowhood she had been every inch a widow, — as far as crape would go, and a quiet life . . .

During this year her child was born, — and she was in every way thrown upon her good behaviour, living with bishops' wives and deans' daughters. Two years of retreat from the world is generally thought to be the proper thing for a widow. Lizzie had not quite accomplished her two years before she re-opened the campaign [of social life] . . . with very small remnants of weeds,[30] and with her crape brought down to a minimum; — but she was young and rich, and the world is aware that a woman of twenty-two can hardly afford to sacrifice two whole years. In the matter of her widowhood, Lizzie did not encounter very much reproach. She was not shunned or so ill spoken of as to have a widely-spread bad name . . .[31]

Finally, Arthur Fletcher in *The Prime Minister* (1875−6), in a hurry to marry Emily Lopez after her catastrophic first marriage, reflects that:

The world has seemed to decide that a widow should take two years before she can bestow herself on a second man without a touch of scandal. But the two years is to include everything, the courtship of the second as well as the burial of the first, — and not only the courtship, but the preparation of the dresses and the wedding itself . . .[32]

Notes

1. J. Austen *Mansfield Park* 1814, Chapter 46ff.
2. *The Times* 12 December 1814, p. 2 col d − p. 3 col e; June 1815, p. 3 col d et al. For divorce procedures at the period see below, Chapter 5. The case for criminal conversation brought by Lord Rosebery against the adulterer Sir John Mildmay was reported at great and unusual length by the *The Times* of 12 December 1814, occupying well over a page of the two pages then given to news by *The Times*. Lord Rosebery had asked for £30,000 damages and received £15,000, among the highest ever given. Sir John Mildmay's own wife had died in 1810, leaving an infant son. He was intimate in the Rosebery household. His wife had been the Countess' sister and a brother of his was married to another sister of hers. There was unease about their relations after an absence of the Earl's and the Earl forbade him the house on his return and took his wife to Scotland. Mildmay grew a beard and, dressed as a sailor, used to climb through a window into the Countess' apartments in the evenings, where he was caught with a brace of pistols in his possession by the Earl's brother and servants. He was made to leave, the Earl refused to see his wife and she was to be sent to relatives but the couple eloped to France with a carriage. A long letter to the *The Times* in June 1815, when the divorce was going through the House of Lords, inter alia complaining of

the Earl of Rosebery's misguided generosity in allowing the Countess £200 per annum in addition to £300 per annum of her own, alluded to the regrettably well known nature of the case.

3. *The Times* 12 December 1814.

4. A. Trollope *The Claverings* 1867, Chapter 12. The plight is nowhere better described than over Lady Glencora's meditated elopement with Burgo Fitzgerald in A. Trollope *Can You Forgive Her?* 1864, vol 2, Chapter 50 et al.: 'Would she be happy, simply because he loved her, when all women should cease to acknowledge her, when men would regard her as one degraded and dishonoured, when society should be closed against her, when she would be driven to live loudly because the softness and graces of quiet life would be denied to her? Burgo knew well what must be the nature of such a woman's life in such circumstances . . . And, under such circumstances was it likely that he would continue to love her?'

5. J. Austen *Pride and Prejudice* 1813, Chapters 46–53, 61.

6. G. Eliot *The Mill on the Floss* 1860, Book 6 Chapter 13, Book 7.

6A. G. Gorer *Death, Grief and Mourning in Contemporary Britain* London 1965.

6B. See below pp. 58–9.

7. Good and probably independent accounts appear in: anonymous *Cassell's Handbook of Etiquette* London 1860; and in Anonymous [Eliza Cheadle] *Manners of Good Society, Being a Book of Etiquette* London 1872.

8. A. Trollope *Framley Parsonage* 1861, Ch. 11.

9. See e.g. A. Trollope *Can You Forgive Her?* 1864, vol 1 Chapter 40: 'The widow was almost gorgeous in her weeds . . . she had not sinned in her dress . . . The materials were those which are devoted to the deepest conjugal grief. There was the widow's cap, generally so hideous . . . There was the dress of deep, clinging, melancholy crape . . . There were the trailing weepers, and widow's kerchief pinned close round her neck . . . But there was that of genius about Mrs. Greenow, that she had turned every seeming disadvantage to some special profit, and had so dressed herself that though she had obeyed the law to the letter, she had thrown the spirit of it to the winds. Her cap sat jauntily on her head . . . Her weepers were bright with newness, and she would waft them aside from her shoulder with an air which turned even them into auxiliaries . . .'

10. A. Trollope *The Duke's Children* 1880, Chapter 28.

10A. There was no legal restriction, even in the case of widows (who in e.g. France are forbidden by law to re-marry for a prescribed period).

11. A. Trollope *The Eustace Diamonds* 1876, Chapter 1.

12. The length of public mourning depended on closeness of relationship of the deceased to the Sovereign. The time for the Sovereign was 12 weeks. It was 8 weeks for Prince Albert, the Queen's husband in 1861 (*London Gazette* 1861 p. 5427), 3 weeks for her mother in 1861 (ibid. 1861, p. 1237), similarly for her daughter Alice, the Princess Royal, in 1878 (ibid. 1878, p. 7193 part 2), and for her son Prince Leopold in 1884 (ibid. 1884, pp. 1511, 1531 part 1). The death of her eldest son's son Prince Albert in 1892 drew 3 weeks (ibid. 1892, p. 315), but for other relatives in the second degree such as a grandson in 1899 it was 2 weeks (ibid. 1899, p. 863). For the Queen's aunt, a third degree relative, it was 10 days in 1889 (ibid. 1889, pp. 2003–7), for her first cousin, the Duke of Cumberland, a fourth degree relative, one week in 1878 (ibid. 1878, p. 3611 part 1).

13. *The Times* 26 May 1910, p. 8 col a.

14. Mrs Massey Lyon *Etiquette. A Guide to Public and Social Life* London 1927, p. 461.

15. *The Times* 12 May 1910, p. 8 col f.

16. Anonymous (A Member of the Aristocracy) *Manners and Rules of Good*

Society 15th edition London 1888, p. 222.

17. L.H. Armstrong *Good Form. A Book of Everyday Etiquette* London 1889, p. 188.

18. Anonymous (A Member of the Aristocracy) *Manners of Rules of Good Society* 1888, p. 222.

19. Ibid. 26th edition 1902, pp. 2–3.

20. *Cassell's Domestic Dictionary. An Encyclopedia for the Household* London [1877–9], pp. 549–50.

21. A. Trollope *Framley Parsonage* 1861, Chapter 11.

22. Lyon *Etiquette* 1927.

23. W. Thackeray *Vanity Fair* 1847–8, Chapters 36, 40–1.

24. M. Edgeworth *Helen. A Tale* London, 1834 Chapter XXII (1896 Macmillan edn., p. 226).

25. Vyvyan Holland *Son of Oscar Wilde* 1954, Penguin 1957, p. 133.

26. G. Eliot *Middlemarch* 1871–2, Chapter 55.

27. A. Trollope *The Prime Minister*.

28. W. Thackeray *Vanity Fair* 1847–8, Chapters 38, 57–62, 66–67.

29. A. Trollope *Can You Forgive Her?* 1864, vol 1 Chapter 7. See above note 9.

30. Widow's weeds were worn by widows for a year and a day. They included a widow's cap, much crêpe and a few articles of clothing peculiar to widows. See above at note 9 for one description.

31. A. Trollope *The Eustace Diamonds* 1876, Chapter 17.

32. A. Trollope *The Prime Minister* 1875–6, Chapter 65.

4 Kinship Terminology and Marriage Preferences

Before returning to kinship customs regulated by law in England, it is worth dwelling briefly on some other conventions which although they are in no way legally enforced, underline the existence of a *system* of kinship.

1. Kinship Terms

Linguistic assimilations and distinctions are generally considered significant as indications of assimilations and distinctions made in thought. I have remarked on the English classification of relatives into the two categories of 'blood' and 'in-law' relatives, or, more formally, 'consanguineous' and 'affinal' relatives, and also on the English treatment of distance of relationship. The organisation of mourning for relatives suggests that the civil law degree reckoning employed by lawyers corresponded to ordinary people's conception of distance and relationship. Mourning was longer and deeper the 'closer' the relation who had died, and 'closeness' followed the civil law reckoning with almost uncanny precision. So-called kinship terminology also requires consideration.

In setting out Parker's Table in Figure 2.3 I employed the terms commonly used when ordinary people talk about their relations. These have several noteworthy features, which tend to support claims I have made about the way relatives were and are classified in England. I use the historic present in what follows.[1]

The first and most obvious point, often commented on in the deceased wife's sister debates, is that the terms in use for relatives by marriage are identical with those in use for the 'same' blood relations, with merely the addition of '-in-law' or the prefix 'step-'.[2] On marriage, husband and wife become 'as one' and call each other's relations by the same terms; a person's spouse's father, mother, sister, brother, uncle and aunt are his 'father-in-law', 'mother-in-law', 'sister-in-law' and so on for the rest, although as we get to more distant relatives 'cousin by marriage'

64

might be more common usage than 'cousin-in-law'. Similarly, when a sister, brother etc. marries, his or her spouse is one's 'brother-in-law', 'sister-in-law' and so on. It used to be the case that if one's father or mother re-married, his or her spouse was spoken of as one's 'father-in-law' or 'mother-in-law'. Thus for instance Mr Murdstone in relation to David Copperfield in Dickens' novel of that name (1849−50), or Mrs Weston to Frank Churchill, her husband's son by his first marriage in Jane Austen's *Emma* (1816) or Mrs Dashwood to Mr John Dashwood, her husband's son (and his wife) in Jane Austen's *Sense and Sensibility* (1811), and commonly in the eighteenth century.[3] But it was always more usual to prefix 'step-', and the alternative 'in-law' usage has by now died out.

The precise line between 'step-' and '-in-law', and their development over the years may be interesting but need not detain us. Roughly, a step-, as opposed to an in-law, relationship comes about through re-marriage on the part of a direct ascendant. The new spouse of a father, mother, grandmother etc. is a 'step-mother', 'step-father' and the like. Reciprocally, someone who marries a person previously married may acquire 'step-children': the children of their spouse's previous marriage.[4] Someone whose parent re-marries may acquire step-brothers or step-sisters; the children of the new spouse by the previous marriage. He or she may also acquire 'half' brothers or sisters, where one and not both parents are in common. The re-marriage of a relation who is not an ascendant, like a brother or a sister or a son, merely brings about more in-law relations. One's son's second wife is no more nor less one's 'daughter-in-law' than his first wife.

The in-law and step- terminology so operates that a husband and wife use basically the same terms for the same persons. A mild exception occurs in that, strictly speaking, there is an in-law relationship only between a person and the blood relations of his or her spouse, or, as it can equally well be described, between a person and the spouse of his or her blood relation. There is strictly speaking no affinity between, for instance, a man and his wife's brother's wife; she is his wife's sister-in-law and not his own. Usage is probably a little hazy in this area, and the different range of relatives thereby in fact possessed by husband and wife is generally played down, to the extent that this relative could well in practice be referred to as a 'sister-in-law'. There is an example in *Vanity Fair* (1848): Becky and Lady Jane, married to two brothers, are referred to as 'sisters-in-law'.[5] A man could marry his wife's brother's wife should it happen that his wife and her brother died. There was a category of mourning, known as 'complimentary mourning' which might be donned for friends or for what were sometimes known as 'connections', who were not exactly relations but, as the term suggests, 'connected' by relationship.[6]

Much more clear-cut and noteworthy is the fact that, with the sole exception of step-brothers and sisters, the blood relatives of one spouse do not describe the blood relatives of the other by any kinship terms. A person's sister's husband's brother, for example, is definitely not a brother-in-law: he is no relation, and has to be described as one's 'sister's brother-in-law' or, more improbably, as one's 'brother-in-law's brother'. One could just think of a term for a sister's husband's brother viz. 'brother-in-law', although it would not be correct to use it. In other cases, even this possibility vanishes. One's son's wife's mother, for instance, is someone for whom one could not even think of an appropriate term. She would be one's 'son's mother-in-law' or one's 'daughter-in-law's mother' according to circumstance, but no relation of one's own. Similarly, a man's brother's wife's father is his brother's father-in-law[7] or sister-in-law's father. It is only the partners to a marriage who have a relationship with the blood relatives on both sides.[8] This was not so in all Christian societies at all times. Witness the fact, important to the plot of Tolstoy's *War and Peace* (1866) that in Russia a man's sister, or brother, could not marry his wife's brother, or sister. Thus if Natasha had married Prince Andrew, his sister Maria could not have married her brother Nicholas, a restriction not found in England.[9] On the other hand in Jane Austen's *Emma*, there is not the least impediment nor even comment when Emma, whose sister is married to Mr Knightley's brother, marries Mr Knightley.[10]

A feature which English kinship terminology shares with some other Western societies, but not with, for instance, the Romans, or most other contemporary societies, is the lack of distinction between maternal and paternal kin. Cousins of whatever sort are just 'cousins', father's and mother's brothers and sisters are undifferentiated as 'uncles' and 'aunts', according to sex, and, reciprocally, one's siblings sons and daughters are all alike one's 'nephews', if male, 'nieces', if female.

The lack of distinction between maternal and paternal relations in the language, and in common thinking about relations, seems less clearly, or less consistently a definite feature of English kinship than for instance the absence of relationship between the blood relations of one spouse and those of the other or than the presence of a relationship between a married couple and the kin on both sides.

Customs associated with relationship, such as non-marriageability or going into mourning, are found between a person and his spouse's relatives, along with use of a definite kinship term, and the conventions mirror those concerning blood relations. The fact that there is no relationship between the blood relations of one spouse and the blood relations of the other is equally clear-cut. The law books are specific on the point. It is probably common knowledge. The language reflects it. Freedom of marriage between, absence of mourning when it was customary between relatives, is consistent with this absence of relationship.

It is not however the case that no distinction at all is made between maternal and paternal relations. Apart from the existence of the terminology, when it is necessary to be specific, 'on my mother's side' or 'my paternal grandfather', there are some definite differences made.

An obvious one is that surnames or 'family' names pass in the male line, except in the case of illegitimate children, who normally take their mother's name. Children born in wedlock have their father's surname, not, as the apparent lack of distinction between paternal and maternal kin might lead one to expect, surnames derived from the names of both parents. It could be argued that children do inherit both parents' name in as much as a woman takes her husband's name at marriage and the children inherit this common name. But there is another important area in which distinction was and is made between paternal and maternal kin. This is in inheritance of property and titles, some of which go entirely in the male line, as with 'entailed' estates or succession in the Peerage. Others, like succession to the throne, go in the male line before the female line. Thus sons of the Sovereign (and their children) are heirs to the throne in order of the sons' ages, before any daughters.[11]

The use of terms for relatives reflects another feature of English kinship: the distinction between the 'direct' line and collateral ones. The 'direct' line is upwards between a person and his parents, parents' parents and so on, his 'ascendants', and downwards between a person and his children and children's children, his 'descendants'. Siblings and their children, parents' siblings and their descendants are 'collateral' relations, and not in the direct line.

English has relatively few uncompounded terms for relatives. Apart from 'husband' and 'wife', and the rarer 'spouses', who are not classed as relations but as a unity or 'as one', there are: 'father' and 'mother', both 'parents'; 'son' and 'daughter', both 'children' (although 'child' unlike 'parent' or 'son' has also a common non-kinship use for the young, as against the 'adult'). We also have 'brother' and 'sister'. 'Sibling' to mean either is not a term much used in common speech; it is more usual to refer to 'brothers and sisters'.[12] There is 'uncle' and 'aunt', the brother and sister respectively of a parent, 'nephew' and 'niece', the son and daughter respectively of a sibling. There is no term comparable to 'parents' to refer to these collectively. They are just 'uncles and aunts' or 'nephews and nieces'. Finally there is 'cousin' used for both male and female relatives of the appropriate nature.

The remaining terms are compounds. The suffix '-in-law' and prefix 'step-' have already been discussed. There are also prefixes indicating distance of relationship: 'grand-' and 'great-', and in the case of cousins 'first', 'second' etc., with suffixes as generation indicators.

A parent's parent is a 'grandparent', a child's child a 'grandchild'. Like 'mother' and 'father' (or 'Mummy', 'Daddy', 'papa', 'mama'), 'Grandfather' and 'grandmother' (or derived diminutives, 'Granny', 'Grandpa') are in common use as terms of address, as well as in referring to these relatives. 'Grandson' and 'granddaughter' would normally not be used as terms of address, the grandchild's christian name being used instead; they are common terms of reference. To go further up or down the direct line 'great' is prefixed without limit on number. Thus a grandparent's parents are 'great-grandparents' and their parents 'great-great-grandparents'. Similarly in the descending line. The sibling of a parent is an uncle or aunt. The sibling of a grandparent is not a 'grand' anything but a 'great-aunt' or 'great-uncle'. Reciprocally, while the child of a sibling is a nephew or niece, the child of this child is a 'great-nephew' or 'great-niece'.[13] It is doubtful if there are great-great aunts or great-great nephews, but if so they

Figure 4.1   Cousins

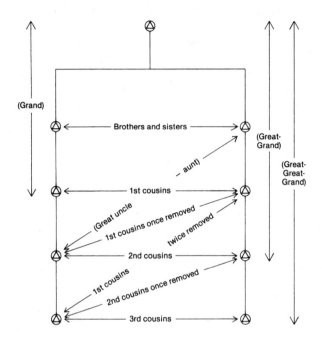

are the sisters of great-grand parents or the great-grandsons of siblings.

The cousin terminology is as such undifferentiated by sex or generation. While I would be my aunt's niece or my son's parent, I am my cousin's cousin. But distance and generation can be indicated. My parents' siblings' children are my first cousins. My parents' siblings' grandchildren or my grandparents' siblings' children are my first cousins once removed. The children of two first cousins are second cousins, of two second cousins third cousins. Cousinhood can continue indefinitely. The nature of the terms can be seen diagrammatically (see Figure 4.1).

2. Marrying Up or Down

Before returning to features of marriage and relationships regulated by law, it is worth mentioning another unregulated feature.

Among English views concerning marriage is the idea that

ideally a marriage is between equals,[14] although the romantic marriage par excellence is between a man of higher and a woman of lower status. The proper marriage in England was and is a 'love match', with due regard, in the past, for the ability of a man to maintain his wife, with or without property brought into the marriage by her. In general it was and still is somewhat 'unmanly' for the husband to live on his wife's property or earnings. Marriages between a man of lower status and a woman of higher status are commonly thought of as mercenary. It was, and still is, also rather dubious for a husband to be younger than his wife. Ideally, husband and wife are more or less of an age, with the husband perhaps a little older, but, while not vying in romantic attraction with the marriage of high status men and lower status women, the marriage of a much older man with a much younger woman was readily tolerated, although most usually thought of as unlikely to be a love match on the woman's side. 'If the man be not more than fifteen years older than the woman the difference in age can hardly be thought of as an obstacle', as Trollope commented on one such marriage in 1878.[15] It is worth noting that the husband should also be taller than his wife but probably not very much taller.

Victorian and earlier English novels are filled with the romantic marriage where a man of high standing marries a woman of low or lower standing. In Richardson's novel *Pamela, or Virtue Rewarded* (1740), Pamela, a young servant, after resisting her master's attempts at seduction, ultimately marries him with her virtue intact and his family approving the marriage.[16] Young Lord Silverbridge in *The Duke's Children* (1880), over a century later, marries a charming American girl, whose grandfather was a dockworker.[17] On the other hand, Lopez is a social climber and a cad when he marries Emily Wharton, a solicitor's daughter, in *The Prime Minister* (1875–6),[18] and, although Trollope does his best, he, like his fictional characters, finds it difficult to justify the perfectly worthy Tregear in *The Duke's Children* (1880), the younger son of a country squire, when he proposes to marry Lady Mary, his friend Silverbridge's sister and the daughter of a wealthy Duke who has been Prime Minister.[19]

This feature of English kinship has attracted even less academic attention than mourning or the kinship terminology, but we can find explicit statements of the thinking behind the preferences. Two main lines of thought can be distinguished.

One is that marriage creates a relationship between a married couple and the kin on both sides, and ideally this relationship carries with it social intercourse, rendered, it was thought, difficult where the kin on either side is of low social status compared to the couple. The other is that within the marriage, the husband is or ought to be superior to, or at least the equal of his wife, the unity of husband and wife being effected by the wife becoming 'part' of her husband.

The point about in-law relationships was commonly employed in literature, among other things in relation to romantic marriages. Examples abound. In Dickens' *David Copperfield* (1849–50), little Emily's fisherman family try to persuade Steerforth's upper-class family that, having seduced her, Steerforth ought to marry her. One objection made by his disagreeable family is that 'her humble connections would render such a thing impossible, if nothing else did'.[20] In Jane Austen's *Pride and Prejudice* (1813), Darcy is shown as trying to dissuade himself from an otherwise suitable marriage to Elizabeth Bennet on account of the 'inferiority of [her] connections' and the 'total want of propriety so frequently, so almost uniformly betrayed' by her nearest relations.[21] ('Connections' is used (instead of 'relations') to moderate the insult as in both cases the points are made directly by the man or his family to the woman or hers.) Lord Silverbridge's younger brother remarks to his sister Lady Mary that 'Silver is going to have an odd sort of a mother-in-law'.[22]

This difficulty is generally depicted as more or less satisfactorily surmountable. In *David Copperfield* Emily's family offer, sadly enough, never to see her again: 'She shall never be disgraced by us.'[23] Darcy and Elizabeth entertain her satisfactory relations, and avoid her unsatisfactory ones.[24] Lady Mary remarks to Silverbridge's brother 'in reply that this would not signify, as the mother-in-law would be in New York'.[25] On the other hand, in another Trollope novel, *Ralph the Heir* (1871), Ralph Newton, heir to the Newton estates, tries to marry the daughter of a breeches-maker to extricate himself from debt and his need to sell his interest in the estate. The misalliance founders on the rock of her father whom he cannot face as an ever present father-in-law and from whom she properly declines to be parted.[26]

A factor important to bear in mind is that when two people married and became as one they set up, or ought as a rule to set up, an independent household.[27] Lopez, among his other sins, will not do so and lives off his wife's father and in his house.[28] 'I'll turn Traffick out, and I suppose he'll take his wife with him', another of Trollope's irate fathers-in-law threatens: 'Augusta made up her mind no doubt to leave her father's house when she married . . .'[29] But ideally the married couple retained contact with both families and it was certainly discreditable for a woman to cut her family on marrying up in the social scale. Griselda Grantley in Trollope's Barsetshire novels, including *The Small House at Allington* (1864) and *The last Chronicle of Barset* (1867), daughter of an Archdeacon, becomes Lady Dumbello, and later Marchioness of Hartletop, 'a splendid matrimonial alliance'.[30] 'She is above them all' a character remarks.[31] 'A Marchioness of Hartletop', Trollope comments, 'has special duties which will hardly permit her to devote herself frequently to the humdrum society of a clerical father and mother . . .',[32] and so on. Probably the easiest of marriages between a man of higher and a woman of lower status was when the woman had in effect or in fact no family.

The question of future relations with in-laws was undoubtedly a factor in favour of marriage between equals. Also, the wife should in fact not be personally inferior to her husband. It is of the greatest importance that Silverbridge's American wife is personally his equal, similarly in the case of Darcy and Elizabeth. Emily is not Steerforth's equal in education or social accomplishment, and Mrs Steerforth says of her son: 'He would disgrace himself . . . she is far below him. She is uneducated and ignorant'.[33] In *Pride and Prejudice* (1813) Mr Bennet, Elizabeth's father, had been foolish enough to marry an ignorant wife of poor understanding and the marriage was not a success.[34] However, in many cases the wife could be brought up to the right level: 'Raise her up,' little Emily's relations say, 'Teach her better.'[35]

This brings us to the second line of thought, the thinking which made marriage between a man of higher status and a woman of lower status acceptable in a way that the reverse situation is not. It subdivides into two views. First, a woman, properly and usually in practice, takes or took her husband's rank or status in a way that a husband does not take his wife's. The King of England's wife becomes Queen of England; the Queen of England's husband does not become King, but only Prince Consort.

Secondly, there is a sense in which a husband is, or was, the wife's superior.

In *Pamela* (1740) Richardson separates and explains these notions. The question is asked 'Where can the difference be between a beggar's son married to a lady, or a beggar's daughter made a gentleman's wife?' Another character supplies the answer: ' "Then I'll tell you: the difference is, a man ennobles the woman he takes, be she *who* she will; and he adopts her into his *own* rank, be *what* it will; but a woman though ever so nobly born, debases herself by a mean marriage, and descends from her *own* rank to *his* she stoops to" ' (Richardson's italics).[36] There are limits: the twice divorced American Mrs Simpson's ineligibility to be Queen of England forced Edward VIII to abdicate when he insisted on marrying her; she could not be raised to his level. There are also exceptions: Queens of England do not lose rank by marrying beneath themselves; but of course if they are to marry and supply heirs to the throne they have difficulty in avoiding marrying below their own rank, except by marriage to foreign royalty.

The propriety, and in normal cases actual fact of a woman taking her husband's rank or status is distinguished by Richardson from another point which also tells against marriage between a man of lower and a woman of higher status: ' ". . . When a Duke marries a private person, is he not still her *head*, by virtue of being her husband? But when a lady descends to marry a groom is not that groom her *head*, being her husband?" ' (Richardson's italics).[37]

The taking of her husband's rank by a woman was and is formalised in only some cases, principally when titles are in question, the wife of the King of England is Queen, the wife of Sir X Y is Lady Y, and so on. But it was otherwise with the idea that a husband was his wife's 'head'. It was part of common sentiment. But as the law stood until changes of the late nineteenth and twentieth centuries, it was also a legal matter, which became subject to criticism.

In *The Subjection of Women*, which John Stuart Mill published in 1869, he compared the lot of women in law, especially that of married women, unfavourably to that of slaves in Rome: 'the wife is the actual bond-servant of her husband: not less so, so far as legal obligation goes, than slaves commonly so called. She vows a lifelong obedience to him at the altar, and is held to it all through her life by law.'[38] Her property, earnings, children belonged to her husband. She could be assaulted and what, in ordinary parlance, would be 'raped' by him (except that in its legal definition 'rape' was almost certainly confined to intercourse without her consent by a man who is *not* her husband).[39] Nor could she leave or change her master: '. . . no amount of ill usage, without adultery superadded, will in England free a wife of her tormentor.'[40] 'I have', Mill added, 'no desire to exaggerate; nor does the case stand in need of exaggeration':

> I have described the wife's legal position, not her actual treatment. The laws of most countries are far worse than the people who execute them, and many of them are only able to remain laws by being seldom or never carried into effect. If married life were all that it might be expected to be, looking to the laws alone, society would be a hell upon earth.[41]

Notes

1. There is a discussion of the development of English kinship terminology in J. Goody *The Development of the Family & Marriage in Europe* CUP 1983, Appendix 3, 'Bilaterality and English Kin Terminology'; and in R.T. Anderson *Changing Kinship in Europe* Kroeber Anthropological Society no 28, Berkeley, California 1963. These probe aspects of its early history back into medieval Christianity, Anglo-Saxons, the Norman Conquest etc. This chapter concentrates on present usage and that of recent centuries.

2. Goody *The Development of the Family* 1983, p. 269 seems to date the use of 'that curious suffix "in-law" ' to the Norman Conquest 1066, as also some other changes. R.T. Anderson *Changing Kinship in Europe* 1963, cited by Goody *The Development of the Family* 1983, says that the words changed; however, 'the classification has not changed in over a thousand years'. He associates the classification with the introduction of Christianity 'which appears to have influenced the terminology through its marriage prohibitions', p. 29.

3. Charles Dickens *David Copperfield* 1848–9, Chapter 14; Jane Austen *Emma* 1816, Chapter 51; Jane Austen *Sense and Sensibility* 1811, Chapters 1, 2, 5.

4. Occasionally we meet the usage 'step-daughter-in-law' for a step-son's wife. See e.g. A. Trollope *John Caldigate* 1879, Chapter 9.

5. W. Thackeray *Vanity Fair* 1848, Chapter 41. In Jane Austen's *Pride and Prejudice* 1813 Chapter 52 a marriage of Darcy to Elizabeth is spoken of as if it would make Darcy 'brother-in-law of Wickham'. Wickham is married to Elizabeth's sister, Lydia. In A. Trollope *The Vicar of Bullhampton* 1870, Chapter 42, Mr Quickenham and Mr Fenwick, married to two sisters, are once referred to as 'brothers-in-law' (Chapter 42) but frequently the reference is to their 'wife's brother in law' (Chapters 42, 55).

6. In Jane Austen *Emma* 1816, Chapter 45 Mr Weston resolves that his

mourning will be as handsome as possible for his first, dead wife's brother's wife (cf *Emma* Chapter 2 for the relationship). Mr Knightley is spoken of as 'particularly connected with the family [of Emma and her father] as the elder brother of Isobella's husband' [Isobella is Emma's sister] *Emma* Chapter 1.

7. See e.g. A. Trollope *Is He Popenjoy?* London 1878, vol 1 Chapter 10.

8. See above Chapter 1. Law books frequently mention the fact. See e.g. J.T. Hammick *The Marriage law of England* 2nd edn. revised and enlarged 1887, p. 37.

9. L. Tolstoy *War and Peace* 1866. Cf vol 3 Chapters 33 and 34 where the point is explicitly stated. Prince Andrew and Natasha are engaged, but Prince Andrew's father insists on a year's delay (vol 2 Book 6 Chapter 23). During this time Natasha falls in love with Kowaguine, elopes, and breaks her engagement (vol 2 Book 8 Chapters 52, 58, 59). Meantime Natasha's brother Nicholas meets Andrew's sister Maria. They fall in love (vol 2 Book 10 Chapter 96). Prince Andrew is mortally wounded (vol 3 Chapter 7) and by chance brought to Natasha's parents' house with other wounded. Their love revives. Nicholas and Maria feel on the footing of relatives (vol 3 Chapters 34, 36). Prince Andrew dies (vol 3 Chapter 36). Ultimately Natasha marries Peter (Epilogue Part I Chapter 5), and Nicholas marries Maria (Epilogue Part I Chapters 6 and 7).

10. Jane Austen *Emma* Chapters 49ff.

11. Succession to ranks and titles and inheritance of property is a vastly complex subject in England as different rules govern different kinds of property and title. With certain exceptions, a person may bequeath his or her own property at death by 'will', i.e. as he or she declares in proper form before death. If someone fails to make a will, that is, dies 'intestate', property descends according to the laws of intestacy which have altered from time to time. Titles, and some property, cannot be bequeathed by will, and pass to heirs in a fashion detailed by law. Succession to the throne, to inherited titles and to entailed estates are the main instances. For some time there have been taxes on property at death, known as 'death duties', and these are varied according to the kinship of the heir, being less the closer the heir. In the inheritance of property and succession to titles in England, there is a preference for descendants over ascendants, for males over females, and for elder over younger. Thus the throne descends to the eldest son and to his progeny before it may go to the next eldest son. If there are no sons nor progeny of sons, the throne goes to the eldest daughter and her progeny and so on. Succession to dukedoms, earldoms, baronetcies and the like, together with 'entailed estates', follows the same rules except that these cannot go to women nor descendants in the female line. 'Primogeniture' in the shape of inheritance by the eldest son, gives rise to patrilineal lines (not 'lineages', as anthropologists use this term), and to the phenomenon of 'younger sons' whose lines get detached from the title/estate.

12. Although relative age affects succession and certain forms of inheritance, there is no terminological distinction between elder and younger siblings.

13. 'Grand-nephew' is occasionally used. In Charles Dickens *David Copperfield* 1848–9, Chapter 15, Miss Trotwood refers to David as her 'grand-nephew'.

14. This was certainly not news. R.A. Houlbrooke *The English Family 1450–1700* London 1984, p. 73ff mentions it for his period: 'The ideal parity between marriage partners was widely emphasised . . . Most important . . . was parity of rank' (p. 75).

15. A. Trollope *Is he Popenjoy?* 1878, Chapter 1.

16. S. Richardson *Pamela, or Virtue Rewarded* 1740.

17. A. Trollope *The Duke's Children* 1880, Chapters 39–40, 47, 52, 53, 61, 68–74.

18. A. Trollope *The Prime Minister* 1875–6, Chapters 1, 3–5, 9–10, 13–14,

23–6, et al.

19. A. Trollope *The Duke's Children* 1880, Chapters 74, 79, 80.

20. Charles Dickens *David Copperfield* Chapter 32.

21. Jane Austen *Pride and Prejudice* London 1813, Chapters 34–5, also Chapter 10. Cf also notes 34 and 24.

22. A. Trollope *The Duke's Children* Chapter 74.

23. Charles Dickens *David Copperfield* Chapter 32.

24. Jane Austen *Pride and Prejudice*, Chapters 60–1, cf notes 21 and 34.

25. A. Trollope *The Duke's Children* Chapter 74.

26. A. Trollope *Ralph the Heir* 1871, Chapters 24, 53.

27. It is worth noting the nuance in Jane Austen's *Emma* when Mr Knightley reflects that 'A man should always wish to give a woman a better home than the one he takes her from, and he who can do it, where there is no doubt of her regard, must I think be the happiest of mortals' (Chapter 49).

28. A. Trollope *The Prime Minister* 1875–6, Chapters 39, 40, 48–9, 52–3, 55, 58–60.

29. A. Trollope *Ayala's Angel* 1881, Chapter 13.

30. A. Trollope *The Last Chronicle of Barset* 1867, Chapter 2.

31. A. Trollope *The Small House at Allington* 1864, Chapter 16.

32. A. Trollope *The Last Chronicle of Barset* 1867, Chapter 2.

33. Charles Dickens *David Copperfield* Chapter 32.

34. Jane Austen *Pride and Prejudice* Chapter 42, cf notes 21 and 24.

35. Charles Dickens *David Copperfield* Chapter 32.

36. S. Richardson *Pamela* 1740, Tuesday Morning (Dent edition 1914, reprinted 1955, vol 1, p. 381).

37. Ibid.

38. J.S. Mill *The Subjection of Women* 1869, Chapter 2.

39. This was a knotty legal point. See below Chapter 6, Section 2.

40. Mill *The Subjection of Women* Chapter 2.

41. Ibid.

5   Divorce

At one time it was widely believed that the English household had altered in composition to include only parents and children. In 1940 Malinowski advised the Church of England that the smaller range of relatives living together justified its proposed curtailment of prohibitions of marriage with in-laws.[1] Later the supposed reduction of the household was attributed to the industrial revolution.[2] Later still, the myth of the diminished household was exploded with the aid of statistics.[3] Before as well as after the industrial revolution, a married couple properly had an independent household, and in the seventeenth and eighteenth century arguments about the proper extent of prohibitions of marriage and sexual intercourse between kin, even those most eager to reduce them never ventured to claim that relatives beyond parents and unmarried children normally lived in the same house.[4] With the ghost of an altered household laid, the most obvious practical change in English kinship in the past two or three centuries has been the introduction and increase of divorce, that is, of dissolving marriages to allow re-marriage. Probably because of the deep-seated view that husband and wife form a unity, and other aspects of the kinship system, the increase in divorce has been accompanied by lament.[5] Its early history is not well known and descriptions are apt to be inaccurate.

1. Early History

Divorce did not exist in any form in England until around 1700. Before the Reformation the Catholic Church forbade it. The Catholic Church did accept many grounds on which marriages could be annulled, that is, an apparent marriage declared to have been no marriage. So many were there that a preamble to a Statute of Henry VIII of 1540 declared that 'none could so surely knit and bounden, but that it should lie in either parties' power . . . to prove a pre-contract, a kindred, an alliance, or a carnal knowledge to defeat the same'.[6] This Statute removed most of the grounds of annulment. After the Reformation there was generally provision for divorce in Protestant countries, including Scotland, which introduced it in 1560 for adultery or malicious desertion by either sex. England was the exception. The Church of England, like the Catholic Church, would not countenance it.

The ecclesiastical courts granted what were called 'divorces *a mensa et thoro*', i.e. from board and bed, for adultery and cruelty. These were available to both sexes but did not permit re-marriage. In 1603 there was a Statute against bigamy,[7] that is going through the acts of marriage while still married, 're-marriages' after divorces *a mensa et thoro* included.[8] Divorces *a mensa et thoro* were not properly 'divorces', which as a matter of definition do permit re-marriage, but only what were later termed 'judicial separations'.

The ecclesiastical courts also granted divorces *a vinculo matrimonii* i.e. from the bonds of marriage, which did allow re-marriage. But these were not divorces either. Like the old annulments, they were granted only if the original 'marriage' was not valid. Legal writers complained of the confused terminology, and pointed out that you cannot dissolve a non-existent marriage.[9] By the nineteenth century, reports in *The Times* of divorces *a vinculo matrimonii*, known as 'a vinculo', almost always referred to them as 'annulments', as distinct from 'divorces'. The most common grounds were lack of consent or non-consummation.[10]

Contracting an invalid 'marriage' was not normally subject to penalties. Even those within the prohibited degrees were not punished: such 'marriages' were simply voidable or later void, that is, no marriages.[11] But going through the acts of marriage with an undissolved marriage on one's hands was different. It was a crime, that of bigamy. Bigamous 'marriages' were not only void but subject to harsh penalties: death, transportation and at the present time two years of imprisonment.[12] In these circumstances, re-marriage with a spouse alive was not something which could come to edge its way in by custom as marriages within the Prohibited Degrees succeeded in doing for several centuries. Divorce entered in a different fashion.

The first dissolution of a marriage generally considered to have been a genuine divorce, in which an existent marriage was dissolved to permit re-marriage, was that of Lord Roos in 1670.

It was obtained by a private Act of Parliament for his wife's adultery. It took eight years to effect and was hailed as a Protestant victory.[13] The next such case was some 28 years later, that of the Earl of Macclesfield in 1698. However, after the Duke of Norfolk's divorce by Act of Parliament in 1700,[14] which took nine years to procure, Parliament decided that the dissolving of marriages to enable re-marriage came within its jurisdiction,[15] and from then until 1857, when the Matrimonial Causes Act made divorce a judicial procedure, divorces were effected by private Act of Parliament. Cases were heard in detail by the House of Lords and then referred to the House of Commons.

The procedure for obtaining a divorce between 1700 and 1857 was not confined to that of obtaining a private Act of Parliament. The House of Lords would agree to consider a divorce Bill only if the petitioner had already secured a divorce *a mensa et thoro* for adultery from the ecclesiastical courts. By the end of the eighteenth century it also came to require that the husband should have brought a successful case for damages against the adulterer for 'criminal conversation', colloquially 'crim. con.', with his wife. These were known as 'verdicts at law' and were dealt with by the King's Bench or other secular courts.[16]

Adultery remained the only grounds for divorce in England until 1937. Until 1923, women were able to procure a divorce only if the husband's adultery was compounded by other off- · ences, until 1857 only incest or bigamy, after 1857 also cruelty, desertion etc.[17] Women were exempt from the need to bring criminal conversation cases;[18] on the other hand, it was only in 1801 that a divorce was first sought by a woman. She was successful,[19] but there were in all only four divorces by women by private Act of Parliament.[20]

The number of divorces remained very low in the initial years after Parliament decided to grant them. There were 13 or 14 between 1700 and 1750.[21] The rate began to rise in the second half of the eighteenth century, when there were 117 or an average of 2.3 per annum. From 1880 to 1857 there were 193, an average of 3.3 a year over these 58 years.[22]

In 1850 a Royal Commission on divorce headed by Lord Campbell was appointed, It reported in 1853.[23] With one dissentient, it favoured the transformation of divorce into a judicial procedure. It gave a picture of divorce as it then was as an upper class or aristocratic domain, cumbersome and slow and out of reach by its expense to all but the wealthy.

This picture has coloured subsequent accounts of English divorce before 1857,[23A] and was achieved only by some signal inaccuracies as to the facts. The number of divorces between 1800 and 1852 was said to be 110, which gave the impression of a falling divorce rate.[24] There were in fact 175 divorces between 1800 and 1852.[24A] Divorce was on the increase. Again, successful appellants for divorces *a mensa et thoro* were said to be prevented by expense from getting a private Act.[25] But a number of those who had obtained private Acts in the exemplar of cases of divorces *a mensa et thoro* in the Consistory Court of London between 1845 and 1850 were stated in an appendix[26] not to have done so, so that it appeared as if only a third instead of half had continued proceedings.[27] Or, to take another example, the cost of obtaining a private Act of Parliament was said to be £200.[28] But this was arrived at from average expenses of £188 4s 6d in a 'List of Divorce Acts since 1837' which included only 26 unidentified Acts.[29] There were in fact 71 Acts during the period.[30] The Commission not only over-stated the total cost of divorce proceedings.[30A] It also omitted to mention that a husband could and often did procure high damages for criminal conversation from the adulterer, that costs were invariably awarded against the adulterer, that by no means all divorces were in the upper classes, much less obtained by aristocrats, or that the total procedure could be, and often was, extremely swift.

One of the first divorces, in 1701, was by a London grocer, one Mr. Box, who, it is true, was married to a baronet's daughter, and the adulterer bore the title 'Esq'.[31] In 1711, the son of a merchant, apprenticed to a wine merchant, who as a minor had married one Sarah Bell 'a woman of bad fame and lewd conversation', procured a divorce.[32] In 1729 a divorce was granted to a Mr. Cobb.[33] A printed page appended to his printed Act stated that his wife was a 'Common Prostitute, Night-Walker and a Notorious Thief' as well as the 'wickedest woman in the World'. The other 10 divorces between 1700 and 1750 were in the upper classes. There were two Dukes, three baronets and one heir to a baronet. There were three gentlemen with the title 'Esq' and a further divorce obtained by a 'gentleman' (not entitled 'Esq'). If the Baronetage is included in the 'aristocracy' along with the Peerage, the 'aristocracy' was obtaining half of the few divorces.

The position changed fairly rapidly. The 'upper classes', taken to include anyone of the Peerage, the Baronetage, with the title 'Esq' or described as a 'gentleman', continued to secure about two-thirds of all divorces, but the share of the 'aristocracy' dwindled, until after 1830 it was only 2.4 per cent of all divorces. Non-upper-class people who procured divorces in the eighteenth century included a farmer, a trimming maker, a riding master. Between 1800 and 1857 a butcher, a vet, a cabinet maker, a master mariner, a flour factor married to a baker's daughter, a linen draper and an oil cooper were among successful appellants.[34] Clergy formed 6 per cent of both aggrieved husbands and adulterers. The Army, Navy and India accounted for a great many successful appellants, both upper-class and not so upper-class.

No regular legal records were kept of criminal conversation cases. Divorce Acts were classified as 'unprinted private Acts': only the manuscript counts as the Act. Many were printed privately but some exist only in manuscript.[35] However, *The Times* took to reporting various stages of divorces, sometimes in great detail and by the 1840s and 1850s omitted few or none. The preambles of private Acts give much information about the parties. Journals of the House of Lords detailed their proceedings. From these various sources it is evident that the 1853 Commission exaggerated in placing the average total cost of a divorce at £700.[36] Doubtless some divorces were expensive. But many were undisputed. Even the 1853 Commission placed the cost of an undisputed divorce *a mensa et thoro* at only £120–£140,[37] and the costs of criminal conversation cases, which in any case were awarded against the adulterer, could be as low as £12.[38]

Private Acts only sometimes specify costs awarded in criminal conversation cases. The highest I have found were £392 in 1825 and £695 in 1850; the average of the costs specified in 17 Private Acts, which are in pounds sterling, was £150.[39] The husband could sue *in forma pauperis* if he had no money: thus Chippindall, Gentleman in 1850.[40] Normally, damages received by the husband for criminal conversation must easily have paid for those parts of the costs which might have fallen on the husband. In the 17 cases between 1754 and 1857, for which Acts specify costs awarded for criminal conversation, damages awarded to husbands averaged £1,439 or £1,289 more than costs the bulk of which they would not normally have had to pay. The highest of the damages in these cases was £5,000 in 1802 and 1825, the lowest was £20 in 1842.

Damages could be much higher. £20,000 was awarded in two criminal conversation cases of 1809 and 1808 specified in Acts of 1810 and 1811.[41] The Earl of Rosebery asked for £30,000 in 1814 and received £15,000.[42] Between 1780 and 1857 damages of over £500 were awarded to injured husbands for criminal conversation in well over half the 223 cases on record which issued in divorce Acts; in 12 per cent the damages were over £5,000[43] and they averaged £8,500. Actions for criminal conversation might be brought for profit as in the unsuccessful case in 1836 by Norton against Lord Melbourne, then Prime Minister.[44]

There are plenty of instances on record where the procuring of a divorce Act was rapid enough. Lord Rosebery discovered his wife's adultery in November 1814 and secured royal assent to his divorce Act on June 28, 1815.[45] A marriage contracted in March 1850, where the adultery was discovered in January 1851, was fully dissolved on August 7th 1851.[46]. Most divorces were accomplished within the year, and the parties were free to re-marry as soon as their Act had received royal assent.

Rejections of pleas for damages or divorce occurred if the adultery could not be proved. In 43 per cent of divorce Acts there is stated to have been either an elopement or a child born which could not have been the spouse's. In some cases, evidence was more troublesome, and consisted of letters or the statements of witnesses such as servants, neighbours, landladies.[47]

Pleas for parliamentary divorce and for divorces *a mensa et thoro* were refused if the plaintiff could be shown to have committed adultery as well, and counter charges on this score were not uncommon.[48] A spouse also could not obtain the relief sought if he or she had condoned the adultery (e.g. by inter-course after discovery of the adultery) or had colluded or connived at it, and there were knotty legal problems about the precise nature of these impediments to divorce.[49] These causes do not seem to have prevented the obtaining of damages for criminal conversation. Thus, Dennis, refused a divorce *a mensa et thoro* in the Consistory Court in 1808 for condoning his wife's adultery and/or because of his own adultery, had procured £5,000 damages at the King's Bench in a criminal conversation case against his own brother for adultery with his wife.[50]

2. The Matrimonial Causes Act of 1857

The Report of the Royal Commission of 1853, headed by Lord Campbell, was clearly both inaccurate and biassed. It would be idle to speculate on the reasons. Perhaps the clerks were incompetent. Perhaps the Commissioners had a strong desire for the change, for this reason or that, without too much particularity about the means. Lord Campbell hailed from Scotland and was on his promotion. The Church of England, which would lose jurisdiction, was becoming a popular target. Reducing expense and opening to the poor what is open to the rich is always a good platform and in the issue of divorce the way had been well paved.

Lord Maule's judgment in a case of bigamy in 1845, widely quoted and still famous, mocked at the current procedures. The culprit, who pleaded that he had re-married without obtaining a divorce because he could not afford a divorce, was castigated for not having spent the necessary £1,000, which he did not possess. Maule lingered with loving detail on the procedures he would have had to go through to obtain a divorce, and pronounced as his sentence for the bigamy one day's imprisonment, already served.[51]

Less well known is the part played by the famous and eccentric Lord Brougham, who had defended Sir John Mildmay in the 1814 Rosebery criminal conversation case[52] and Queen Caroline against George IV's charges of adultery against her in 1820,[53] and had risen to be Lord Chancellor (1830–4). He had raised the issue of divorce reform in Parliament in 1844, averring, among other things, that 'the remedy was at present confined to the rich; no poor man, no man even of moderate means could avail himself of it'.[54] He heard numerous cases in the House of Lords in the 1840s and 1850s[55] and lost no opportunity of publicising divorces which were expensive.

Hartley's divorce of 1850, reported in *The Times* of 8 March 1850[56] was a case in point. Hartley was a Liverpool engineer. Thompson, the adulterer, was also an engineer. Initially he disputed the charge. Hartley had obtained £4,000 damages, and the costs, awarded against Thompson, had amounted to a further '£690 odd', taxed and paid. Lord Brougham, presiding at the House of Lords' hearing for the second reading of the divorce Bill, commented 'Enormous . . . An engineer against an engineer . . . Why, it is perfectly monstrous . . .'. In reply to the point

'But your Lordship must recollect that they are two railway engineers', Lord Brougham rejoined 'I don't care if they were Californian engineers . . . I still say the amount is monstrous . . . Why the thing is preposterous'. Hartley claimed to have expended nearly £3,000 in procuring proofs. In moving for the second reading of his Bill, Lord Brougham made a more general speech: 'he could not but advert to the enormous expense parties were put to in cases of this sort in consequence of the present system . . . Had Mr. Hartley been a poor man . . .it would have been impossible that he should have obtained that remedy to which he was clearly entitled . . . it was monstrous'. In the early summer of the same year, Lord Brougham was delayed in arriving at the House of Lords for the hearing of Chippendall's Bill; he was a poor man, so poor that he was permitted to sue as a pauper.[57] He obtained his remedy nonetheless.

In Hartley's case in 1850 the adulterer certainly paid heavily. It is not clear that the husband, Hartley, was out of pocket, even though, unlike for instance the Earl of Rosebery in 1814−15, he was probably not richer. A more general problem had however developed. Whereas divorces had on the whole been financially advantageous to husbands and financially punitive to the adulterer, the courts were awarding lower damages for criminal conversation than they had done in the late eighteenth and early nineteenth century, and a good many adulterers were escaping altogether. Between 1800 and 1820 damages of £500 or more were awarded in 38 out of 50 cases, 76 per cent, at an average figure of £4,568, between 1820 and 1830 in 16 out of 25 cases, 64 per cent, at an average figure of £2,687, between 1830 and 1857 in 44 out of 114 cases, only 38 per cent and at a reduced average of £1,640.[58] In other words, the proportion of criminal conversation cases in which damages over £500 were awarded had halved and where they were awarded it was at about a third of the level of 30 years earlier. Moreover the chance of receiving damages at all was much reduced.

The need for a verdict at law in a criminal conversation case in order to petition for a divorce Bill had always been waived if it could be shown that none could be brought because the adulterer was, for example, unknown, dead, bankrupt, out of jurisdiction. The requirement that the damages awarded should have been paid was similarly waived if it could be shown to be impossible to collect them. Between 1800 and 1820 there were only two instances out of 50 divorce Acts in which no criminal conversation case had been possible, in one because it was a wife's divorce. In the 1820s, which sported four instances of damages over £5,000 and ten between £1,000 and £5,000, it proved impossible to collect the damages in one of the former and four of the latter, and in two further instances no case was possible, making seven out of 25 divorces or 28 per cent in which no damages nor probably costs could be procured. No criminal conversation case could be brought in about a quarter of the 114 cases after 1830. Adulterers increasingly went abroad out of jurisdiction, and the expense would then fall on the husband.[59] Hartley's case was unusual in the costs incurred, but by 1850 he was perhaps fortunate not to have to pay anything himself.

It is tempting to suppose that the reduced damages awarded were connected with a drop in social class of those obtaining divorces in the same period. However, the aristocracy had had no monopoly of high damages nor indeed always obtained them. The 26 instances of damages over £5,000 cited in divorce Acts were evenly divided between aristocracy, those entitled 'Esq' and others.[60] Lower-class appellants tended to be awarded relatively low damages. On the other hand, there is no evidence of a general drop in the social class of successful appellants between the 1750s and 1850s, and certainly not one commensurate with the drop in the level of damages. It seems more likely that the courts were awarding lower damages because, for instance, divorce had become a more routine part of the social scene.

Criminal conversation cases were not much alluded to in Parliamentary Debates of the Matrimonial Causes Bill except as infamously notorious abroad and a scandal of English life, 'that foul opprobrium upon our judicial system, that stain upon our national character, the abominable action of crim. con.'[61] Advocates of the measure did not remark on the gradual breakdown of the system which had prevailed, where adultery with another man's wife had been an expensive pastime and the husband relatively protected financially. It may have been sufficiently slow to have escaped notice. In any case in promoting the Matrimonial Causes Act, Members of Parliament preferred to cite the 1853 Commisssion's facts and figures, and to recommend a simpler, less expensive process, as in Scotland. The almost invariable claim was that no change was to take place except in procedure: criminal conversation cases were to be abolished, as were ecclesiastical and parliamentary divorce. Divorces *a mensa et thoro* became judicial separations, private Acts were replaced by judicial divorces, and all was administered by a single court.[62]

Opposition to the Matrimonial Causes Bill was strong but ineffective. Prominent among its opponents was Gladstone, then member of Parliament for the University of Oxford.[63] He is reputed to have made a hundred speeches on the subject in the 1857 debates. To its opponents, the Matrimonial Causes Act would not merely change the procedure for procuring divorces. It would legalise it and do away with the 'indissoluble marriage to which we have adhered since England was England'.[64] The clergy were up in arms, and won only the right to refuse Church marriage to divorced persons, a right which the Church continued to exercise until 1985[65] but which was worth less because secular marriage in Registry Offices had been introduced in 1836[66] and by 1857 already accounted for 5 per cent of marriages.[67]

Women and their advocates were also hostile to the measure. The reason for this was that substantially the same grounds for divorce that were used in passing private Acts were to become statutory, viz. that a man could procure a divorce for simple adultery but a woman could obtain one only if the husband's adultery was compounded by other offences. In 1857 to be a woman divorced for adultery was to become a social outcast: 'she is driven from society, she has no refuge, no-one will receive her'.[68] Unrepresented in Parliament, women brought a petition against the Bill, signed by 16,000.[69] Gladstone in particular spoke on their behalf and on the unfortunate inequality between husband and wife which he claimed that the new legislation would promote:

> . . . for my part I shall always assert the principle of equal rights. It is impossible to do a greater mischief than to begin now, in the middle of the nineteenth century, to undo with regard to womankind that which has already been done on their behalf, by slow degrees, in the preceding eighteen centuries, and to say that the husband shall be authorized to dismiss his wife on grounds for which the wife shall not be authorized to dismiss her husband. If there is one broad and palpable result of Christianity which we ought to regard as precious, it is that has placed the seal of God Almighty upon

the equality of man and woman with respect to everything that relates to those rights; and I will offer the utmost resistance to any attempt to induce this House to adopt a measure which, I believe, would lead to the degradation of woman.[70]

When the House of Lords refused divorces to women for their husband's adultery in the first part of the nineteenth century, it was sometimes commented that divorces would rise uncontrollably if women could divorce their husbands for adultery. Thus the Duke of Norfolk in 1811: '. . . their Lordships would be opening such a door to divorces that they would go beyond number and their Lordships would have nothing else to do than to grant them . . .'[71] The stigma which attached to divorce would go for reasons detailed by Lord Brougham in Mrs Hall's case of 1850, viz. that husband and wife would be able to agree on the husband's giving grounds for a divorce which could then be procured by the wife: men did not lose their rank and station for breaking their marriage vows in the fashion that women did.[72]

In Parliamentary Debates it was more common to defend the difference made between husband and wife by drawing a distinction between adultery as committed by husbands and wives: 'It was possible for a wife to pardon a husband who had committed adultery; but it was hardly possible for a husband ever really to pardon the adultery of a wife'[73] or 'in all ages it had been felt that the adultery of the wife brought ruin on the married state, but not so the simple unfaithfulness of the husband'.[74] Since it was being claimed that the change to be made was but a procedural one, it would not have been consistent radically to alter the grounds of divorce, which allowing women to procure divorces for simple adultery would have been. It should however be noted that nearly 70 years were to elapse before they could do so.[75]

There were accurate forecasts made of the divorce rate if the Matrimonial Causes Bill became law, that, judging by Scottish figures, it would rise from its present figure (3.3 per annum), represented as 2 a year, to about 100–150 per annum. In reply to the favourite argument that what was open to the rich should be open to the poor, opponents like Gladstone, pointed out that if indeed it had this effect, this was a substantial change, if only because the constraints of Society afforded a protection against divorce in the upper classes which would be lacking in other classes. He did not note, as a member only of the House of

Figure 5.1   Divorces enacted and decrees absolute, England (1730−1980)*

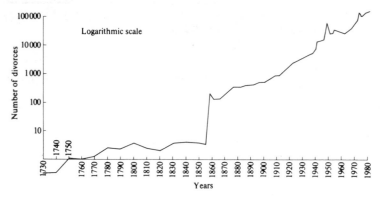

(Figures are given in ten-yearly averages until 1857, then in five-yearly averages. See also Chapter 5, Appendices 1 and 2.)

* Compiled from a count of divorce Acts until 1857 and from 1858 onwards from data in Royal Commissions 1912−13 and 1956, HMSO *Social Trends* (1981). Sources do not quite tally, and all figures after 1857 should be treated as approximate *passim*. The logarithmic graph plots the number of divorces on a scale which becomes steadily more compressed in order that equal percentage changes are represented as equal distance on the vertical axis. The upward tendency of the curve indicates an exponential increase in the number of divorces, its fairly steady gradient a fairly steady rate of increase over time. Where the gradient is identical the rate of increase is the same. The rise from *c.* 3.3 divorces per annum to *c.* 150 per annum after the 1857 Act, a 46-fold (or 4,545 per cent) increase in a year, is conspicuous with this mode of presentation but because the absolute figures are comparatively so low, it cannot readily be seen in the ordinary graphs of Appendix 5.2, especially B−D, scaled to incorporate 150,000 divorces per annum.

Commons he probably did not know, the extent to which divorce had already travelled downwards in the social hierarchy.

One hundred fifty a year was not a vast figure in a married population of about 6 million. By 1900 there were still only around 500 divorces a year in a married population of about 11 million. However by 1980 there were 150,000 divorces a year, or 1 in 11 of the married population each year a matter of 1,000 times as many as when divorce was legalised some 120 years earlier. A logarithmic graph of divorce rates from 1730 to 1980 highlights the probable importance of the 1857 Act in the growth of English divorce. The rate of increase was as great in the second half of the eighteenth century as in the second half of the nineteenth century, and 1857 stands out clearly as a watershed. The other marked departure from a fairly steady rate of increase was in World War II; the high divorce rate then is popularly attributed to hurried war marriages, the prolonged absence of husbands and the stationing of foreign troops, especially American, all over England, with chocolate, charm and nylon stockings to offer.[76]

Until 1923, when women could for the first time get divorces for simple adultery by their husbands, 60 per cent of divorces were procured by husbands. Thereafter the proportions reversed and it was wives who obtained 60 per cent of the divorces. The exception was the two World Wars, 1914–18 and 1939–45, when 70 per cent of divorces were instituted by husbands.[77]

The Matrimonial Causes Act of 1937[78] made desertion and cruelty independent grounds for divorce. Desertion soon accounted for about half the divorces.[79] The 1937 Act was preceded by a period of 'hotel' cases. The *Encyclopedia Britannica* of 1929 attributed these to the 1923 Act: 'one result of equalizing the grounds of divorce [between the sexes] was the marked increase in the number of wives' suits in which the charge was based on a solitary incident in a hotel.'[80] The husband would 'act the gentleman' and spend a weekend in a hotel with a hired person, shoes outside the door. A.P. Herbert's novel *Holy Deadlock* (1934) depicts such a case, and A.P. Herbert, then member of Parliament for the University of Oxford, was the introducer of the Bill which became the Matrimonial Causes Act of 1937. In 1969 a further step was taken. The Divorce Reform Act of that year introduced divorce by consent, rather than as previously only for an offence, by treating the 'irretrievable breakdown' of a marriage as grounds for dissolving it.[81]

A stigma continued to attach to divorce for at least a century after its 'legalisation' in 1857. In 1957 Graveson was writing:

> Society has become increasingly accustomed to divorce as a normal social institution. The divorced person is no longer a social outcast but acceptable *in all but the most exclusive circles of Society*. (my italics)[82]

It was, for example, only in the 1950s that divorced persons were allowed into the Royal Enclosure at the Royal Ascot races, and Prince Charles's wedding in 1981 was the first such ceremonial occasion which could be attended by divorced persons. It is doubtful whether even at that date the heir to the English throne could have married a divorced woman, although he could by then marry the daughter of divorced parents. A new note was struck in 1984 with the claim that 'divorce is now a major health hazard'.[83] In 1985 it was 'Marriages of unemployed and unskilled more likely to end in divorce'.[84]

During the debates leading to the Matrimonial Causes Act of 1857 countries with high and increasing divorce rates were often cited: the United States, Prussia, and France after the Revolution were favourite examples.[85] The Bishop of Oxford warned:

> It might be long before the people would take advantage of the new law, for such changes seldom appeared in their full effects all at once; but slowly, step by step, it might change the whole moral aspect of the nation.[86]

But for all their words about how the Church vows of cleaving 'until death us do part' would become 'until we do quarrel'[87] even opponents of the 1857 Act probably did not seriously expect quite the increase in divorce which ultimately took place. This is further depicted in Appendix 5.2 to this chapter. Chapter 7, Section 2 discusses some explanations.

Notes

1. B. Malinowski 'A sociological analysis of the rationale of the prohibited Degrees of Marriage'. Appendix 3 in the Church of England Commission *Kindred and Affinity as Impediments to Marriage* London 1940.

2. E.g. P. Laslett (ed.) *Household & Family in Past Time* CUP 1972.

3. See e.g. L. Stone *The Family, Sex and Marriage in England 1500–1800* London 1977, revised edition 1979, p. 416ff; R. Houlbrooke *The English Family 1450–1700* London 1984, especially pp. 10ff, 15.

4. See Chapter 8, Section 1 for examples.

5. For examples see Chapter 7, Section 2.

6. 32 H 8 c 38 re-enacted 1 Eliz 1 c 1.

7. 1 Jac 1 c 11, repealed and re-enacted 9 Geo 4 c 31 sec 22.

8. Whether marriage after a divorce *a mensa et thoro* constituted bigamy has been a debated point. 1 Jac 1 c 11 made the proviso that the penalty (of death) was not to apply to persons divorced by a sentence of the ecclesiastical court. But

it has been argued that marriages between such persons were nevertheless included as bigamy (subject only to lesser ecclesiastical penalties), and were certainly not valid. In 1605 Lady Rich, after receiving a divorce *a mensa et thoro* 'married' Montjoy, Earl of Devonshire. The 'marriage' was performed by Laud, later Archbishop of Canterbury, then the Earl's chaplain, and nearly cost Laud his career. According to G. Craik *The Romance of the Peerage* London 1848, 'the marriage drew forth instantly an outcry of horror and indignation' (vol 1, p. 277), which the earlier adulteries of the parties had not done. The Earl fell from 'honour to contempt', which 'broke the poor Earl's heart. He died . . . on the 3rd of April 1606, within little more than three months after his marriage' (Craik *The Romance of the Peerage* vol 1, p. 282). Cf Craik *The Romance of the Peerage* vol 1, pp. 417−19 for more general discussion of the point. See also e.g. T.D. Woolsey *Essay on Divorce and Divorce Legislation* New York 1869, pp. 171−2, 289−292.

9. See e.g. J.F. MacQueen *A Practical Treatise on the Appellate Jurisdiction of the House of Lords and Privy Council together with the Practice on Parliamentary Divorce* London 1842, p. 465 note (b); P.M. Bromley *Family Law* 6th edn. 1981, p. 187 note 2.

10. See e.g. *The Times* 18 December 1815, Archer page 3, col e, Cresswell.

11. Although J.T. Hammick *The Marriage Law of England* 2nd revision and enlarged edition 1887, p. 139 mentions perjury as an offence for which someone could be indicted if he or she knew there was an impediment and did not declare it.

12. According to Hammick *The Marriage Law of England*, p. 24 'A second marriage whilst the former (undivorced) husband or wife is known to be living constitutes . . . bigamy'. 'The offence of bigamy was exclusively of ecclesiastical cognizance until the year 1603, when it was made a felony' . . . 'By 1 Jac c 11, repealed and re-enacted by 9 Geo c 31, sec 22, which enactment was treated in the same way by 24 & 25 Vict c 100, s 57' (Hammick ibid. who says also that 'In the proposed alteration of laws under the Commonwealth, it was proposed in accordance with the severity of Puritan notions, that bigamy should be punished with death'.) The Offences against the Person Act, 24 & 25 Vic c 100 sec 57 (1861) put the penalty for the felony of bigamy at penal servitude not exceeding 7 years or imprisonment with or without hard labour for 2 years. It applied to British subjects anywhere, excluding cases where the previous marriage was void (though not where it was only voidable) or a divorce had taken place. Bigamous 'marriages' are void but there is no relief from the penalty if the 'marriage' would have been void for other reasons, e.g. being within the Prohibited Degrees.

13. See e.g. MacQueen *A Practical Treatise*, p. 471; G. Howard *A History of Matrimonial Institutions* Chicago 1904, reprinted 1964, vol 2, pp. 103−4 differs, and considers the earliest real divorces to be those of the Earl of Macclesfield in 1698 and of the Duke of Norfolk in 1700.

14. Duke of Norfolk 11 & 12 Gul 3 *c 2*.

15. MacQueen *A Practical Treatise*, p. 473; F. Clifford *A History of Private Bill Legislation* London 1885, vol 1, pp. 411−12.

16. All 322 divorce Acts between 1700 and 1857 mention a previous divorce *a mensa et thoro*. Before 1750 over two-thirds of divorce Acts did not mention any verdict at law. Between 1750 and 1780 about a third did not. In the 1790s all but 3 of 42 Acts did. Standing Orders in Parliament, Lords 28 March 1798, no 168, regularised the requirement for a verdict at law, if it was possible, as well as for an ecclesiastical 'divorce'. See S. Wolfram 'Divorce in England 1700−1857' *Oxford Journal of Legal Studies* 1985, vol 5 no 2, especially Table 2 and pp. 159−60.

17. Matrimonial Causes Act 1857, 20 & 21 Vic c 85; section 27 specified the

aggravations of adultery for which women could get divorces. The Matrimonial Causes Act 1923 13 & 14 Geo c 19 (repealed and re-enacted 1925) allowed women to obtain divorces for adultery *simpliciter*, the Matrimonial Causes Act 1937 I Ed 8 & Geo 6 c 57 introduced desertion and cruelty as separate grounds for divorce.

18. They were almost certainly unable to. Cf MacQueen *A Practical Treatise*, p. 492 ('There can be no precedent to support an action for criminal conversation by a wife against the seducer of her husband') and Wolfram 'Divorce in England', p. 159 note 17.

19. An Act to dissolve the marriage of *Jane Campbell* with *Edward Addison* her now husband on Account of Incestuous Adultery with the Sister of the said Jane Campbell 1801, 41 Geo 3 *c 102*.

20. The other three were Mrs Turton 1831, 1 & 2 W 4 *c 35* (incestuous adultery), Mrs Battersby 1840, 3 & 4 Vic *c 48* (adultery and bigamy), Mrs Hall 1850 13 & 14 Vic *c 25* (adultery and bigamy). Mrs Teush 1805, Mrs Moffat 1832 and Mrs Dawson 1848 were unable to get divorce acts for simple adultery. Cf MacQueen *A Practical Treatise*, pp. 480−4; Clifford *A History of Private Bill Legislation* vol 1, pp. 416−18; Wolfram 'Divorce in England', pp. 174−5.

21. Fourteen are recorded but only thirteen appear to exist (see Appendix 5.1A to this chapter).

22. Divorce Acts, 123 − sess 2, May − June 1857, reprinted in *British Parliamentary Papers* Irish University Press vol 3 1971, p. 117, is the most accurate official annual return of English divorces before 1857. I have been unable to find any trace of one recorded for 1714. The return omitted 7 Acts between 1750 and 1857, and 5 more were passed after it was printed. See Appendix 5.1A to this chapter (reproduced from Wolfram 'Divorce in England', p. 181).

23. *First Report of the Commissioners appointed by her Majesty to enquire into the law of divorce & more particularly into the mode of obtaining divorces a vinculo*, 1853, reprinted in *British Parliamentary Papers* vol 1 1969.

23A. See below, e.g. notes 24, 25, 30 and references in Wolfram 'Divorce in England'.

24. *First Report of the Commissioners . . . into the law of divorce*, p. 10. The 1853 Commission's figures reappear in the later Royal Commissions on divorce of 1912−13 and 1956 and seem to be the source of the incorrect figure of *c.* 250 divorces before 1858, commonly found (70 fewer than there were). L. Holcombe *Wives and Property. Reform of the Married Women's Property Law in Nineteenth-Century England* Toronto and Oxford 1983 gives 90 instead of 193 for 1800−57, possibly following W.S. Holdsworth *A History of English Law* 1922 vol 1, p. 623, who gives this figure for 1800−52. Fuller details of these errors are given in Wolfram 'Divorce in England' especially note 3 and Appendix 1B, reproduced in Appendix 5.1B to this chapter.

24A. See Appendix 5.1A to this chapter.

25. The view had already been expressed by Lord Brougham in Parliament in 1844 (*Hansard*, 3rd series, lxiii, 694−700) and Judge Maule in R. v. Hall 1845, and continues into modern legal textbooks, e.g. S.M. Cretney *Principles of Family Law* 3rd edn. 1979, p. 97; P.M. Bromley *Family Law* 6th edn 1981, p. 187; B.M. Hoggett and D.S. Pearl *The Family, Law and Society* London 1983 Chapter 5 Section 1, e.g. p. 140; and historical writings, e.g. M.L. Shanley ' "One must ride behind". Married Women's Property & the Divorce Act of 1857', *Victorian Studies* vol 25, 1982, p. 357; Holcombe *Wives and Property*, p. 96. See Wolfram 'Divorce in England' especially note 4, p. 157 for other examples.

26. pp. 29−31.

27. Britten (p. 29), Caton, Faussett, Ashby & Tayleur (p. 31) were stated not

to have obtained divorce Acts. Britten obtained one in 1845, Faussett in 1849, Ashby in 1850, Tayleur in 1851. Caton's was in 1854, after the Commission reported. It recorded 32 husbands obtaining divorces *a mensa et thoro* for adultery (and one for cruelty), and 21 wives (one of whom obtained a divorce Act). The Consistory Court of London was not the only court to grant these divorces.

28. *First Report of the Commissioners . . . into the law of divorce*, pp. 18 and 33. Holcombe *Wives and Property*, p. 96, speaks as if this part of the procedure was said to cost £600–£800, the figure normally given for the total proceedings, i.e. including the preliminaries of divorces *a mensa et thoro* and actions for criminal conversation. See also below note 37.

29. No names or chapter numbers are given. S. Anderson has succeeded in identifying them through the solicitors used who were named. See S. Anderson 'Legislative Divorce — Law for the Aristocracy?' in G. Rubin and D. Sugarman (eds) *Law, Society and Economy. Essays in Legal History* 1984 note 100.

30. See Appendix 5.1A to this chapter.

30A. See below pp. 81–2.

31. Box 1701 12 & 13 W 3 *c 18*.

32. Jermyn 1711 MS 9 Anne *c 30*.

33. Cobb 1729 2 Geo 2 *c 31*.

34. These occupations are listed as they are specified in the divorce Acts. Further details are given in Wolfram 'Divorce in England', p. 164 Table 3, and in the section 'Divorce and the Aristocracy', pp. 162–6; other details may be found in Anderson 'Legislative Divorce', pp. 414, 426–35 (commented on by Wolfram 'Divorce in England', p. 162 note 25). See Appendices 5.1C and 5.1D to this chapter for a summary of ranks and occupations of husbands and adulterers. Peerage and Baronetage are combined as 'Titled', 'Esq' (= Esquire) ranks higher than 'gentleman'. It seems not unreasonable to take these as the 'upper classes'. But the intricacies of the class system and lack of extensive data about individuals necessary to ascertain their exact social position makes it impossible for any summary to be anything but crude.

The nature of the problem is easily seen for instance by taking the personnel in novels by Anthony Trollope (1815–82), a great expert on the nuances of social stratification. *Doctor Thorne* 1858 is as good an example as any. Doctor Thorne himself, of good family, is the village doctor, without other means. He is an intimate friend of the local squire Mr Gresham. Mr Gresham is married to Lady Arabella, 'sister of the great Whig Earl' (de Courcy) (the de Courcys are shown as a rather stupid bunch). He becomes heavily in debt to the wealthy Sir Roger Scratchard, previously in a 'low rank of life . . . a journeyman stone-mason', whose sister, while engaged to a respectable tradesman, was seduced under promises of marriage and probably with the aid of drugs, by Doctor Thorne's villainous brother. Roger Scratchard killed the seducer and was imprisoned for 6 months. The daughter of the illicit union, brought up by Doctor Thorne as his niece Mary Thorne, and educated with the Gresham children, is unquestionably a lady. Ultimately she inherits Sir Roger's money (which cancels out the misfortune of her birth) and marries Frank Gresham, eldest son and heir of Mr Gresham, who has long been intent on marriage with her. Sir Roger Scratchard is a remarkable man but decidedly not a gentleman, his wife even less a lady, and his son, Sir Louis, is also no gentleman: as Trollope says elsewhere, that operation with the sow's ear rarely succeeds in the first generation. The clergyman in *Dr Thorne*, Mr Oriel, is a gentleman, with private means. Plenty of Trollope's clergymen are not (e.g. Mr Slope in *Barchester Towers* 1857 or Mr Maguire in *Miss Mackenzie* 1864); others are excessively poor e.g. Mr Crawley especially in *Framley Parsonage* 1861 and *The last Chronicle of Barset* 1867. There is no purpose in further labouring the point that the applicants for divorce could not be more than approximately divided into social class.

Anderson employs previously devised social stratifications with some qualifications (p. 416 note 11). The proportion of 'upper class' petitioning comes out fairly close to Appendix 5.1C, at about half mid-eighteenth to mid-nineteenth century. Anderson claims that no petitioners for a statutory divorce came from the lower orders (p. 417) but this conclusion seems open to question.

35. The original handwritten Acts are preserved in the House of Lords Records Office at London and are the only documents which rate as official.

36. L 700 or L 800 *First Report of the Commissioners . . . into the law of divorce*, p. 18 section XLIV.

37. Ibid., p. 18. Contested cases were put at £300−£500. Holcombe *Wives and Property*, p. 95, says incorrectly that 'In the 1850s it was estimated that an uncontested [sic] divorce *a mensa et thoro* cost between £300 and £500, while if the divorce was contested the cost might run into thousands of pounds'. (Holcombe's account of the procedures pp. 93−6 is confusing and somewhat inaccurate.)

38. Chippindall 1850 13 & 14 Vic *c 22*.

39. In 1820 arrangements were made for the conduct of divorces *a mensa et thoro* and of criminal conversation cases in India, 1 Geo 4 c 101. Cf MacQueen *A Practical Treatise*, pp. 547, Appendix IX, 796−7. Damages were then assessed in rupees. There were 16 such cases between 1820 and 1857. Damages ranged from 2,000 to 25,000 rupees. Costs are given once at 831 rupees: Cheape's divorce Act 1844 7 & 8 Vic *c 47* (damages 3,000 rupees). See also S. Anderson 'Legislative Divorce', p. 436ff, who in a very detailed study of costs, using ecclesiastical records, concludes that '75% paid less than £250' (p. 441).

40. 13 & 14 Vic *c 22*.

41. These were to the Rt. Hon Henry Wellesley against Lord Paget for the adultery of his wife Lady Charlotte Cadogan in 1809 (Divorce Act: 50 Geo 3 *c 1*, 1810), and Lord Cloncurry against Sir John Piers Bt in 1808 (Divorce Act: 51 Geo 3 *c 73*, 1811).

42. 55 Geo 3 *c 104*. See above Chapter 3 note 2. The criminal conversation case in December 1914 against Sir John Mildmay was reported at length in *The Times*, 12 December 1814 p. 2 col d − p. 3 col e. The divorce Act received Royal Assent on 28 June 1815.

43. In 26 cases damages of over £5,000 were awarded, in 68 between £1,000 and £5,000, in 32 between £500 and £1,000. See Wolfram 'Divorce in England', Table 4 and Section 'Damages and Costs', pp. 166−72 and Appendix 5.1E to this chapter. ˙

44. See e.g. *Dictionary of National Biography* 'Caroline Norton', p. 207; David Cecil *Melbourne* 1965 edn. Part 4, Chapter 13 (4).

45. See above note 42 and Chapter 3, note 2.

46. Webster 1851 14 & 15 Vic *c 25*.

47. See e.g. Lismore's case *The Times* 2 May 1826, p. 4 vol f (7 Geo 4 c 55, 1826); Dillon's case Consistory Court 1842 reported in *The Times* 28 January 1842, p. 6 col f − p. 7 col a, 23 April, p. 6 col f et seq; Hill's case 1849 House of Lords *The Times* 27 July 1849, p. 7 col c, 30 July, p. 8 col d (12 & 13 Vic *c 34*, 1849); Ashby's case 1850 House of Lords *The Times* 23 March, p. 7 col b (13 & 14 Vic *c 23*, 1850); Talbot's case House of Lords, reported in *The Times* 13 March 1856, p. 10 col d−e, 5 May, p. 10 col c, 23 May, p. 5 col a (19 & 20 Vic *c 16*, 1856). See Wolfram 'Divorce in England', p. 173 Table 6 and p. 174 for details.

48. This was not so initially. The Duke of Norfolk procured his divorce in 1700 for the Duchess' adultery despite his well-known profligacy (MacQueen *A Practical Treatise*, p. 572; Clifford *A History of Private Bill Legislation*, vol 1 p. 408 note 2). But it was quite clear later. See e.g. Dennis 1808 *The Times* 26 January,

p. 3 col c; he secured damages of £5000 at the King's Bench against his own brother but was refused a divorce *a mensa et thoro* in the Consistory Court in 1808 (cf note 43). See also e.g. King's case 1850 in the Consistory Court *The Times* 15 July 1850, p. 7 col b, 9 December col a−b where the principle was stated that a husband could not get a divorce *a mensa et thoro* for his wife's adultery if himself guilty of adultery.

49. See e.g. Lismore's case 1825 Consistory Court *The Times* 10 November 1825, p. 3 cols e−f, 17 November, p. 3 col a (7 Geo *c 55*, 1826); (Mrs) Turton's case 1830 Consistory Court *The Times* 2 July 1830, p. 3 col f − p. 4 col b, 8 July, p. 6 col b, 19 July, p. 3 col f (1 & 2 W 4 *c 35*, 1831); Ashby's case 1850 *The Times* 2 March 1850, p. 7 col a (13 & 14 Vic *c 23*, 1850); Campbell's case 1857 Consistory Court, *The Times* 23 April 1857, p. 7 cols b−c, House of Lords 23, 26, 29 May, 5 June (20 & 21 Vic *c 10* 1857).

50. *The Times* 26 January 1808, p. 3 col c (cf note 41). Dennis failed, having violated his conjugal vows and been conducive to his own dishonour by leaving his wife in his profligate brother's company. There were counter-charges of both condoning and his adultery. The latter was not pursued since the former was proved and was sufficient to prevent the divorce of his wife which he sought.

51. In R. v. Hall. It is cited, with slight variation in many places including *The Times* 3 April 1845, Lord Campbell *Hansard* 3rd series vol 134, cols 14−15, *Royal Commission on Divorce & Matrimonial Causes* HMSO CMD 6478, 1912−13, p. 12 para 20, Graveson in R.H. Graveson and F.R. Crane (eds) *A Century of Family Law* London 1957, pp. 7−8; 'Divorce' *Encyclopedia Britannica* 1967 vol 7, p. 515. It is sometimes said to have been responsible for the Matrimonial Causes Act of 1857 but I have been unable to find any evidence for this.

52. Reported in *The Times* 12 December 1814, p. 2 col d − p. 3 col e. See Chapter 3 note 2 for details of the case. Sir John Mildmay admitted guilt. Brougham pleaded the mitigations of youth and passion and Mildmay's straitened means at the time, as well as the punishment he and his paramour would bear by public opinion.

53. George IV brought charges of adultery against his wife, then Princess of Wales, and tried to stop her being crowned. Public sympathy was much with her, and she died soon after. See especially H. Brougham *Speeches of Henry, Lord Brougham upon Questions relating to Public Rights, Duties, and Interests; with Historical Introduction and a Critical Dissertation upon the eloquence of the Ancients* Edinburgh 1838 (4 vols) vol 1 'Queen Caroline' [1820] pp. 86−256 and 'Queen Caroline's right to be crowned with the King' 1821, pp. 256−304. Brougham claimed that the charges were trumped up and without evidence.

54. House of Lords *Hansard* 3rd series 8 March 1844 vol 73, pp. 694−9.

55. Some examples were: Matthyson *The Times* 3 July 1846, p. 7 col d; 4 July, p. 7 col c; Humphreys *The Times* 31 July 1846, p. 7 col a; Waldy *The Times* 6 March 1849, p. 7 col a; Hill *The Times* 27 July 1849, p. 7 col c; 30 July, p. 8 col d; Cripps *The Times* 14 July 1849, p, 7 col d; Mrs Hall *The Times* 27 July 1850, p. 7 col d; 3 August, p. 6 col f; Talbot *The Times* 13 March, p. 10 col d; 5 May, p. 10 col c; 23 May, p. 5 col a.

56. *The Times* 8 March 1850, p. 6 col e et seq.

57. Chippindall, Gentleman, 1850 13 & 14 Vic c 22, *The Times* 16 May 1850, p. 7 col d.

58. Calculated from data in private divorce Acts. See Appendix 5.1E to this chapter, and Wolfram 'Divorce in England', pp. 169−72.

59. Derived from data in private divorce Acts. See Appendix 5.1E to this chapter (reproduced from Wolfram 'Divorce in England', Table 4, p. 170), and Wolfram 'Divorce in England', p. 169.

60. Wolfram 'Divorce in England', Table 5, p. 173. Between 1790 and 1830,

eight titled persons (five peers and three baronets), eight 'Esqs' and eight with no titles nor described as 'gentlemen' each received £5,000 or more in damages. A further person entitled 'Esq' obtained £8,000 in 1845 and one with no title £5,000 in 1846. Plenty of titled people were awarded low damages. For instance, Lord Viscount Bolingbroke Viscount St John got £500 for the adultery of his wife, Lady Diana Spenser, eldest daughter of the Duke of Marlborough, 1768, the Hon Pownoll Pellew Esq, heir to the Rt. Hon Lord Viscount Exmouth £250 in 1820, Viscount Lismore nominal damages from the Hon R. Bingham 1826. The butchers and bakers who procured divorces tended to be awarded low damages but not invariably: a flour factor secured £400 against a surgeon for the adultery of his wife, a baker's daughter, in 1840. See Wolfram 'Divorce in England', pp. 169–72 for more details. According to C.G. Addison *Wrongs and their Remedies* (3rd and subsequent editions *Addison on the Law of Torts*) first edn. 1860, pp. 689–92 the courts were permitted to take the position in life of the adulterer but not his means into account in assessing damages. Small worth of the wife or bad conduct of the husband reduced awards.

61. *The Times* 6 March 1857, p. 7 col a. See also e.g. *Hansard* 3rd series 17 May 1857, House of Lords, vol 145, p. 536.

62. 'Criminal conversation' was abolished in sec 59 but sec 33 of the Act says: 'Any Husband may, either in a Petition for Dissolution of Marriage or for Judicial Separation, or in a Petition limited to such Object only, claim Damages from any Person on the Ground of his having committed Adultery with the Wife of such Petitioner . . . the Claim made by every such Petition shall be heard and tried on the same Principles, in the same Manner, and subject to the same or the like Rules and Regulations as Actions for Criminal Conversation are now tried and decided.' That is, the adulterer still paid damages. However, 'after the Verdict has been given the Court shall have power to direct in what Manner such Damages shall be paid or applied, and to direct that the whole or any Part thereof shall be settled for the Benefit of the Children (if any) of the Marriage, or as a Provision for the Maintenance of the Wife.' It was thus no longer possible to claim damages except in the course of obtaining a divorce and the husband might not keep the damages.

63. Gladstone, Chancellor of the Exchequer until 1855 and after 1859 (Prime Minister in 1863 et seq) was in the opposition in 1857.

64. Gladstone in House of Commons, 27 July 1857 *Hansard* 3rd series vol 147, p. 389.

65. The General Synod of the Church of England finally decided to try a scheme whereby some divorced persons would be able to marry in church in July 1983. *The Times* 15 July 1983, p. 1 col 3. But it proved contenious and by 1985 had still not been accepted. See above Chapter 2.

66. An Act for Marriages in England 1836, 6 & 7 W c 85.

67. Figures for secular marriages are given in 'Marriages (England and Wales)' 1857, 106–1–Sess 2.

68. Lord Lyndhurst in House of Lords *Hansard* 3rd series vol 142, 20 May 1856, p. 410. See above Chapter 3.

69. *Hansard* 3rd series 4 August 1857, vol 147, p. 1031.

70. Gladstone, House of Commons *Hansard* 3rd series 24 June 1857, vol 147, p. 393.

71. Reported *The Times* 2 March 1811, p. 2 col 3.

72. *The Times* 3 August 1850, p. 6 col f.

73. Lord Chancellor, House of Lords, *Hansard* 3rd series 19 May 1857, vol 145, p. 490.

74. Buxton, House of Commons, *Hansard* 3rd series 7 August 1857, vol 147, p. 1280.

75. See Chapter 7, Section 2 on the fact that women did in fact get increased grounds for divorce by the addition of desertion as a compounding offence of adultery as new grounds: after 1857 women procured 40 per cent of divorces, a far higher proportion than before.

76. Table 5.1 is not corrected for population. (See Appendix 5.2 for some population related divorce figures.) It is compiled from divorce Acts until 1857 and from 1858 on from data in the *Royal Commission on Divorce & Matrimonial Causes* HMSO Cmd 6478, 1912–13, Appendix III, Tables 1 & 2, pp. 27–8 and Table VI, p. 30, *Royal Commission on Marriage and Divorce* HMSO Cmd 9678, 1956, Appendix 2, p. 373, Diagram A and HMSO *Social Trends* 11, 1981 (published December 1980), p. 33 Table 2.13. Sources do not quite tally and figures after 1857 must be treated as approximate. See also Appendix 5.2 to this chapter. 'England' includes Wales and (until 1857) Ireland, but not Scotland, In Ireland divorce continued to be by private Act after 1857: cf Clifford *A History of Private Bill Legislation*, vol 1 London 1885, p. 451 note 3.

77. Calculated from figures in *Royal Commission* 1912–13 vol B Appendix III, Tables I–III, pp. 27–8, *Royal Commission* 1956 Appendix II, Table I, pp. 355–7, HMSO *Social Trends* 1981, Table 2.13, p. 33.

78. 1 Edw 8 & 1 Geo 6 c 57.

79. *Royal Commission* 1956 Appendix II Table 2, p. 356.

80. 'Divorce' *Encyclopedia Britannica* 14th edition 1929, vol 7, p. 457.

81. Eliz II 1969 c 55.

82. Graveson in Graveson and Crane (eds) *A Century of Family Law*, p. 13.

83. *The Times* 29 March 1984, p. 3 cols a–c. Cf below Chapter 7, Section 2.

84. *The Times* 10 January 1985.

85. See e.g. *Hansard* 3rd series vol 145, 19 May 1857, pp. 534–5; vol 147, 30 July, pp. 749, 757, 770.

86. *Hansard* 3rd series vol 145, 19 May 1857, p. 530.

87. Gladstone House of Commons *Hansard* 3rd series 31 July 1858, vol 147, p. 828 and *The Times* 1 August 1857, p. 6 col d.

Appendix 5.1A

Divorce Acts in England, before 1858, annual return (123 — Sess. 2: 28 and 29 May 1857, ordered to be printed 23 June 1857)

Return of the number of Acts of Parliament since the Reformation to the present time, dissolving marriage and enabling the parties to marry again; distinguishing the years in which such Acts passed.

Year in which Act passed	Number of Acts in each Year	Year in which Act passed	Number of Acts in each Year	Year in which Act passed	Number of Acts in each Year	Year in which Act passed	Number of Acts in each Year
1540	1	1765	1	1799	10	1829	7
1551	1†	1766	2	1800	1	1830	9
1670	1	1767	1	1801	5	1831	4
1690	1	1768	3	1802	1	1832	2
1698	1	1769	2	1803	2 +1	1833	1
1700	1	1771	1	1804	1 −1	1834	2 +1
1701	2	1772	7	1805	4	1835	5
1711	1	1773	4	1806	2	1836	1
1714§	1	1774	2	1807	1	1837	1
1724	1	1775	+1	1808	1	1838	1
1725	1	1776	6 −1	1809	5	1839	8
1729	1	1777	2 +1	1810	2	1840	8
1733	1	1778	5	1811	2	1841	5
1738	1	1779	6	1812	2	1842	8 +1
1743‡	1*	1782	1	1813	1	1843	5
1745	1	1783	3	1814	5	1844	4
1747	1	1784	1	1815	3	1845	4
1748‡	1	1785	1	1816	3	1846	6
1750	1	1787	2	1817	3	1847	2
1752	2	1788	2	1818	+1	1848	4 +1
1753	2	1789	2	1819	5	1849	7
1754	3	1790	1	1820	1	1850	7
1755	1	1791	2 +1	1821	1	1851	3
1756	1	1792	3	1822	1	1852	1
1757	2	1793	5	1823	2	1853	3
1758	2	1794	1	1824	1	1854	2
1759	1	1795§	1	1825	6	1855	5 +1
1760	2	1796	9	1826	3	1856	2
1763	1	1797	5 +1	1827	2	1857	+5
1764	1	1798	4	1828	1		317

*Public Act.
†Afterwards repealed, 1 Mary.

Note: This appears to be the most accurate official return of divorce Acts on record. Corrections are indicated as follows. §No trace; ‡Date of Acts in fact 1744 and 1749; +1 = there is one additional Act in that year; date and number = number of Acts in a year for which there was no return. It is hoped but cannot be guaranteed that corrections are complete. A correct annual return of divorce Acts for 1824–43 can be found in the Lords' *Sessional Papers* (1844) Vol. X (43) 144.

Appendix 5.1B   Cited Divorce Figures (to 1858)

The Royal Commission of 1853 gave figures for divorce Acts between 1715 and 1852 totalling 244 (instead of 300, not including one untraceable Act). This figure was repeated in the Royal Commissions of 1912–13, vol 3, 11, and 1956, 4, para 18, and in other works, sometimes extended to all divorces before 1858. Graveson (1957) *A Century of Family Law*, 5 says that 'In the two centuries before 1858 the sum total of divorces did not exceed two hundred and fifty'. Bromley (1981) *Family Law* 6th edition, 187, note 3 speaks of 'fewer than two divorces by statute a year'. Holdsworth (1922) *A History of English Law*, vol 1, 623, note 4, while citing the 1853 Commission's other figures gave 90 for 1800–50 (actual figure 172). L. Holcombe, *Wives and Property* (Toronto and Oxford 1983) 96 gives a figure of 90 for the century before 1857 (instead of 193). G. Howard (1904) *A History of Matrimonial Institutions* vol 2, 106–7, adding the Commission's other figures to '14 between 1775 and 1780' (actual figure 20) and omitting 1780–1800, arrived at a total 'for the century and a half during which the practice prevailed' of 'perhaps not more than two hundred'. Sometimes the figures err the other way. Clifford (1885) *A History of Private Bill Legislation* vol 1, 451, again citing the Commission's other figures, gave 196 for 1805–57 (actual figure 183). Shanley (1982) ' "One Must Ride Behind". Married Women's Property & the Divorce Act of 1857' *Victorian Studies* vol 25, 357 says that 'by the nineteenth century some ten private acts for divorce passed parliament each year' (actual figure 3.3 per annum). A probable source for this is a speech by Lord Brougham (1844) 3H lxxiii 695 cited by Shanley ' "One Must Ride Behind". Married Women's Property & the Divorce Act of 1857' *Victorian Studies* vol 25, 357 note 4; this gave 170 divorces for 1700–1835 (in fact 227–9) and 'In the last five years on an average nine every year' in fact an average of 7 per annum 1839–43 (1835–43 average: 4.75 per annum). Some recent works give 317, e.g. *Encyclopedia Britannica* (1967) vol 7 p 515 — without source. L. Stone *The Family, Sex and Marriage in England 1500–1800* (London 1977) 38–9 and 52, and Hoggett and Pearl (1983) *The Family, Law & Society* cite the return reproduced in Appendix 5.1A.

Appendix 5.1C

Rank/occupation of husbands in divorce Acts (1750–1857)

	1750–9 (No.)	(%)	1760–9 (No.)	(%)	1770–9 (No.)	(%)	1780–9 (No.)	(%)	1790–9 (No.)	(%)	1800–9 (No.)	(%)	1810–19 (No.)	(%)	1820–9 (No.)	(%)	1830–9 (No.)	(%)	1840–9 (No.)	(%)	1850–7 (No.)	(%)	Total (No.)	Average (%)
Titled	1	7	2	15·4	7	20·5	1	8	6	14·3	4	17·5	6	22	6	24	1	3	0	0	1	3·5	35	11·5
Esq.	8	53	4	30·7	10	29	5	41	19	45·2	10	43·5	13	48	13	52	23	66	30	55	14	48	148	47·8
Gentleman	4	27	3	23	4	11·75	1	8	3	7·1	2	9	1	4	1	4	2	6	1	2	4	14	26	8·4
'Upper classes' total	13	87	9	69·2	21	61·25	7	57	28	66·6	16	70	20	74	20	80	26	75	31	57	19	65·5	209	67·5
Clergy			1	7·7	3	9			3	7·1	2	9	1	4	1	4	3	8	3	6	1	3·5	18	6
Merchant	2	13	1	7·7	4	11·75			1	2·3	2	9	1	4			1	3	2	4	2	7	15	5
Surgeon/Doctor of Physic			1	7·7	2	6	1	8	2	5	1	4							2	4			8	3
Armed forces (not with title, 'Esq.')†							1	8			1	4	1	4	4	16			2	4	1	3	14•	5 (14)•
Others (not with title, 'Esq.')			1	7·7	1	3			3	7·1	1	4	2	7			2	6	4	7	4	14	20	6·5
No information except that no title of Esq. etc.					3	9	3	25	4	9·5			2	7			3	8	10	18	2	7	22	7
Total	15	100	13	100	34	100	12	100	42	100	23	100	27	100	25	100	35	100	54	100	29	100	309‡	100

•Twenty-nine of those listed as 'Esq.' were also in the army or navy.
†Mixed ranks.
‡One untraceable Act omitted.

Appendix 5.1D Rank/occupation of adulterers in divorce Acts (1750–1857)

	1750-9	1760-9	1770-9	1780-9	1790-9	1800-09	1810-19	1820-9	1830-9	1840-9	1850-7	Total (No.)	(%)
Title†	1	2	5	2	2	3	4	5	3•	1	2	30	10·6
Esq.†	5	2	8	6	13	5	5	4	6	4	3	61	21·7
Gentleman			1		1	1	1					4	1·4
'Upper class' total	6	4	14	8	16	9	10	9	9	5	5	95	33·8
Clergy		2	2		2	1	2	3	1	1		11	4
Merchant		1	1		1	1		1			1	6	2
Surgeon/Doctor of Physic					1		1	1		3	1	8	3
Armed forces (not with title/'Esq.')	1	1	1	2	7	1	2	5	6	11	8	44†	15·7 (22)†
Others (not with title/'Esq.')	5	2	5		4	8	3	1	2	7	4	41	14·6
No information (but no title)	2	5	6	1	6	2	9	5	14	21	5	76	27
Total	14	11	29	11	37	22	27	25	32	49	24	281	100
Wives' cases						1			1	1	1	4	
Foreign	1	1			2			2	2	3	2	10	
Unknown	1	1	5	1	3					1	2	13	

'Others' include:
1750s: Two servants of husband, warehouseman, flax dresser, jeweller/yeoman.
1760s: Teacher of music, lodger, secretary to Spanish ambassador.
1770s: Chemist, servant, soapmaker/miller, instructor, attorney.
1790s: Servant of husband, surgeon's assistant, banker.
1800s: Attorney, dentist, gold and silverman, wine merchant.
1810s: Barrister, auditor, steward of husband's estate.
1820s: Wholesale grocer.
1830s: Accountant, 'professional man'.
1840s: Barrister, oilman, solicitor, artist, civil servant.
1850s: Civil engineer, husband's usher, coachman, clerk in HM customs.

•Two foreign †Eighteen of those listed 'Esq.' were also in the army or navy.

Appendix 5.1E   Damages awarded for criminal conversation (1780–1857) cited in divorce Acts

Damages awarded	1780–9 (No.)	(%)	1790–9 (No.)	(%)	1800–9 (No.)	(%)	1810–19 (No.)	(%)	1820–9 (No.)	(%)	1830–9 (No.)	(%)	1840–9 (No.)	(%)	1850–7 (No.)	(%)	Total (No.)	Total (%)
£5000 or more	0	0	7	25	8	35	5	18	4•	16	0	0	2	4	0	0	26	12
£1000–£5000	3	50	11	39	8	35	12	44	10†	40	9	26	8	16	7	24	68	30·5
£500–£1000	3	50	3	11	1	4	4	15	2	8	3	9	8	16	7	24	32	14
£500 or more	6	100	21	75	17	74	21	77	16	64	12	35	18	36	14	48	126	56·5
Under £500			5	18	5	22	3	11	2	8	11	31	11	22	4	14	40	18
Nominal									2	8	1	3	2	4			7	3·1
Rupees							2	8	3	12	3	8	7	14	3	10	16	7·2
No case possible			2	7	(1)	4	1	4	2	8	7 (+1)	23	11 (+1)	24	7 (+1)	28	30 (+4)	15·2
Damages not specified	(5)		(11)															
Total Cases	6	100	28‡	100	23	100	27	100	25	100	35	100	50§	100	29	100	223	100

These are cases followed by divorce Acts, and the dates are those of divorce Acts.

• Damages not possible to collect in one case.

† Damages not possible to collect in four cases (all 1829).

‡ No action in three cases (unexplained).

§ No action in four cases (unexplained).

( ) Wife's case.

Appendix 5.2A

Divorces in hundreds per annum — England (1853–1908)

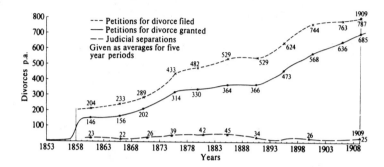

Compiled from figures in *Royal Commission on Divorces and Matrimonial Causes* 1912–1913 Appendix III, Tables 1 and 2 27–8 and Table VI, 30.

Appendix 5.2B

Divorces in thousands per annum — England (1858—1980)

Compiled from *Royal Commission of 1912—13 as in Appendix 5.2A, Royal Commission on marriage and divorce* (1956) Appendix 2, 373 Diagram A, HMSO *Social Trends 11* (1981) 33, Table 8.13.

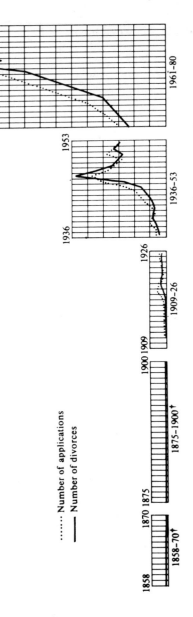

...... Number of applications
—— Number of divorces

† Absolute numbers so low that graphic illustration not possible.

Appendix 5.2C

Divorces granted in England per annum per 10,000 of the married
population (1860–1950)

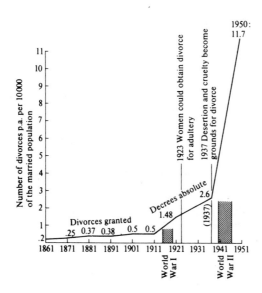

Compiled from figures in *Royal Commission* (1912) Appendix III, Table V
(which contains a misprint), *Royal Commission* (1956) Appendix II, Tables 6
and 7.

Appendix 5.2D

Divorces granted per annum in England per 1000 of the married
population (1850–1980)

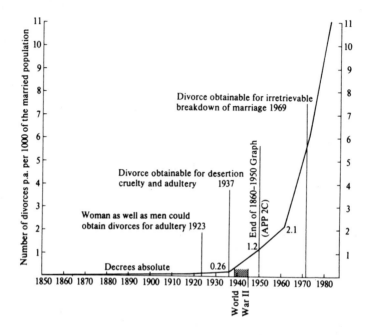

Compiled from *Royal Commission*, see Appendix 5.2C, and HMSO, see
Appendix 5.2B.

6 The Marriage Bond

Women's rights, the legal status of wives and the doctrine of the unity of husband and wife are often entangled, almost to the extent of being treated as the same phenomenon. The most common context for this conflation is in discussions of property in nineteenth-century England. Thus from the United States in 1982:

> Under the Common law a married woman had no legal identity apart from her husband. This was known as the doctrine of spousal unity . . . This meant that a man assumed legal rights over his wife's property at marriage.[1]

Or from Mill's pen in *The Subjection of Women* in 1869:

> The two are called 'one person in law', for the purpose of inferring that whatever is hers is his, but the parallel inference is never drawn that whatever is his is hers.[2]

Another book called *Woman's Work and Woman's Culture*, in hand when *The Subjection of Women* appeared, and also published in 1869, included a long article entitled 'The Property disabilities of a married woman, and other legal effects of marriage', and the article contained the comment that 'the very being or legal existence of the woman is by common law superseded during marriage; or at least, it is incorporated and consolidated into that of the husband'.[3] Or more succinctly in a contemporary aphorism: 'Husband and wife are one person, and that person is the husband.'[4]

The rights of women, and their development, are obviously not confined to the legal status of wives, nor did the legal status of wife versus husband exhaust the doctrine of the unity of husband and wife. However, rights over property are important, and the Married Women's Property Acts of 1870 and the early 1880s were significant changes in all these areas, and require some discussion of their own.

1. Property

By 1887, in the 2nd edition of *The Marriage law of England*, Hammick was writing:

> In England, an important principle arising from the marriage contract was . . . based on the maxim that husband and wife were one person in law. The wife's existence was regarded as having merged in that of her husband, and she was held to be incapable of holding separate property, or of performing separate legal acts. But the principle has been modified by recent legislation to so great an extent that it can scarcely be said to operate at the present time.[5]

The principal legislation consisted of the Married Women's Property Acts of 1870[6] and the early 1880s, especially the Married Women's Property Act 1882,[7] which made first the earnings of a married woman, and next any property she brought into the marriage or acquired during it her own. Mill, as member of Parliament for Westminster 1865−8 was one of the promoters of the 1870 Act, and the literature of 1869 must be seen as literature in a cause, that of effecting the passage of the Married Women's Property Bill, which had failed in 1868. Before 1870, the property of a married couple was entirely in the hands of the husband, except where marriage settlements had been made.

Marriage settlements were instituted in the sixteenth century, and took the form of settling property 'for her separate use' on the wife (and/or her children). Readers of English fiction will be familiar with the phenomenon; such settlements were a preliminary to virtually any marriage among the wealthy or merely well to do.

The fact was well known: 'under the present law [1869] every woman of property (unless she be singularly destitute of good advisers) has her fortune settled when she marries'.[8] The property might be settled on a wife by her own family or by her future husband, and the latter was a common occurrence in 'romantic marriages', where a wealthy man married a penniless girl, who might thereby, as in the case of Trollope's Lizzie Greystock, be transformed into a very wealthy widow.[9] On the other hand, any property not settled on the wife was the property of the husband. Many a man became rich by marriage, and there were 'peculiar temptations to scheming and unprincipled men to secure the affections of ladies with large fortunes'.[10] A wise father, of course, took his precautions, especially if he had doubts about his prospective son-in-law's motives at marriage or likely future conduct. Trollope's villainous Lopez, for instance, succeeds in getting no money with his wife.[11]

Marriage settlements were so common and institutionalised that they were much spoken of in the committees and debates leading to the 1870 Act. They were administered by the Courts of Equity, as opposed to those of Common Law.[11A] Thus we may read (1868):

> . . . at Common Law the wife had no separate existence from that of her husband . . . She and her husband were considered as one person; but that person was not a combination of the two, but was represented by the husband alone . . . No man of position or wealth would dream of allowing his daughter to marry under the simple condition of the Common Law, no matter how favourable appearances might be. He would very properly insist upon a marriage settlement . . .[12]

As might be expected, the incursions made on the Common Law by the practice of the Courts of Equity, furnished the perfect platform for securing the change: 'The Courts of Common Law and the Courts of Equity administer two distinct systems of law . . . there is one law for the rich, another for the poor' (1868).[13] 'The wealthy classes escape from the operation of the Common Law by means of marriage settlements . . . the wealthy as a rule set aside the law . . . [the humbler classes] were without the protection from the Common Law which the wealthy had found so necessary . . .' (1868).[14]

In *Wives and Property* (1983),[15] Holcombe has detailed the events leading to the 1878 Act and the more radical one of 1882.

In the 1850s an organised movement for women's rights sprang up, which put as its first goal the reform of the law of married women's property. There were publications, and women formed a committee. This held public meetings and enlisted the aid of such figures as Lord Brougham,[16] among his other roles President of the Law Amendment Society. It collected evidence of the wrongs of women, made the most of Florence Nightingale's famous work in the Crimean War (1854–6) as an example of what women could achieve, and collected 26,000 signatures for a petition, [16A] including those of such well known literary figures as Elizabeth Barrett Browning and Mrs Gaskell.[17] The petition was presented in Parliament in 1856 by Lord Brougham in the House of Lords and Sir Erskine Perry in the House of Commons.[18]

Bills were introduced both before and after the General Election of 1857 but were put on one side as a result, or by means, of the Bill which issued in the Matrimonial Causes Act of August 1857. This Act included some protection of the property of divorced, separated and deserted wives and thereby as it was put took 'the wind out of the sails' of the Feminist movement.[19]

The movement revived in the second half of the 1860s under the aegis of John Stuart Mill, elected to Parliament in 1865[20] who initiated the campaign for women's suffrage i.e. for women to have 'the vote', that is be able to vote for Members of Parliament.[21] Petitions for votes for women were presented in Parliament in 1866 and 1867, during the debates of the Reform Bill, designed to extend male suffrage; and Mill moved an amendment to include women in the new suffrage.[22]

In 1868 a Married Women's Property Bill was introduced in Parliament similar to the post-election Bill of 1857, giving married women substantially the same property rights as men and single women.[23] A new, grander Married Women's Property Committee was founded, this time with men as well as women members.[24] It renewed interest in the reform by publications, petitions, public meetings. A number of eminent members of Parliament took up the cause.[25] However it was only partly successful.

In 1868 a Parliamentary Select Committee to which the Married Women's Property Bill was referred recommended that it should go to another Select Committee in the next session. In the following year, 1869, it became too late in the session to get the Bill through all its Parliamentary states. In 1870, thanks in part to a rival, much more limited Bill introduced by the opposition, the House of Lords re-wrote the Bill, limiting it largely to married women's earnings, and it was this much modified Bill which passed *faute de mieux*,[26] and became the Married Women's Property Act of 1870.

After 1870 the impetus for reform was reduced, although the Judicature Act of 1873,[26A] which merged all the superior courts into a new Supreme Court of Judicature and ruled that where

Equity and Common Law conflicted, Equity was to prevail, made it probably inevitable that in the end all married women would enjoy the property rights that many already had under marriage settlements.[27] In 1877 an Act resembling the 1870 English Married Women's Property Act was passed for Scotland.[28] After the Liberals returned to power in the General Election of 1880 success finally greeted the protracted campaign, and Married Women's Property Acts of a more extensive nature were passed, first for Scotland in 1881[29] and then in 1882 for England.[30]

Thereafter all married women were to have all property they acquired or became entitled to before or after marriage 'for their separate use'. With a few limitations, they could dispose of it by will or otherwise, sue or be sued, carry out separate trades or businesses. Married women were made liable for debts contracted before marriage (a much troubled subject) and for the maintenance of their spouse and descendants in the same fashion as their husbands. Husbands and wives also became able to institute civil and criminal proceedings against each other with respect to property; criminal proceedings were limited to acts committed after or at the point of desertion.

The Married Women's Property Act of 1882 was hailed as a milestone in the 'emancipation' of women and, by giving wives statutory rights to property distinct from their husband's, as a nail in the coffin of the unity of husband and wife.

Holcombe stresses[31] that the 1882 Act used the model of marriage settlements, as well as the vocabulary: 'her separate property'. But subsequent legislation made further inroads on the unity of husband and wife so far as their property was concerned and also reduced the differences in their rights and obligations to each other and *vis-à-vis* the outside world. For instance, in 1925 husband and wife counted as two instead of one in receiving gifts from a third party.[32] In 1935[33] 'married women's property' replaced 'her separate property', married women became responsible for all torts and were given the same rights in bequeathing their property as their husbands.[34] In 1968 husbands and wives could bring criminal charges against each other for theft.[35]

But it is important to note that a century after the Married Women's Property Acts, the relation between a husband and wife regarding property is still substantially different from that between any other two people. Marriage entails particular conditions about income and property, which cannot be varied by intending spouses, and if terminated by divorce a division has to be made.

One area in which 'married couples' remain a separate category is that of taxation. Holcombe [36] claims, a little rashly and not perhaps quite consistently, that the law of taxation is the only part of the law of property where 'the old . . . rule of identity of husband and wife lingers on'.[37]

Until 1971 a wife's income, apart from an 'earned income allowance', was taxed as if it were 'part' of her husband's. With taxation at higher rates the higher the income, this aggregation entailed heavier taxation of two married people than of two unmarried ones (and at one time was a strong incentive to 'living in sin'). The husband's income was taken first, and the wife's as an addition, so that the wife's income was taxed at an effectively higher rate than her husband's. The husband also received a married man's allowance which reduced the portion of his income liable to taxation.

After 1971[38] a married couple could elect to have the wife's earnings taxed as if she were a single woman. But income from investment continued to be treated as the husband's, even if the property was in every other respect the wife's. Taxation on investment income is at the husband's rate and he is liable for its payment. Barring very special provisions, the husband also remained responsible for the annual tax declaration of his own and his wife's income. In commenting on the Budget of 1985, *The Times* said 'One change that the Treasury will be pressing is the separate taxation of husband and wife. However, any action on that is unlikely before 1990'.[38A]

For a time division of property between husband and wife in the event of divorce followed legal ownership. Each took his or her 'own' property. But, as Holcombe explains,[39] this principle was replaced by one peculiar to the married state. In 1967 the 'matrimonial home', construed as existing for the duration of the marriage (viz. until terminated by death or divorce) gained protection from acts of the other spouse or third parties.[40] The Matrimonial Proceedings and Property Act of 1970[41] ruled that in a divorce the 'matrimonial property' or 'family assets' were to be aggregated and then 'fairly' divided between the spouses. 'Fair' division in the 1970s normally consisted of two-thirds of the assets going to the husband, one third to the wife.[42]

The Married Women's Property Acts of the 1870s and 1880s

were lobbied for by organisations promoted by women in pursuit of women's rights. But even by the time of the 1870 Act and increasingly thereafter, there were other women's causes and other organisations dedicated to their promotion. Thus for instance the National Society for Women's Suffrage. Rights for Women did not mean just rights of married women against their husbands, but included votes for women, and their education.

Women's education, already promoted by the founding in the 1850s of what became famous girls' schools[43] and of Bedford College at the University of London was furthered in the 1870s by compulsory general education[43A] and by the founding of colleges, with staff as well as students composed entirely of women, at Oxford and Cambridge.[44] In *The Subjection of Women*, written in 1861 and published in 1869, Mill was as eloquent about women's capacities and education as he was on the subject of wives' ownership of property distinct from their husband's.[45] In Trollope's fictional London Rights of Women Institute in *Is he Popenjoy?* (1878), it is the entry of women into the professions on which interest is focused.[46]

The right to vote, first proposed by Mill in Parliament in 1868 ran into problems, not least from strife within the ranks of its promoters as to whether all women or only those without husbands should enjoy the right. The right of women to vote in municipal elections was soon achieved, by the Municipal Franchise Act of 1869.[47] But a Queen's Bench decision[48] in 1872 construed it as limited to propertied women who were single. It was 1894 before married women achieved the right.[49] The right of women, single and married, to vote in Parliamentary elections[49A] or enter Parliament[49B] followed only in 1918. Holcombe claims that both the major political parties feared for themselves with so large a body of new voters,[50] 'even though in debate many of them tried to laugh it off as ridiculous or to scorn it as subversive'[51]: 'Reforms, after all, are not carried through by debates but by the machinery controlled by political parties and their leaders.'[52] In a similar vein, Holcombe is inclined to attribute the passage of the Married Women's Property Act in 1882 to the fact that the Lord Chancellor, Selbourne, promoted it.[53] This was not, he says, because Selbourne favoured women or their causes, which he did not, but because he was a strong advocate of reform of the judiciary, which included subordination of Common Law to Equity. And what the 1882 Act did was for the future to make statutory a provision with respect to the property of married couples, different from that which had prevailed under Common Law but which, due to the practice of the Courts of Equity, had been possible, and effected for many marriages, by the use of marriage settlements. Holcombe altogether eschews the notion that a change in 'intellectual climate' played any part in this legislation or in the enfranchisement of women.

I shall return to the 'intellectual climate'. But it is worth adding a few comments on the ridicule to which Holcombe refers and which no doubt was used as a political weapon.

There are social conventions about uses of ridicule: when, about what, by whom it may be applied, which are different in different societies or at different times, and are themselves informative. For instance, a member of Parliament in nineteenth century England could make fun of women 'wearing the trousers' but there would certainly have been more than cries of 'shame' had he ridiculed e.g. the virtue or purity of English women. In England of that period this was sacrosanct. In *The Last Chronicle of Barset* (1867), Trollope depicted Grace Crawley's learning and that of her younger sister Jane, derived from their poverty stricken clergyman father's education, without the remotest hint of mockery whether his own or on the part of his characters. Grace's excellent education is admired by other characters; Trollope mentions in passing that Jane 'was only sixteen, and had as yet read nothing but Latin and Greek — unless we are to count the twelve books of Euclid and Wood's Algebra and sundry smaller exercises of the same description'.[54] The women's movements, on the other hand, then as later, went to extremes and formed an acceptable target.

Thus, the Institute in the Marylebone Road in Trollope's *Is He Popenjoy?* (1878), for instance in Chapter 17, a chapter called 'The Disabilities':

> The real and full name of the College . . . was . . . 'Rights of Women Institute. Established for the Relief of the Disabilities of Females'. By friendly tongues to friendly ears, 'The College' or 'The Institute' was the pleasant name used; but the irreverent public was apt to speak of the building generally as the 'Female Disabilities'. And the title was made even shorter. Omnibuses were desired to stop at the 'Disabilities'; and it had become notorious that it was just a mile from King's Cross to the 'Disabilities'.

The heroine, Mary, otherwise Lady George, daughter of the Dean of Brotherton, is advised not to 'go in for it' but is taken along one evening when the German Baroness Banmann is to address it about women architects. One Miss Doctor Olivia Q. Fleabody from Vermont eventually steals the thunder to the chagrin of the Baroness. The Baroness opens her address with the words 'De manifest infairiority of de tyrant saix':

> . . . There was renewed applause . . . it seemed that the men were specially charmed with this commencement of the Baroness's oration. It was so good that she repeated it . . . Lady George, with considerable trouble, was able to follow the first sentence or two . . . But . . . [then] found . . . that she could not understand two words consecutively . . . But the audience applauded throughout . . . Then came a loud rolling sentence, with the old words as an audible termination, 'de manifest infairiority of de tyrant saix' . . . Lady George became very tired of it all. It was worse than the longest and the worst sermon she had ever heard . . .'[54A]

2. Sex

By depicting the doctrine of the unity of husband and wife as an instrument of male domination over women, the promoters of the Married Women's Property Acts did not present it in a favourable light. The picture has travelled down the generations,[55] and it has become necessary to make clear what any contemporary would have known: that the idea that husband and wife are as one had many other aspects and implications. Among them was that husband and wife are 'one flesh', and that sexual intercourse should take place between and only between husband and wife.[56]

'Marriage' and its inception varies widely from one society to another and some details of English practices are relevant.

In England, a marriage is very simple, and inexpensive, to contract. It requires (3 weeks) notice or license, and a brief, theoretically public ceremony and the signing of a register, followed by 'consummation' i.e. an act of sexual intercourse. Various Statutes over the centuries have regulated the necessary ingredients of the marriage ceremony, where, when and by whom it may be conducted, as well as the circumstances in which a man and woman may marry.[56A]

The vast majority of marriages used to take place in a Church, the service (appended to this chapter) being conducted by a clergyman, with a minority in other specified places of worship. In 1836 it became possible to marry in a Registry Office, and by now this is the most common place of marriage.[57]

The main conditions which have to be satisfied by intending spouses, apart from the fact that they must be of opposite sexes, are that they must be old enough, of sound mind, consenting parties, not within the Prohibited Degrees nor currently married to anyone else, and, if minors, that they have their parent's or guardian's consent. Stating that any of these rules is in danger of being breached can prevent a marriage ceremony from being performed. Thus the famous scene in Charlotte Brontë's *Jane Eyre* (1847)[58] when the ceremony to marry Rochester to Jane Eyre is interrupted by the declaration that he has a wife still living. Some breaches of the rules are felonies, some also or instead invalidate the marriage, although if the ceremony has been performed, legal proceedings are necessary for the marriage to be pronounced void. Breaches of some rules are neither felonies nor invalidating factors. If parents do not prevent the marriage ceremony, its performance between minors gives rise to a valid marriage.[58A]

By custom a wedding normally consists of more than a marriage ceremony. The marriage ceremony is usually followed by provision of food and drink by the bride's family to invited guests, who would as a rule include the bridegroom's family.[59] 'Wedding presents' are given to the married couple before the wedding and may be displayed on the day. The bride used to be supplied with a trousseau — clothes and household linen. Omission of these aspects of weddings in no way invalidates a marriage. It might cause social comment, more particularly as such omission was proper in cases like that of Lydia Bennet's, in *Pride and Prejudice* (1813)[60] who lives with Wickham before a marriage is patched up. Mrs Bennet

> found, with amazement and horror, that her husband would not advance a guinea to buy clothes for his daughter . . . She was more alive to the disgrace which her want of new clothes must reflect on her daughter's nuptials than to any sense of

shame at her eloping and living with Wickham a fortnight before they took place.[61]

Weddings could and can be very splendid. Thus Silverbridge's in Trollope's *The Duke's Children* (1880):

> One of the most brilliant remembered in the metropolis . . .
> There had been a . . . general feeling that the bride of the heir
> of the house of Omnium should be produced to the world
> amidst a blaze of trumpets and a glare of torches.[62]

The same might be said of the 'fairy tale' wedding of Prince Charles, heir to the English throne, to Lady Diana Spencer a century later in 1981. Weddings might also be very quiet and intimate. So for example that of Silverbridge's sister, Mary:

> Both the Duke and Mary were determined that this wedding
> should be different. It was to take place at Matching, and none
> would be present but they who were staying in the house, or
> who lived around . . . It was very pretty . . . they all walked
> . . . After the breakfast — which was by no means a grand
> repast . . . the happy couple were sent away in a modest
> chariot . . .'[63]

The wedding night, i.e. the night following the wedding day, was considered the proper time for intercourse consummating the marriage.

In the nineteenth century, a marriage was normally preceded by an 'engagement', made public, and with each family receiving the intended spouse. The engagement was initiated by the man asking the woman to marry him, and seeking her father's consent (or first seeking it and then asking her) and the woman agreeing. In the nineteenth century an engaged couple might kiss each other, and kissing was virtually the symbol of an engagement. With a few exceptions,[63A], kissing was not meant to take place except between actual or intending spouses, and in their case only were prolonged embraces with kissing on the lips proper, in private. An engaged couple was not supposed to have sexual intercourse, a view now radically altered.[64]

An engagement could be broken off, especially by mutual consent. Theoretically, if unilaterally done ('jilting'), the injured party could bring a case for damages for breach of promise.[64A] In practice, this was rare, and frowned on, and a man who broke an engagement without justification would be more likely to be thrashed and cold-shouldered, after it became impossible to 'call him out' i.e. fight a duel with him.[65] Thus Crosbie, when he jilts Lily Dale in favour of an Earl's daughter in Trollope's *The Small House at Allington* (1864).[66] Engagements varied greatly in length, and were not necessary except in so far as 21 days notice had, and still has, to be given of a marriage, unless it is performed by 'special license', and time might be wanted for marriage settlements.

A single act of sexual intercourse after the marriage ceremony is necessary and sufficient to validate the marriage so long as there is no impediment such as one spouse being already married or the parties being within the Prohibited Degrees. Sexual intercourse between one party to an engagement and a third party discovered during the engagement would certainly have justified, and still would justify, breaking it off. There does not appear to have been any redress if such sexual intercourse took place before the marriage but was discovered only after it. Certainly it did not invalidate the marriage or constitute grounds for separation or divorce.[66A]

However, sexual intercourse between either spouse and someone else during the marriage was grounds for divorce *a mensa et thoro* (i.e. separation)[67] and between 1700 and 1937 became the only grounds for divorce. A single proven act of sexual intercourse between his wife and someone else enabled a husband to divorce his wife or a wife to secure a divorce *a mensa et thoro*. For a divorce proper a wife had to have further grounds viz. that the adultery was incestuous or bigamous, or, after 1857, coupled with desertion etc. No husband or wife was obliged to separate from or divorce the other for adultery, and if there was sexual intercourse between them after adultery by either was known to the other, the adultery was considered to have been condoned, and was no longer grounds for divorce, unless fresh acts of adultery were committed.[68]

Adultery might be proved by the guilty couple being caught red-handed, as with Mildmay and the Countess of Rosebery,[69] by elopements, or other direct evidence of intercourse. The bearing of a child by the wife when the husband could have had no access to her at a possible time of conception was also considered proof of adultery. Eighteenth-century divorce Acts commonly contained clauses bastardising children born a year after separation of husband and wife.[70]

During most of the period, adultery by the party bringing the divorce (or *a mensa et thoro*) suit might well prevent success. Sexual intercourse between a spouse and someone else was an offence against the other spouse for which he (or in suitable circumstances, she) was justified in casting the other off, and given the means to do so, provided, however, that the technically innocent spouse was not himself (or herself) to blame. That adultery was for so long the only offence for which divorce was possible is strong evidence of the importance attached to sexual faithfulness in marriage in England, especially on the part of the wife.[71]

There is ample other evidence.[72] But a distinction needs to be drawn between a husband's, or wife's, right to sexual faithfulness on the part of the wife (or husband) and the exercise of the right. The right to divorce a spouse for adultery continues, although adultery is no longer the only nor even the most important ground. However, by the late nineteenth century, and at some earlier periods, such as probably the later eighteenth century, the right was frequently not exercised, and adultery, even by women, became a very much less heinous offence than it had been, to judge by plays put on the London stage in the 1890s, especially among the upper classes.[73]

The central place of sexual intercourse in marriage is shown not only by the attitude to intercourse outside marriage, but also by the attitude to intercourse within it. We have seen that a single act of sexual intercourse after the marriage ceremony is necessary, and, in normal circumstances, sufficient to validate the marriage. By mutual consent the husband and wife might never engage in any further acts of intercourse. This would certainly not be regarded as desirable.[73A] The Church of England wedding service, which dates from 1662, speaks of the procreation of children as the first purpose of marriage. And the law intervenes to the extent that what would constitute rape, if committed by a man against a woman not his wife, does not constitute rape if the man is her husband. Rape, i.e. a man having intercourse with a woman without her consent, or, as it used to be put, by force, fear or fraud, is a serious criminal offence, punishable at law since at least the seventeenth century.[74] A famous judgment of

1888, R. v. Clarence, held that a husband was not guilty of rape even though he knew he had venereal disease, and his wife, who did not know, contracted it, since by marrying she had consented to sexual intercourse.[75] Other judgments confirmed this position, except in some cases of separation orders with non-molestation clauses or decrees nisi (a divorce not yet made absolute).[76] In its 1984 final report on Sexual Offences, the Criminal Law Revision Committee pointed out that a husband could be indicted for assault or assault causing harm etc., offences for which there are prison sentences by an Act of 1861,[77] and recommended that between those married and cohabiting, there should continue to be no possibility of rape.

The laws and customs governing sexual intercourse in England have sometimes been supposed to result in some way from the idea made explicit in the wedding service that marriage is designed for the procreation of children. That sexual intercourse was responsible for conception was certainly known for many centuries, together with the approximate period of gestation, although it was the 1870s before the mechanism (of the male sperm fertilising the female ovum) was established, and 1900 before heredity was attributed to the transmission of genes rather than of blood.[78] Children were properly conceived only by sexual intercourse of married parents, and sexual intercourse outside marriage might result in particular tragedy if a child was born. So for instance Hetty's plight in George Eliot's *Adam Bede* (1859). Hetty is a respectable girl, niece of farmers. But she is seduced by the squire's son, Arthur, and conceives a child. She runs away rather than face the shame, cannot find Arthur, bears the child in secret, abandons it in the hope of concealing its existence and is finally transported for infanticide.[79]

A hundred years later little or no shame attached to premarital sexual relations, especially of a stable nature, and at first glance this might seem to be attributable to more effective contraception, making the procreation of children a more avoidable consequence of sexual intercourse. According to Stone in 1979:

> Premarital sexual experimentation has become increasingly respectable, thanks partly to a dramatic improvement in contraceptive technology which has at last more or less successfully isolated sexual pleasure from procreation, and partly

to a shift of attitude to one favourable first to contraception and now also to abortion.[80]

However, closer inspection makes it doubtful whether either the old or the new rules relating to sexual intercourse can be satisfactorily accounted for in terms of the object of marriage being the procreation of children.

In the first place, English marriage is not in general well adapted to this end. In particular, failure to procreate children has never been grounds for annulling or terminating a marriage, even when production of an heir to titles, entailed estates or the throne might assume critical importance. There are societies where it is. In certain African societies, for example, childlessness is grounds for dissolving a marriage, or a childless widow may be required to have intercourse, with e.g. her husband's brother, in order that the dead man may have children. The ceremonies of marriage may take place over a protracted period, such that a child is conceived before the marriage is finalised. Nepal supplies one instance. The brief ceremony followed by a single act of intercourse which creates a marriage in England is a poor method of ensuring that marriages will result in children.[81] If production of children is the object of marriage, one might expect pre-nuptial intercourse between engaged couples and conception before marriage to have been favoured, instead of which, in most classes at most periods, it was a matter of shame, and indeed would not have occurred between any persons of principle in the nineteenth century. The bride's wedding dress was white, a symbol of her purity. Again, there has never been any bar to marriage by women past child-bearing age nor in later times to the availability of contraception to either party of a childless marriage. In England (unlike, for instance, France) medical examination before marriage is not customary.

By English law a husband is presumed to be the father of any child born to his wife unless it can be proved that he is not its natural father. And the fact that a woman's adultery was considered worse than a man's was sometimes atrributed to the fact that she could introduce spurious offspring. However, adultery from which no child resulted, or perhaps even could result (the woman was e.g. barren or past child-bearing age) would not render her less liable to divorce for adultery. If the heinousness of a woman's adultery was due to the possible introduction of spurious offspring, this is difficult to understand. So is the fact that in England, (unlike, for instance, France) there is no legal prohibition on the re-marriage of a widow during the time she might be pregnant by her first husband. The conventional prohibition of re-marriage during two years of mourning for a spouse bore on a man as well as a woman,[82] and in any case no one supposed that a pregnancy could last so long. No child followed the seduction of Carry Brattle, the unmarried daughter of a miller, in the *Vicar of Bullhampton* (1870) but her disgrace is little if at all, less.[83] Again, and very difficult for Stone's hypothesis to accommodate, it is not only sexual intercourse between the unmarried or them openly setting up house together which has become accepted in recent decades but also the production of illegitimate children. These are little distinguished from children born in wedlock whose families have become 'one-parent families' as a result of their parents' divorce. On the other hand, in 1983, Parkinson, a married man with grown up children, had to resign from the Cabinet when his affaire with an unmarried woman, pregnant by him, became public knowledge.[84]

There is no doubt that a desire that children should be conceived and born in and only in wedlock accompanied the view that sexual intercourse should take place between and only between the married. But there is no serious evidence that the connection between them was that the wish for legitimate children was responsible for the restriction of sexual intercourse to marriage. It is at least as plausible to claim that the stigma which attached to conception outside marriage was due to the fact that it supplied public proof of extra-marital sexual intercourse and that the fundamental precept was that sexual intercourse was a form of intimacy properly existing between those and only those 'as one' i.e. united by marriage. Hence, too the related impropriety of kissing, or of certain forms of conversation, between the unmarried or someone and the spouse of another. Arguably, latter-day acceptance of both intercourse outside marriage and conception between those not married have the same root: dwindling of the singular unity of husband and wife.

Notes

1. M.L. Shanley '"One must ride behind": Married Women's rights and the Divorce Act of 1857' *Victorian Studies* vol 25 1982, p. 360.

2. J.S. Mill *The Subjection of Women* 1869, Chapter 2.

3. H.N. Mozley 'The Property disabilities of a married woman and other legal effects of Marriage' in J.E. Butler (ed.) *Women's Work and Women's Culture* London 1869, p. 187.

4. See e.g. *On Married Women's Property Bill*, Special Report 17 July 1868, para 2, reprinted in *British Parliamentary Papers: Marriage and Divorce* vol 2, 1970, p. ix.

5. J.T. Hammick *The Marriage law of England. A Practical Treatise* 2nd edition, revised and enlarged, London 1887, p. 3.

6. Married Women's Property Act 1870 33 & 34 V c 93.

7. The Married Women's Property Act 1882 45 & 46 V c 75.

8. Mozley 'The Property disabilities of a married woman', p. 212.

9. A Trollope *The Eustace Diamonds* 1876, Chapters 1–2.

10. Mozley 'The Property disabilities of a married woman', p. 208.

11. A. Trollope *The Prime Minister* 1875, Chapters 24–6, 35, 39–40, 44, 52.

11A. The 'Common Law', which originated in medieval times, as 'royal law' was administered by (unpaid) Justices of the Peace, lesser cases being heard at 'petty' or 'quarter' sessions, important cases by three superior courts in London: the Court of Queen's Bench and Court of Common Pleas, each headed by a Chief Justice, and the Court of Exchequer, headed by a chief Baron. These Chief Justices held life peerages and were members of the House of Lords. Final appeal was to the House of Lords. The Central Criminal Court, established in 1834, was part of the Common Law system.

Equity, which acquired jurisdiction later, particularly in the seventeenth and eighteenth centuries, e.g. over bankruptcy, intestate estates, guardianship of lunatics and minors, was administered by the Court of Chancery, headed by the Lord Chancellor, also with right of appeal to the House of Lords. By the nineteenth century the Lord Chancellor was the highest judicial official.

The courts differed not only in jurisdiction but in proceedings: oral evidence and the use of juries typified the Common Law Courts, written dispositions and decision by the Judge(s) the Courts of Equity.

The ecclesiastical courts [see Chapter 2, note 9] formed a third set of courts and there was also maritime law, administered by the High Court of Admiralty. See e.g. L. Holcombe *Wives and Property. Reform of the Married Women's Property Law in Nineteenth-Century England* Toronto and Oxford 1983, pp. 9–17 for further detail, and Chapters 2 and 3 for Common Law and Equity in relation to married women.

12. Shaw-Lefevre, House of Commons, 21 April 1868, *Hansard* 3rd series vol 191, pp. 1017–19.

13. *On Married Women's Property Bill* Special Report 1868 paras 2, 6 (see note 4).

14. Shaw-Lefevre 21 April 1868 *Hansard* 3rd series vol 191.

15. L. Holcombe *Wives and Property*.

16. Ibid. p. 62.

16A. Ibid. p. 70.

17. Ibid. p. 73.

18. Ibid. p. 86.

19. Ibid. p. 108.

20. Ibid. p. 111.

21. Not achieved until 1918, after the suffragette movement and World War I.

22. Ibid. pp. 115—16.
23. Ibid. pp. 125—6.
24. Ibid. pp. 126—42.
25. Ibid. pp. 143—7.
26. Ibid. pp. 148—83.
26A. Judicature Act 1873 36 & 37 Vic c 66.
27. Holcombe *Wives and Property*, pp. 185—90.
28. Married Women's Property (Scotland) Act 1877 40 & 41 V c 29. See Holcombe *Wives and Property*, pp. 191—3.
29. Married Women's Property (Scotland) Act 1881 44 & 45 V c 21. Cf Holcombe *Wives and Property*, p. 193.
30. Married Women's Property Act 1882 45 & 46 V c 75. Holcombe *Wives and Property*, pp. 193—205.
31. Holcombe *Wives and Property*, e.g. p. 224.
32. Law of Property Act 1925, 15 & 16 Geo 5. c 20. Cf Holcombe *Wives and Property*, p. 222.
33. Law Reform (Married Womens and Tortfeasors) Act 1935 25 & 26 Geo 5 c 30.
34. Cf Holcombe *Wives and Property*, p. 238.
35. Theft Act 1968 c 60 s 30. Cf Holcombe *Wives and Property*, p. 220.
36. Holcombe *Wives and Property* p. 230.
37. The position over taxation is also not quite accurately described.
38. Finance Act c 68, 1971.
38A. *The Times* 20 March 1985, p. 1 col h. Also p. 1 col a, p. 5 col 2, p. 10 col 5. See O.M. Stone *Family Law. An Account of the Law of Domestic Relations in England and Wales in the last quarter of the twentieth century with some Comparisons* London 1977, pp. 79—83 for a good account as at 1977.
40. Matrimonial Homes Act 1967 c 75. Cf Holcombe *Wives and Property*, pp. 26—7, 233.   •
41. Matrimonial Proceedings and Property Act 1970 c 45.
42. Holcombe *Wives and Property*, p. 233.
43. Miss Buss started North London Collegiate School for girls in 1850. Cheltenham Ladies' College was founded in 1854. See e.g. R.C.K. Ensor *England 1870—1914* Oxford 1936, p. 149ff.
43A. The Elementary Education Act 1870 33 & 34 V c 75 introduced compulsory education for both sexes; reference is the 'child'/'children' throughout.
44. Girton College, founded at Hitchen in 1869, was transferred to Cambridge in 1872, Newnham College, Cambridge was founded in 1871, Lady Margaret Hall, Oxford in 1878, Somerville College, Oxford 1879. The members of these, and women's colleges of later foundation, achieved *de facto* rights in the Universities fairly rapidly, e.g. to sit examinations. Full equal status with the all-male colleges was a slower process. Men's colleges began to admit women in the 1970s and after 1979 virtually all 'single sex' colleges in both Universities went 'mixed' i.e. admitted staff and students of both sexes. (See e.g. *The Times* 10 August 1984, p. 4 cols a—c on the adverse effect to the remaining women's as well as ex-women's colleges.)
45. Mill *The Subjection of Women*, Chapter 3 et al.
46. A. Trollope *Is he Popenjoy?* 1878, especially Chapters 16 and 17.
47. Municipal Franchise Act 1869 32 & 33 V c 55 s 9 enacts that in this and related Acts 'wherever words occur which import the masculine gender the same shall be held to include females . . . [in] the right to vote in the election of councillors, auditors and assessors'.
48. R. v. Harrald 1872 QBD vol 7.
49. Local Government Act 1894, 56 & 57 V c 73 and for Scotland 57 & 58 V

c 58. Cf Holcombe *Wives and Property*, pp. 210–17.

49A. Representation of the People Act 1918 7 & 8 Geo 5 c 64. Until 1928 (Representation of the People (Equal Franchise) Act 1928 18 & 19 Geo 5 c 12) women had to be older (30 years of age) than men (who could vote at 21) to vote. The age is now 18 years for both sexes.

49B. The Qualification of Women Act 1918 8 & 9 Geo 5 c 47 allowed women to sit in the House of Commons. The Sex Disqualification (Removal) Act, 1919 9 & 10 Geo 5 c 71 added that 'A person shall not be disqualified by sex or marriage from the exercise of any public function . . . [etc]'.

50. Holcombe *Wives and Property*, pp. 215–17 citing C. Rover *Women's Suffrage and Party Politics in Britain 1866–1914* Toronto and London 1967.

51. Holcombe *Wives and Property*, p. 217.

52. Ibid. p. 215.

53. Ibid. pp. 210, 197–201.

54. A. Trollope *The Last Chronicle of Barset* 1867, Chapter 63.

54A. A. Trollope *Is he Popenjoy?*, Chapter 17.

55. See e.g. Holcombe *Wives and Property*, pp. 18–19: '. . .the common law, embodying the idea that marriage was for husbands a profitable guardianship of their wives' person and property, merely reflected the economics and social realities of the position of women in the middle ages, when the law developed . . .'

56. The Criminal Law Revision Committee reporting in 1984 used the term 'unlawful sexual intercourse' for intercourse outside marriage, although by then attitudes and practices were very different, and in any case such intercourse had never as such been contrary to the law of the land. This is in connection with rape and following the Sexual Offences (Amendment) Act 1976, HMSO Cmd 9213 15th Report *Sexual Offences* sec 2.57, p. 19.

56A. Thus, inter alia, Canons of the Church of England 1603 required 3 weeks notice, that marriages should be solemnised by a Minister in a Church with open doors between eight and twelve in the forenoon (unless by special license). The Marriages Act of 1836 6 & 7 W 4 c 85 added registry offices, fixed the fee at 5s or 10s by license (cl. 22) and laid down necessary wording to be included. Age of consent (when a marriage might be contracted) was 14 years males, 12 years females. The Marriage Act of 1753, 26 Geo 2 c 33, known as Lord Hardwicke's Act, intended to prevent clandestine marriages and instituting registration of marriages, required the consent of parent or guardian for the marriage of anyone under 21 years, the presence of two credible witnesses, as well as due publication of bans, and declared marriages not in accordance with its procedures void. Changes include e.g. lengthening the hours when marriages may take place (8 am – 6 pm) — Marriage Act 1949 12, 13 & 14 Geo 6 c 76 ss 4 & 75 (1) (a). See O.M. Stone *Family Law. An Account of the Law of Domestic Relations*, Chapter 2 for other details.

57. The Marriage Act 1836, 6 & 7 W 4 c 85 sec 21 et seq. By 1977 *c.* 60 per cent of marriages took place in registry offices (O.M. Stone *Family Law. An Account of the Law of Domestic Relations*, p. 32).

58. C. Brontë *Jane Eyre* 1847, Chapter 26.

58A. See e.g. O.M. Stone *Family Law. An Account of the Law of Domestic Relations*, pp. 33–4.

59. The terms 'bride' and 'bridegroom' are used to refer to the spouses on their wedding day both before and after they are married.

60. J. Austen *Pride and Prejudice* 1813.

61. Ibid. Chapter 50.

62. A. Trollope *The Duke's Children* 1880, Chapters 79–80.

63. Ibid. Chapter 80.

63A. Such as greetings and farewells, between close relatives, or in particular circumstances: under the mistletoe at Christmas, or the bridegroom's 'best man' kissing the bride in the vestry after the service. The kissing was not supposed to be of the passionate quality enjoyed by intending or actual spouses. In A. Trollope *Can You Forgive Her?* 1864−5 Alice foolishly gets re-engaged to her rascally cousin George Vavasseur and Trollope makes much play of the fact that she refuses to kiss him e.g. Chapters 34, 35, 46; when ultimately she gets re-engaged to John Gray, whom she marries, 'no other touch had profaned those lips since last he had pressed them' (Chapter 74). The 1970s BBC TV version of *The Pallisers* did not get the point, and Alice and George kiss on the screen.

64. According to L. Stone (L. Stone *The Family, Sex and Marriage in England 1500−1800* London 1977, rev. edn. 1979), Chapter 12, on admittedly necessarily slender evidence and not specific to England, prenuptial conception in the lower classes became higher in the last half of the eighteenth century and Stone believed that 'almost all brides below the social elite had experienced sexual intercourse with their future husbands before marriage' (p. 388). 'Later still, in the very late eighteenth and the nineteenth centuries, a new wave of sexual prudery spread downwards . . .' (p. 395).

64A. Abolished 1970: Law Reform (Miscellaneous Provisions) Act 1970, c 33.

65. The *Encyclopedia Britannica* of 1929 defines a duel as a 'prearranged encounter between two persons [in fact virtually always men (one between females in France is recorded in the Times Index 1828)], with deadly weapons, in accordance with conventional rules, with the object of voiding a personal quarrel or of deciding a point of honour' vol 7, p. 711. Duelling entered England in the sixteenth century (a century later than France) but was rare before the seventeenth century. It was still common in the early decades of the nineteenth century. Thus *The Times* reported on 129 duels in the 1820s, 37 of which were fought in England (a further one in Scotland and nine in Ireland), an average of 3.7−4.7 per annum in England/UK. It was technically murder and punishable by death for one man to kill another in a duel but in practice juries generally refused to convict. By the 1830s duelling was less favourably viewed, and by the late 1840s the number had diminished, especially in England. *The Times* reported on 37 duels in the 5 years 1845−9, 10 of which were stated to be between foreigners and only 6 of which were fought in England (and a further one in Ireland), at most 1.4 per annum. Between 1850 and 1856 there were reports of five duels fought in England and one in Ireland: 1 per annum. No more duels are reported in England after 1856, though the practice persisted into the 1930s in some European countries. Other sources corroborate this picture of the decline of duelling in England. In *The Claverings* 1867 Chapter 28 Trollope refers to the past possibility of duelling for jilting: 'thirty years since . . . unless the sinner were a clergyman, he [could take] . . . a pistol in his hand . . .'. The old Squire in *The Small House at Allington* 1864, Chapter 31 remarks that in the days of his youth 'a gentleman might have a fellow out who treated him as he [Crosbie] has treated us'. In the 1840s the Army had tightened its sanctions against duelling, and by the 1860s duelling seemed ridiculous (Trollope *The Small House at Allington*, Chapter 31) or at least eccentric (cf A. Trollope *Phineas Finn* 1869 where a duel is fought secretly abroad, Chapter 38 et seq).

66. A. Trollope *The Small House at Allington* 1864, Chapters 30, 31, 34, 35−6. Crosbie gets engaged to an Earl's daughter and breaks his open engagement with Lily Dale. The question arises 'What is to be his punishment?' As in *The Claverings* (1867) there is none ('There are evils which a man may do, and no one can punish him'), apart from, they hoped, 'the scorn which men and women will feel for him': 'You would not have Lily's name brought before a tribunal of law?'; 'I will not have Bernard [her cousin, and nearest young male relation on whom

the duty would devolve] calling him out. Indeed, it would be for nothing; for in these days a man is not expected to fight duels'. 'He [Crosbie] ought to have every bone in his skin broken' (Chapter 31). Cousin Bernard does nothing but when Crosbie gets into the same railway compartment as Johnny Eames, an old friend and aspiring suitor of Lily's, Johnny gives him a black eye on the railway station as they get out; Crosbie avoids making charges against him (Chapter 34).

66A. Both majority and minority reports of the Divorce Commission of 1912 clearly felt that this should be remedied. They recommended that 'where a woman is found to be pregnant at the time of marriage, her condition being due to intercourse with some man other than her husband, and such condition being undisclosed by her to her husband who is ignorant of the fact at the time of marriage', the husband should be entitled to petition for nullity (within a year of the marriage and provided there was 'no marital intercourse' after the discovery): *The Divorce Commission. The Majority and Minority Reports Summarised* London 1912, pp. 38–9, 69. It was remedied in 1937 and 1973: pregnancy *per alium* became grounds on which a marriage could be voided (O.M. Stone, *Family Law. An Account of the Law of Domestic Relations*, p. 47).

67. Along with cruelty.

68. Mrs Addison in 1801 had some problems on this score and it was the renewed adultery between her husband and sister after forgiveness for their earlier adulteries which made her able to obtain her divorce. In 1984 a Mrs Stansfield's divorce was similarly jeopardised by reconciliation after a decree nisi for her husband's adultery but his subsequent adulteries were finally held to make it permissible to grant the decree absolute required to complete the divorce. *The Times* 22 August 1984, p. 3 col d.

69. See above Chapters 3 and 5.

70. Cf Chapter 5 and S. Wolfram 'Divorce in England 1700–1857' *Oxford Journal of Legal Studies* 1985, vol 5 no 2. These were an almost invariable inclusion in divorce Acts before 1780 and rare thereafter. Heathcote's divorce Act of 1851, 14 & 15 V *c 24* included one; the wife's adultery had been with her full brother.

71. On this point, as on others, nothing follows about other parts of Europe or the US. It was well known in England that the French, for instance, had a different view.

72. See above Chapter 3.

73. L. Stone *The Family, Sex and Marriage*, p. 423, claims that middle-class attitudes had already begun slowly to change in the 1870s and spread to the elite in the 1890s. Trollope's novels of the 1870s do not corroborate this supposed change in middle-class attitudes, nor therefore Stone's hypothesis that attitudes spread from the middle class to the elite.

73A. Absence of sexual intercourse after marriage is not regarded as desirable.

74. Definition of rape has never been simple. Cf e.g. The Criminal Law Revision Committee 15th Report *Sexual Offences* London 1984 HMSO Cmd 9213, Part II. At present the maximum penalty is imprisonment for life (p. 16).

75. R. v. Clarence 1888: (1889) R. v. Clarence 22 QBD vol 22.

76. Criminal Law Revision Committee 15th Report *Sexual Offences*, pp. 17–19.

77. Ibid. p. 18. Offences against the Person Act of 1861, 24 & 25 Vic c 100.

78. T. Dobzhansky *Evolution, Genetics, and Man* New York 1955, pp. 25, 45 etc.

79. G. Eliot *Adam Bede* 1859, Chapters 6–7, 12–15, 27, 31, 35ff.

80. L. Stone *The Family, Sex and Marriage*, p. 423.

81. According to Stone (ibid.), p. 385 'the chances of conception from a single

random act of intercourse of a healthy young couple are only between two and four per cent . . .'. This is rather recherché information. But it was certainly known that single acts of sexual intercourse might or might not result in pregnancy. (The Trobriand Islanders used this fact to demonstrate Malinowski's folly in insisting that sexual intercourse caused conception. See e.g. B. Malinowksi 'Baloma; The Spirits of the Dead in the Trobiand Islands' *Journal of the Royal Anthropological Institute* reprinted in B. Malinowski *Magic, Science and Religion and other Essays* 1948, especially pp. 209–11.)

82. See above Chapter 3.

83. A. Trollope *The Vicar of Bullhampton* 1870. In his preface Trollope remarks that 'no fault among us is punished so heavily as that fault, often so light in itself but so terrible in its consequences to the less faulty of the two offenders, by which a woman falls . . . All her own sex is against her . . . She . . . remains in her abject, pitiless, unutterable misery because this sentence of the world has placed her beyond the helping hand of Love and Friendship . . . This punishment is horrible beyond the conception of those who have not regarded it closely . . .'

Carry Brattle was seduced by a lieutenant, her father (a miller) 'had left him all but lifeless' (Chapter 5), no one dared mention her name to her father — who does however ultimately allow her home again. Cf especially Chapters 7, 25, 27, 28, 39–41, 46, 52–3, 66, 69, 73.

84. See e.g. *The Times* front pages 10–16 October 1983.

THE FORM OF
SOLEMNIZATION OF MATRIMONY

¶ *First the Banns of all that are to be married together must be published in the Church three several Sundays, during the time of Morning Service, or of Evening Service, (if there be no Morning Service) immediately after the second Lesson; the Curate saying after the accustomed manner,*

I PUBLISH the Banns of Marriage between M. of — and N. of —. If any of you know cause, or just impediment, why these two persons should not be joined together in holy Matrimony, ye are to declare it. This is the first [second, or third] time of asking.

¶ *And if the persons that are to be married dwell in divers Parishes, the Banns must be asked in both Parishes; and the Curate of the one Parish shall not solemnize Matrimony betwixt them, without a Certificate of the Banns being thrice asked, from the Curate of the other Parish.*

¶ *At the day and time appointed for solemnization of Matrimony, the persons to be married shall come into the body of the Church with their friends and neighbours: and there standing together, the Man on the right hand, and the Woman on the left, the Priest shall say,*

DEARLY beloved, we are gathered together here in the sight of God, and in the face of this congregation, to join together this Man and this Woman in holy Matrimony; which is an honourable estate, instituted of God in the time of man's innocency, signifying unto us the mystical union that is betwixt Christ and his Church; which holy estate Christ adorned and beautified with his presence, and first miracle that he wrought, in Cana of Galilee; and is commended of Saint Paul to be honourable among all men: and therefore is not by any to be enterprised, nor taken in hand, unadvisedly, lightly, or wantonly, to satisfy men's carnal lusts and appetites, like brute beasts that have no understanding; but reverently, discreetly, advisedly, soberly, and in the fear of God; duly considering the causes for which Matrimony was ordained.

First, It was ordained for the procreation of children, to be brought up in the fear and nurture of the Lord and to the praise of his holy Name.

Secondly, It was ordained for a remedy against sin, and to avoid fornication; that such persons as have not the gift of continency might marry, and keep themselves undefiled members of Christ's body.

Thirdly, It was ordained for the mutual society, help, and comfort, that the one ought to have of the other, both in prosperity and adversity. Into which holy estate these two persons present come now to be joined. Therefore if any man can shew any just cause, why they may not lawfully be joined together, let him now speak, or else hereafter for ever hold his peace.

¶ *And also, speaking unto the persons that shall be married, he shall say,*

I REQUIRE and charge you both, as ye will answer at the dreadful day of judgement when the secrets of all hearts shall be disclosed, that if either of you know any impediment, why ye may not be lawfully joined together in Matrimony, ye do now confess it. For ye be well assured, that so many as are coupled together otherwise than God's Word doth allow are not joined together by God; neither is their Matrimony lawful.

¶ *At which day of Marriage, if any man do allege and declare any impediment, why they may not be coupled together in Matrimony, by God's Law, or the Laws of this Realm; and will be bound, and sufficient sureties with him, to the parties; or else put in a Caution (to the full value of such charges as the persons to be married do thereby sustain) to prove his allegation: then the solemnization must be deferred, until such time as the truth be tried.*

¶ *If no impediment be alleged, then shall the Curate say unto the Man,*

M. WILT thou have this Woman to thy wedded wife, to live together after God's ordinance in the holy estate of Matrimony? Wilt thou love her, comfort her, honour, and keep her in sickness and in health; and, forsaking all other, keep thee only unto her, so long as ye both shall live?

¶ *The Man shall answer,*

I will.

¶ *Then shall the Priest say unto the Woman,*

N. WILT thou have this Man to thy wedded husband, to live together after God's ordinance in the holy estate of Matrimony? Wilt thou obey him, and serve him, love, honour, and keep him in sickness and in health; and, forsaking all other, keep thee only unto him, so long as ye both shall live?

¶ *The Woman shall answer,*

I will.

¶ *Then shall the Minister say,*

Who giveth this Woman to be married to this Man?

¶ *Then shall they give their troth to each other in this manner. The Minister, receiving the woman at her father's or friend's hands, shall cause the Man with his right hand to take the woman by her right hand, and to say after him as followeth,*

I M. take thee N. to my wedded wife, to have and to hold from this day forward, for better for worse, for richer for poorer, in sickness and in health, to love and to cherish, till death us do part, according to God's holy ordinance; and thereto I plight thee my troth.

¶ *Then shall they loose their hands; and the Woman, with her right hand taking the Man by his right hand, shall likewise say after the Minister,*

I N. take thee M. to my wedded husband, to have and to hold from this day forward, for better for worse, for richer for poorer, in sickness and in health, to love, cherish, and to obey, till death us do part, according to God's holy ordinance; and thereto I give thee my troth.

¶ *Then shall they again loose their hands; and the Man shall give unto the woman a Ring, laying the same upon the book with the accustomed duty to the Priest and Clerk. And the Priest, taking the Ring, shall deliver it unto the Man, to put it upon the fourth finger of the Woman's left hand. And the Man holding the Ring there, and taught by the Priest, shall say,*

WITH this Ring I thee wed, with my body I thee worship, and with all my worldly goods I thee endow: In the Name of the Father, and of the Son, and of the Holy Ghost. Amen.

¶ *Then the Man leaving the Ring upon the fourth finger of the woman's left hand, they shall both kneel down; and the Minister shall say,*

Let us pray.

O ETERNAL God, Creator and Preserver of all mankind, Giver of all spiritual grace, the Author of everlasting life; Send thy blessing upon these thy servants, this man and this woman, whom we bless in thy Name; that, as Isaac and Rebecca lived faithfully together, so these persons may surely perform and keep the vow and covenant betwixt them made, (whereof this Ring given and received is a token and pledge,) and may ever remain in perfect love and peace together, and live according to thy laws; through Jesus Christ our Lord. *Amen.*

¶ *Then shall the Priest join their right hands together, and say,*

Those whom God hath joined together let no man put asunder.

¶ *Then shall the Minister speak unto the people.*

FORASMUCH as *M.* and *N.* have consented together in holy wedlock, and have witnessed the same before God and this company, and thereto have given and pledged their troth either to other, and have declared the same by giving and receiving of a Ring, and by joining of hands; I pronounce that they be Man and Wife together, In the Name of the Father, and of the Son, and of the Holy Ghost. Amen.

¶ *And the Minister shall add this Blessing.*

GOD the Father, God the Son, God the Holy Ghost, bless, preserve, and keep you; the Lord mercifully with his favour look upon you; and so fill you with all spiritual benediction and grace, that he may so live together in this life, that in the world to come ye may have life everlasting. *Amen.*
¶ *Then the Minister or Clerks, going to the Lord's Table, shall say or sing this Psalm following.*

Beati omnes. Psalm cxxviii.

BLESSED are all they that fear the Lord: and walk in his ways.
For Thou shalt eat the labour of thine hands: O well is thee, and happy shalt thou be.

Thy wife shall be as the fruitful vine: upon the walls of thine house;
Thy children like the olive-branches: round about thy table.
Lo, thus shall the man be blessed: that feareth the Lord.
The Lord from out of Sion shall so bless thee: that thou shalt see Jerusalem in prosperity all thy life long;
Yea, that thou shalt see thy children's children: and peace upon Israel.
Glory be to the Father, and to the Son: and to the Holy Ghost;
As it was in the beginning, is now, and ever shall be: world without end. Amen.

¶ *Or this Psalm.*

Deus misereatur. Psalm lxvii.

GOD be merciful unto us, and bless us: and shew us the light of his countenance, and be merciful unto us.
That thy way may be known upon earth: thy saving health among all nations.
Let the people praise thee, O God: yea, let all the people praise thee.
O let the nations rejoice and be glad: for thou shalt judge the folk righteously, and govern the nations upon earth.
Let the people praise thee, O God: yea, let all the people praise thee.
Then shall the earth bring forth her increase: and God, even our own God, shall give us his blessing.
God shall bless us: and all the ends of the world shall fear him.

Glory be to the Father, and to the Son: and to the Holy Ghost;

As it was in the beginning, is now, and ever shall be: world without end. Amen.

¶ *The Psalm ended, and the Man and the Woman kneeling before the Lord's Table, the Priest standing at the Table, and turning his face towards them, shall say,*

Lord, have mercy upon us.

Answer. Christ, have mercy upon us.

Minister. Lord, have mercy upon us.

OUR Father, which art in heaven, Hallowed be thy Name. Thy kingdom come. Thy will be done in earth, As it is in heaven. Give us this day our daily bread. And forgive us our trespasses, As we forgive them that trespass against us. And lead us not into temptation; But deliver us from evil. Amen.

Minister. O Lord, save thy servant, and thy handmaid;

Answer. Who put their trust in thee.

Minister. O Lord, send them help from thy holy place;

Answer. And evermore defend them.

Minister. Be unto them a tower of strength,

Answer. From the face of their enemy.

Minister. O Lord, hear our prayer.

Answer. And let out cry come unto thee.

Minister.

O GOD of Abraham, God of Isaac, God of Jacob, bless these thy servants, and sow the seed of eternal life in their hearts; that whatsoever in thy holy Word they shall profitably learn, they may indeed fulfil the same. Look, O Lord, mercifully upon them from heaven, and bless them. And as thou didst send thy blessing upon Abraham and Sarah, to their great comfort, so vouchsafe to send thy blessing upon these thy servants; that they obeying thy will, and always being in safety under thy protection, may abide in thy love unto their lives' end; through Jesus Christ our Lord. *Amen.*

¶ *This Prayer next following shall be omitted, where the Woman is past child-bearing.*

O MERCIFUL Lord, and heavenly Father, by whose gracious gift mankind is increased; We beseech thee, assist with thy blessing these two persons, that they may both be fruitful in procreation of children, and also live together so long in godly love and honesty, that they may see their children christianly and virtuously brought up, to they praise and honour; through Jesus Christ our Lord. *Amen.*

O GOD, who by thy mighty power hast made all things of nothing; who also (after other things set in order) didst appoint, that out of man (created after thine own image and similitude) woman should take her beginning; and, knitting them together, didst teach that it should never be lawful to put asunder those whom thou by Matrimony hadst made one: O God, who hast consecrated the state of Matrimony to such an excellent mystery, that in it is signified and represented the spiritual marriage and unity betwixt Christ and his Church; Look mercifully upon these thy servants, that both this man may love his wife, according to thy Word, (as Christ did love his spouse the Church, who gave himself for it, loving and cherishing it even as his own flesh,) and also that this woman may be loving and amiable, faithful and obedient to her husband; and in all quietness, sobriety, and peace, be a follower of holy and godly matrons. O Lord, bless them both, and grant them to inherit thy everlasting kingdom; through Jesus Christ our Lord. *Amen.*

¶ *Then shall the Priest say,*

ALMIGHTY God, who at the beginning did create out first parents, Adam and Eve, and did sanctify and join them together in marriage; Pour upon you the riches of his grace, sanctify and bless you, that ye may please him both in body and soul, and live together in holy love unto your lives' end. *Amen.*

¶ *After which, if there be no Sermon declaring the duties of Man and Wife, the Minister shall read as followeth.*

ALL ye that are married, or that intend to take the holy estate of Matrimony upon you, hear what the holy Scripture doth say as touching the duty of husbands towards their wives, and wives towards their husbands.

Saint Paul, in his epistle to the Ephesians, the fifth Chapter, doth give this commandment to all married men; Husbands, love your wives, even as Christ also loved the Church, and gave himself for it, that he might present it to himself a glorious Church, not having spot, or wrinkle, or any such thing; but that it should be holy, and without blemish. So ought men to love their wives as their own bodies. He that loveth his wife loveth himself: for no man ever yet hated his own flesh, but nourisheth and cherisheth it; even as the Lord the Church: for we are members of his body, of his flesh, and of his bones. For this cause shall a man leave his father and mother, and shall be joined unto his wife; and they two shall be one flesh. This is a great mystery; but I speak concerning Christ and

the Church. Nevertheless, let every one of you in particular so love his wife, even as himself.

Likewise the same Saint Paul, writing to the Colossians, speaketh thus to all men that are married; Husbands, love your wives, and be not bitter against them.

Hear also what Saint Peter, the Apostle of Christ, who was himself a married man, saith unto them that are married; Ye husbands, dwell with your wives according to knowledge; giving honour unto the wife, as unto the weaker vessel, and as being heirs together of the grace of life, that your prayers be not hindered.

Hitherto ye have heard the duty of the husband toward the wife. Now likewise, ye wives, hear and learn your duties toward your husbands, even as it is plainly set forth in holy Scripture.

Saint Paul, in the aforenamed Epistle to the Ephesians, teacheth you thus; Wives, submit yourselves unto your own husbands, as unto the Lord. For the husband is the head of the wife, even as Christ is the head of the Church: and he is the Saviour of the body. Therefore as the Church is subject unto Christ, so let the wives be to their own husbands in everything. And again he saith, Let the wife see that she reverence her husband.

And in his Epistle to the Colossians, Saint Paul giveth you this short lesson; Wives, submit yourselves unto your own husbands, as it is fit in the Lord.

Saint Peter also doth instruct you very well, thus saying; Ye wives, be in subjection to your own husbands; that, if any obey not the Word, they also may without the Word be won by the conversation of the wives; while they behold your chaste conversation coupled with fear. Whose adorning, let it not be that outward adorning of plaiting the hear, and of wearing of gold, or of putting on of apparel; but let it be the hidden man of the heart, in that which is not corruptible; even the ornament of a meek and quiet spirit, which is in the sight of God of great price. For after this manner in the old time the holy women also, who trusted in God, adorned themselves, being in subjection unto their own husbands; even as Sara obeyed Abraham, calling him lord; whose daughters ye are as long as ye do well, and are not afraid with any amazement.

¶ *It is convenient that the new-married persons should receive the holy Communion at the time of their Marriage, or at the first opportunity after their Marriage.*

Part 2

7 Popular Explanations

In England, as in most societies, there exist more or less elaborate popular and expert theories on many aspects of kinship. During the nineteenth century there was a general shift in the style of acceptable explanation or justification away from ones in religious terms to 'scientific' ones, but explanations continued to be of two main logical types: a rule, custom, law, habit was said to serve some purpose and/or its existence was attributed to some causal mechanism. Roughly, and with some qualification, desirable customs are said to have a purpose, undesirable ones to result from the operation of causes. Many of the theories are false, sometimes blatantly so. In later chapters I shall attempt some explanation for the existence of these theories, as well as giving alternative accounts of aspects of kinship in question.

An obvious preliminary to positive claims of these sorts is to make good the contention that the theories themselves are not well founded. To do this thoroughly would require several volumes, and I shall content myself with a few examples, some of which have already been touched on.

In this chapter, I shall examine two theories, which are 'popular' in the sense of being held by most members of the society. One, that the rise in divorce is attributable to the emancipation of women, is held by experts as well as the non-expert. The other, that prohibitions of incest are designed to prevent the ill-effects of in-breeding, is a belief firmly entrenched in the society but altogether eschewed by some sets of experts — lawyers and theologians in the past, and social anthropologists in this century. A number of other theories on the subject have been widely debated among experts but this one is even not often criticised in detail, so certain has it seemed to these classes of experts that it is false.

1. Incest and In-breeding

Ordinary English people who have made no study of the matter almost invariably attribute prohibitions of marriage and inter-course between relatives to the ill-effects of in-breeding. It is widely believed that the children of incestuous unions will be mentally defective, and that the purpose of forbidding 'incest' is to prevent the birth of idiot children.

Popular beliefs are difficult to date but it is probable that belief that 'in-breeding' has ill effects on the progeny is an old one in England and related societies. In 1908 we may read: 'Idiocy, perhaps more than any other disease or defect has long been connected in the popular mind with the marriage of cousins'.[1] Bibliographies of 1875 and 1887 have extensive entries on 'Consanguineous marriages physiologically considered' from the 1850s onwards, as well as a handful of earlier date.[2] Bakewell (1725−95) is said to have been reticent about his 'deliberate and intense use of in-breeding' to improve his livestock because 'at that time [viz. eighteenth century] there was even more prejudice against in-breeding than there is today [1943]'.[3]

In 1980 the Criminal Law Revision Committee spoke of the 'high risk' to children of father−daughter and brother−sister unions: 'nearly one chance in two, of being born with serious defects' and said that 'The chance of transmission of a hereditary defect decreases but does not disappear as relationship becomes more distant'.[4] However, in spite of the popular belief, this theory has not often appeared in documents of this kind until very recently. In particular, the ill-effects to the progeny of incestuous unions scarcely featured in the Parliamentary Debates leading to the Punishment of Incest Act of 1908. This introduced harsh penalties for 'incest', construed as sexual unions between parents and children and siblings (full and half, whether legitimate or not), and made such intercourse a criminal offence in England for the first time.[5] It might be expected that eugenic considerations would have been used. But in fact they were not.

The genetic dangers of incest went unmentioned when the Bill was first, and unsuccessfully introduced in 1903. In 1908, when it came up again, this time successfully, there were tentative passing mentions of 'physical deterioration'[6] and 'consequences of a disastrous kind to the offspring which sometimes followed such intercourse'.[7] But debate centred on other issues. The Bill was promoted as a modest measure to reduce the incidence of incest among the over-crowded poor and help to bring England more in line with Scotland.[8]

The failure to advance eugenic considerations in 1908 has puzzled some later writers imbued with the popular belief. They have ascribed it, *faute de mieux* and incorrectly, to ignorance of these factors at the time. The Criminal Law Revision Committee of 1980 was 'surprised to find how few medical studies there have been of the genetic risk for the offspring of incestuous unions'.[9] An article of 1979 about the 1908 Act in the *Criminal Law Review* claimed that 'Despite the work on heredity by Mendel and Galton, there were no published studies before 1908 of the effect of consanguinity upon inherited characteristics',[10] and that 'reliable tests of the genetic effects on children of incestuous unions . . . [only] appeared . . . after the legislation [of 1908].[11]

Huth's 1887 bibliography on 'Consanguineous marriages physiologically considered' occupies 16 pages and contains 159 items, including several books. There were statistical studies of the effects of cousin marriage on idiocy, lunacy, deaf mutism and a variety of other ills. Debate ranged between France, Italy, England and the US in reputable medical and anthropological journals and from time to time reached less specialist journals like the *Westminster Review*, the *Fortnightly Review*, the *Athenaeum*. Huth has 51 entries for 1862−3. A sample page indicates the style of publication on the physiological effects of in-breeding in the 1870s:

BIBLIOGRAPHY

1875   'The Marriage of Near Kin,' etc. In the Indian Medical Gazette, pp. 105−107, April 1, 1876. 4to.
A Review on the above.

'In-and-In-Breeding.' In the Live Stock Journal and Fancier's Gazette, etc. vol. viii. p. 374; and in the Literary Supplement, No. 240, for November 8. 4to. London, 1878.
A Review on the above.

'The Marriage of Near Kin,' etc. In the Medical Press and Circular, new series, vol. xix. p. 330, No. 1914, for October 20. 4to. London, 1875.
A Review on the above.

'The Marriage of Near Kin,' etc. By Eduard Reich. In the Athenaeum, Monatsschrift für Anthropologie, etc. 1st year, 8th and 9th parts, pp. 544−547. 8vo. Jena, 1875.
A Review on the above.

'Heredity and Consanguinity.' by John Todhunter. In the Dublin Journal of Medical Science, third series, Part II. No. 55, for July. pp. 20−40. 8vo. Dublin, 1876.
A Review on the above, and Ribot's Heredity.

'The Marriage of Near Kin,' etc. In the Westminster Review, new series, vol. xlviii. pp. 299−317, No. 96, for October, Art. I, 8vo. London, 1875.
A Review on the above.

'Die Ehe zwischen Blutsverwandten.' By Otto Zacharias. In the Illustrirte Zeitung, vol. lxvi. No. 1696, for January, 1, p. 11; and No. 1697, for January 8, p. 31. Fol. Leipzig, 1876.
Reprinted in Zur Entwickelungstheorie, pp. 73−82. 8vo. Jena, 1876.
A Review on the above.

A Leading Article on Consanguineous Marriage in the Lancet, pp. 378, 379, No. 11, for March 13. 4to. London, 1875.
'Marriages of Consanguinity.' A Letter to the Lancet by 'Prudence.' p. 668, No. 19, for May 8. 4to. London, 1875.
With the Editor's Reply.

'Marriages of Consanguinity.' A Letter to the Lancet, by 'a Physiologist,' p. 745, No. 21, for May 22. 4to. London, 1875.
1876   The Effects of Cross- and Self-Fertilisation in the Vegetable Kingdom. By Charles Darwin. 8vo. London, 1876.

In 1900 wide publicity was given to what has since been known as 'genetic' or 'Mendelian' theory. De Vries and others published their own findings. Mendel's paper of 1865−6 was re-discovered and became news.[11A] If we add this to the existent popular belief about incest, it is impossible to credit that eugenic considerations had not percolated to Parliament or that ignorance in the first decade of the twentieth century was the reason why they played so little part in making incest a crime in England. It is more probable that for some reason it would have been injudicious to advance genetic arguments. Two likely reasons come to hand.

One is that the experts of the period were by no means agreed on the evils of in-breeding. Its possible virtues had been demonstrated by agriculturists in England in the eighteenth century who, led by Bakewell, dramatically improved farm animals by close in-breeding of selected stock.[12] In 1875 Huth, himself a landowner,[13] was writing:

> the statistics on which so much reliance has been placed, as a proof of the harmfulness of consanguineous marriage, are, when not absolutely false, miserably misleading and defective[14]

and

> any deterioration . . . practically does not occur oftener than in other marriages, or it would be more easily demonstrated.[15]

Arner expressed an equally favoured view when he wrote in 1908:

> Degeneracy does in some cases follow from the marriage of near kin . . . But likewise . . . many of the world's greatest men have been the products of close in-breeding.[16]

Or more generally,

> the most important physiological effect of consanguineous marriage is to intensify . . . inheritable family characteristics . . . by double inheritance.[17]

In other words, the genetic ill effects of in-breeding were disputed and would not have been likely to supply a reliable platform for promoting a harsh new penalty.

Another perhaps even more potent reason for not mentioning genetic considerations as a justification for making incest a crime was the state of affairs in the then closely related domain of the Prohibited Degrees.

When the Punishment of Incest Bill made its first appearances in 1903, the controversy about allowing marriage with a deceased wife's sister, which had begun in 1842, was still unresolved.[18] Opposition was strong, in particular because it was believed, rightly as history has shown, that it would make an end to affinity as a bar to marriage and also impair the unity of husband and wife which lay at the heart of the English kinship system and justified treating affinity like consanguinity. Such was opinion at the time that, to the end, supporters of legalising marriage with a deceased wife's sister insisted that there was no intention to extend this to any other in-laws. In this climate, references to consanguinity as a suitable basis for the law relating to the Prohibited Degrees were rare: 8 mentions in 46 sessions of debate.[19] And when marriage with a deceased wife's sister was legalised in 1907, intercourse with a living wife's sister was specifically still included as incestuous (and thus grounds on which a woman might divorce her husband).[20]

In 1903 the Punishment of Incest Bill foundered on the rock of affinity. Amendments were made to include affinal relatives, in particular step-daughters but also at one point all affinal relatives within the Prohibited Degrees.[21] The Solicitor-General's plea that this would make ' "incest" that which was not incest at present' was greeted with apparent incredulity. the 'hon. and learned Gentleman' was asked if he 'had looked at the table of consanguinity and affinity in the prayer-book, or the Matrimonial Causes Act'.[22]

There were no allusions to affinity when the Punishment of Incest Bill came up again in 1908, the year after marriage with a deceased wife's sister was legalised, and this was when there were some mild references to physiological considerations. But it might well have seemed unwise to dwell much on them if the Bill was to have an uncontroversial passage, as indeed it had in 1908.

It does not seem then that it was because biological factors were unknown that they were not used to further the 1908 Act but rather that what was known was not wholly favourable to the proposed legislation and did not fit with the old and still widely supported system in which affinity was classed with consanguinity. But it might nevertheless appear that the 1908 Act, and that of 1907, marked the beginning of a new stage in which biological considerations became paramount.

There can be no doubt that English law has moved towards consanguinity as a basis of prohibition. There may have been a fortuitous element in the disappearance of the old category of 'incest', viz. sexual relations within the Prohibited Degrees of consanguinity and affinity. It was a consequence of the Church of England's loss of its jurisdiction over matrimonial cases by the Matrimonial Causes Act of 1857 that 'incest' ceased to be punishable by the ecclesiastical courts.[23] It survived as 'incestuous adultery', one of the few grounds for which a woman could divorce her husband under the new judicial procedure set up by the 1857 Act.[24] 'Incestuous adultery' itself ceased to be a category in 1923 because a woman was then enabled to divorce her husband for adultery simpliciter.[25] But there was nothing incidental about the legislation which allowed increasing classes of affinal relatives to marry. This pursued a systematic course. Marriage with a deceased wife's sister was legalised in 1907. It was permitted with a brother's widow in 1921,[26] with all other relatives of a deceased spouse, except those in the 'direct line' in 1931,[27] with the same relatives of a divorced spouse in 1960.[28] Attempts to remove the few remaining restrictions, in the 'direct line' (with step-parents and children and parents and children-in-law) since 1978 seem likely to complete the process begun in 1907 (or 1842) viz. to eliminate prohibitions against unions between affinal relatives.[29] The concept of 'incest' as sexual relations within the Prohibited Degrees of consanguinity and affinity has already disappeared from popular consciousness as well as from English law. 'Incest' is invariably thought of as occurring only between close blood relatives.[30]

This course of events might seem to suggest that social anthropologists have been mistaken in dismissing the biological ill effects of in-breeding as an explanation of prohibitions of incest and marriage between relatives, at least so far as England is concerned. That there are these ill effects is a popular belief. May it not have been this belief (whether right or wrong) which has been responsible for the changes of this century? The fairly steady removal of prohibitions on unions between affines favours the hypothesis, and the silence on the subject in Parliament early in the century could be due simply to the inadvisability of voicing the real consideration in debate, when others, less likely to arouse opposition, e.g. in the Church of England, were at hand.

While it does appear likely that there is a connection between the changes which have taken place and the popular belief or its position, it does not seem probable that the popular belief is the cause of the change.

One difficulty about such a hypothesis is that the disappearance of restrictions on unions between affinal relations has not been

matched by equally steady progress towards making blood relationship the basis of prohibitions. On the one hand, certain non-
blood relations have been added to forbidden relatives, notably
adoptive relatives: the law decrees that they should count for all
purposes as blood relatives. On the other hand, the treatment of
blood relationship has been somewhat erratic. There is, for
instance, no apparent intention either to remove the prohibition
on the marriage of uncles and nieces or aunts and nephews, nor
to return them to the fold of blood relations between whom
intercourse is incest.[31] In 1984 the Criminal Law Revision Committee caused some consternation when it recommended that
sexual relations between brothers and sisters over 21 years of
age should cease to rate as incest:

> It should remain the offence of incest for brother and sister to
> have sexual intercourse with each other but it should cease
> to be an offence where they have both reached the age of 21.[32]

In defiance of normal English categories[33] and genetic theory,
the Criminal Law Revision Committee persisted in classing
brothers and sisters as in the 'first degree' along with parents and
children.[34] But in the section entitled 'The genetic risks of incest'
in its 1984 report[35] it also proceeded to dispute its own earlier
conclusions on the biological ill effects of 'incest':

> According to a small survey . . . [in 1967], the risk is 28%
> higher than in the case of non-incestuous births. The figure of
> one in two [children born to incestuous unions suffering
> serious defects] mentioned in the working paper [of 1980] now
> seems too high.[36]

The Committee pointed out that 'Society does not yet prohibit
sexual intercourse in other circumstances in which there is a high
genetic risk of abnormality in the offspring of a relationship, for
example with hereditary diseases . . .'[36A] and concluded that:
'Although the genetic factor remains an argument we do not
think that on its own it would justify retaining an offence of
incest'.[37] The Criminal Law Revision Committee had also become persuaded that 'step-children need the protection of a separate offence analogous to incest'[38] and recommended that 'a
separate offence should be created of unlawful sexual intercourse

with a step-child under 21'.[38A] Recommendations are not of course necessarily put into practice but they are some evidence of trends of thought.

Even if English law had moved more clearly than it has towards forbidding unions betwen particular blood relatives, and these only, there would be another difficulty about attributing twentieth century changes to popular eugenic beliefs. Such a shift might have created a presumption that the law had acquired a biological basis but it would not be sufficient to prove it, since there could be quite different reasons for the change.[39] Evidence would be needed of the causal role of biological beliefs. And the available evidence is not particularly favourable.

Thus, the fact that the 1908 Incest Act, apart from being confined to blood relatives included illegitimate ones, which has been adduced by some to help demonstrate new biological influence,[40] will not bear this construction. Prohibitions of marriage and 'incest' had included illegitimate, as well as legitimate, blood relations since before the Reformation, and Henry VIII's Statutes and Parker's Table reaffirmed the position. They had also included illegitimate blood relations of a spouse as forbidden affinal relatives along with legitimate ones, and until a fairly late date affinity itself was created by sexual intercourse as well as by marriage.[41]

When ordinary English people today attribute prohibitions of unions to the ill effects of in-breeding, specifically that it results in idiot children, this is supposed to be by biological or genetic mechanisms. However, in the past the belief that in-breeding results in idiot children had a different basis which was not biological: 'when idiocy did follow consanguineous marriages, as it sometimes would, it was believed to be the fit punishment of some divine law'.[42] Thus it is said that Bakewell was initially secretive about his use of in-breeding to improve his lifestock because in the eighteenth century his methods verged on the sacrilegious.[43] By the time that the supposed ill effects of in-breeding were ascribed to biological mechanisms, rather than to the wrath of God, the ill effects were themselves in doubt. Bakewell's successful experiments, studies of cousin marriage and the like from the 1850s onwards, and finally genetic theory suggested that in-breeding intensifies characteristics, but good as well as bad.[44]

Ordinary English people not only believe that 'incest' results in idiot children and now attribute this to biological mechanisms. They also embrace the belief that the results of a union depend on the excellence or otherwise of the original stock. Short of subsidiary hypotheses, such as that only bad stock engages in incestuous unions[45] or that bad genes are transmitted differently from good,[46] the beliefs are inconsistent. Some philosophers have insisted that apparently inconsistent beliefs are never actually so; only one or other is the genuine belief.[47] In this case it would certainly be difficult to say which, since both appear to have been held concurrently in the society at large for a substantial period of time. They are commonly put forward by the same people. Experiment reveals that pointing out the inconsistency fails to dislodge either, even temporarily. Typically, the point about intensification is conceded, but the view that incest produces idiot children is repeated. If pressure is put, some means are found of ending the conversation.

The popular belief that incest produces idiot children has acquired a scientific as opposed to religious rationale, in the sense that it is biological factors rather than operations of the Deity which are supposed to be responsible. But it has proved impervious to what would normally be regarded as scientific evidence, such as that supplied by genetic experiment. Since it pre-dates and is inconsistent with biological theory, it would certainly not be easy to maintain that it is a consequence of scientific influences.

The view comes to the fore in political settings to defend or promote restrictions on unions between consanguineous relatives or to assist in removing or avoid extending restrictions on unions between non-blood relatives. But the use of the biological ill effects of in-breeding in political settings followed, rather than preceded, the replacement of the old categories of consanguinity and affinity by consanguinity alone as the basis for prohibition, and it seems likely that the voicing of the belief, if not the belief itself, was a consequence of the severing of affinity from consanguinity. The sequence of events is not that scientific discovery created the belief in the biological ill effects of in-breeding and the belief in turn altered the law and common thinking towards resting the law on consanguinity (alone). Rather, after the law and popular conceptions of kinship had changed, an old belief (that incest produces idiot children) in a new scientific guise (that this occurs by biological mechanisms), became a useful tool. The inconsistency of the old belief with the belief that in-breeding may or may not be harmful (depending on the original stock) gives it all the powers of retreat when, as in the 1984 Criminal Law Revision Committee report, reduction in restrictions on unions between blood relations is itself in question.

2. Divorce and the Emancipation of Women

The whys and wherefores of restrictions on unions between relatives have exercised a perennial fascination and the abundant crop of theories it has produced are further considered in Chapter 8. The English popular belief, which has considerable ramifications of its own, is a minor theory so far as the expert is concerned.

Divorce presents a very different picture. Here there has been little serious attempt at explanation either of variation between societies or of English practices.

Divorce in England raises many interesting questions.[48] Why should divorce have been forbidden in England for centuries, and then been made progressively easier to obtain? Scotland allowed both sexes to obtain divorces for adultery or desertion from 1560 onwards. Why did England reach this position only in 1937? Why, on the other hand, was the passage of the 1857 Divorce Act relatively so swift when measures like legalisation of marriage with a Deceased Wife's Sister or the Married Women's Property Acts took decade after decade to effect? Why were there a thousand times as many divorces in England in 1980 as in 1858? Is there any way of explaining the exponential increase in the divorce rate, at a fairly steady 3–6 per cent a year, since 1730? These questions are seldom asked and yet more rarely answered.

It is generally agreed that the increase in divorce is a major change. The change is generally deplored. This has been so since its early days. Thus the Archbishop of Canterbury's lament in 1809, when divorces had risen to 3 a year, about the:

> pollution of divorce bills now daily more frequent. So common indeed were they, that . . . they seemed to be considered as the proper fruits of marriage . . . It was impossible that such things could last long.[49]

The Royal Commission of 1956 expressed similar views: the then 28,000 divorces a year, it said, were a 'matter of grave concern' and 'grave anxiety',[50] '[endangering] the whole stability of marriage'.[51] The sentiment was echoed in the volume published the following year to mark the centenary of the 1857 Divorce Act. Lord Evershed, Master of the Rolls, wrote of the 'present terrible volume of matrimonial cases',[52] adding that

> carried to their logical conclusions, such tendencies would . . . lead to the result . . . that . . . the family could no longer survive as the essential unit of society.[53]

There is constant comment in newspapers and elsewhere about the ever-rising divorce rate. By 1984 statistical research was being cited to prove that 'the evidence that divorce is a major health hazard is now overwhelming . . . It carries increased risks of mental and physical illness, suicide, heart disease and other conditions'[54] — including lung cancer, a disease more often attributed to cigarette smoking (a previously fashionable activity which has fallen into disrepute). Any decline in divorces is noted as an improvement, every rise as a further misfortune.[55]

Despite this attitude to divorce, legislation for the past two or three centuries has largely consisted of making divorces easier to obtain. This was the avowed object of the 1857 Act: it was to open to the poor remedies said to be available only to the rich. It simplified the procedure, and slightly widened the grounds for which divorce could be obtained by allowing women to procure it for adultery compounded by desertion as well as by incest or bigamy. Subsequent legislation progressively added to the grounds for which 'relief' might be sought and tried to reduce the financial impediments. In 1923 women could obtain divorces for simple adultery i.e. adultery uncompounded by other offences. In 1937 desertion and cruelty became independent grounds for divorce by either sex. In 1969 separation and agreement by both parties effectively became sufficient. The refrain that 'divorce should be possible for the poor, as well as the rich'[56] sounded long after 1857. The Royal Commission on Divorce of 1912 was still referring to 'the practical exclusion of the poorer classes from the remedy . . . of . . . the well-to-do'.[57] According to Holcombe, it was the Legal Aid and Advice Act of 1949,[58] nearly a century after the 1857 Act, which (by increasing aid for meeting legal costs) made '. . . divorce proceedings readily accessible to poorer classes for the first time'.[59]

By far the most common explanation of the increase in the frequency of divorce, if sometimes accompanied by subsidiary hypotheses, is that it is due to the emancipation of women. Thus Evershed in 1957:

> Looking back to the year 1857, the most significant change which has affected our society (greater even than the abasement of the landed estate) has been the change in the status of women . . . The two things, the multiplicity of divorces and the emancipated status of women have gone necessarily hand in hand.[60]

The theory predominates both popularly and among experts but it is seldom spelt out in detail, supported with evidence or the connecting mechanism clarified, and its vagueness is a major difficulty in evaluating it. Nor is this the only problem.

The conviction that the increase in divorce is caused by the emancipation of women is commonly supplemented by what must be regarded as a different theory, viz. that the successive changes in divorce law are due to deficiencies in the previous state of the law. This is rarely proffered as explicit explanation. But it appears implicit in many commentaries on divorce legislation: defects of the law before the piece of legislation under consideration are detailed, as if they explained why the law was changed. So for instance Dicey in 1914:

> The Divorce Act of 1857 was a triumph of individualistic liberalism and of common justice. It did away with the iniquity of a law which theoretically prohibited divorce, but in reality conceded to the rich a right denied to the poor.[61]

Since the changes have all been directed towards making divorce easier to obtain (by widening the grounds, simplifying the procedures, reducing financial constraints etc.) we have a paradox. Each new relaxation is seen as a better state of the law than the one before. Apparently, greater ease in procuring a divorce is applauded. Yet it is also evidently likely to help to increase the number of divorces, and the increasing divorce rate is not normally applauded. This quandary is sometimes resolved by claiming that the real misfortune is marital breakdown: 'it is useless to maintain a tie in theory which is broken in fact',[62] 'divorce is not a disease but a remedy for a disease'.[63] Better divorce and happy re-marriage than merely separated or etc. couples. In this connection we may read of masked or artificially lowered divorce rates. For example, Holcombe cites 'well over 7,000 maintenance orders' issued each year by magistrates courts to wives securing separation orders in the early twentieth century, when there were approximately 800 divorces a year, as indicating 'how many more people would have sought relief in the Divorce Court . . . had its proceedings been equally expeditious and inexpensive'.[64]

A more complex issue arises in the realm of explanation. If the individual changes of for instance 1857, 1923, 1937, 1949, 1969 are each to be explained as reforms of particular previous defects in the law, and each is responsible for a higher rate of (actual) divorce, how do these explanations relate to the more global explanation of the increased frequency of divorce as a product of the emancipation of women?

Possibilities are numerous. These could be two competing explanations. According to one, it was relaxation of the divorce laws which caused the rising rate of divorce. According to the other it was not legal changes but the emancipation of women which was responsible. But there are also a variety of ways of conjoining the theories. For example, the progressive relaxation of the divorce law might itself have been caused by the progressive emancipation of women. Perhaps the emancipation of women put pressure on the law by increasing the frequency of divorce or separation, or perhaps it created pressure in other ways, and the relaxations of the law were the immediate causes of the increasing rate of divorce. Alternatively, the changes in divorce law might have been independent of the emancipation of women, and the raised rate due to a combination of the two. Part of the increase might be attributable to the one, part to the other, or the rise sometimes due to the one, sometimes to the other. Or the legal changes provided the means of securing divorces while the emancipation of women caused the marital breakdowns leading to the desire for divorces.

The literature reflects the rather bewildering array of possibilities. Thus in the 1956 *Royal Commission on Marriage and Divorce*:

Greater demands are now made of marriage, consequent on the spread of education, higher standards of living and the social and economic emancipation of women. The last is probably the most important. Women are no longer content to endure the treatment which in past times their inferior position obliged them to suffer . . . There is a further factor . . . There is a tendency to take the duties and responsibilities of marriage less seriously . . . The result of this outlook is that . . . there is an increasing disposition to regard divorce, not as the last resort, but as the obvious way out when things begin to go wrong.[65]

Or Evershed in 1957:

The [multiplicity of divorces] . . . could not have happened without the [emancipated status of women]: both may be said to have raced helter skelter and side by side, before the impulses of the calamities of the last two generations . . . I am sufficiently advanced in years to remember vividly the some-what extravagant antics . . . of the militant suffragettes immediately before the First World War.[66]

Again, we may read in one of Dicey's lectures (1914) that the 1857 Act opened to the poor what was open to the rich,[67] in another that the 1857 Act 'and the feelings it fostered' were

closely related to the Married Women's Property Acts 1870–1893. Nor can anyone doubt that these enactments have in their turn given strength to the belief that women ought . . . in the eyes of the law, to stand substantially on an equality with men . . . Law and opinion . . . are here so intermixed that it is difficult to say whether opinion has done most to produce legislation or laws to create the state of legislative opinion.[68]

There is clearly a sense in which the Married Women's Property Acts can both be attributed to the 'emancipation of women' and be said to have contributed towards this emancipation. 'Emancipated' women formed the movements, which, ridiculed though they might be, undoubtedly had a causal role. They might not have been sufficient, but it seems unlikely that the Acts would have been passed without them, or at least not so soon.

The Acts themselves contributed to women's 'emancipation' by making more women financially more independent. There were connections between these Acts and the 1857 Divorce Act. The passage of the Divorce Act, with its clauses about divorced women's property, reduced the impetus of the women's movement, and probably delayed the Married Women's Property Acts.[69] The introduction of a Bill about Married Women's Property in 1857, at the instigation of women, may have helped to achieve a majority for the Divorce Act in that year.[70]

However, there are many other possible candidates for explaining the passage of the 1857 Divorce Act, and if the Act helped to 'emancipate' women it was not in the direct fashion of the Married Women's Property Acts. Far from campaigning for it, women were opposed to the Divorce Act[71] which did not give them the same rights as men in securing divorces themselves, and appeared to make it easier for them to be divorced. They did in fact gain in the power to obtain divorces. The House of Lords had recognised only adultery compounded by incest or bigamy as adequate grounds. The 1857 Act added further compounding grounds, notably desertion. Only 4 of the 193 divorces between 1800 and 1857 were procured by women: 2 per cent of divorces. When the divorce rate jumped to over 150 per annum after the 1857 Act, 40 per cent of divorces were instituted by the wife.

Further connections can be found between one or another aspect of the 'emancipation' of women and the relaxation of the divorce laws or rising divorce rate, notably perhaps in the case of the Divorce Act of 1923. This was passed soon after World War I and the enfranchisement of women in 1918. It put women on a footing with men by allowing them to divorce their husbands for adultery simpliciter and thereafter the proportion of men and women obtaining divorces reversed. Except during World War II, when 70 per cent were instituted by husbands, wives obtained 60 per cent of the divorces instead of 40 per cent as before. The 1923 Act gave rise to the notorious 'hotel' cases, which in turn assisted the promoters of the 1937 Act, the Act whereby grounds for divorce were extended beyond sexual infidelity, to desertion or cruelty.[72] But, while such connections may be adduced, an explanation of the growth of divorce in terms of the emancipation of women is unsatisfactory unless it fulfils more stringent conditions. In particular, something more systematic than the occasional link is needed to establish a causal connection between the emancipation of women and the growth of divorce, and the putative cause, 'the emancipation of women', requires a less wandering definition than is usual.

The exact interpretation to be put on the term 'emancipation of women' is seldom clarified, and there are many possibilities. Women can be said to be more 'emancipated' if they go about more freely, are educated outside the home, work more or in higher places, enjoy greater financial independence, if they indulge in freer sexual habits, have more legal rights in marriage or in other spheres, or are considered or behave more like men.[73] Each of these ingredients could be further broken down, and doubtless there are further factors which could be included. It would be difficult to dispute that women have become more 'emancipated' both in their role in marriage and in the society at large. On the other hand this is not the only change, and the claim that the relaxation of the divorce laws or the increase in divorce rates is due to this factor or set of factors does not appear plausible.

Among its difficulties is that such major legal changes as the 1857 Divorce Act, or those of 1937 or 1969, cannot reasonably be ascribed to any factor included in the 'emancipation of women'. The 1857 Act is indeed only rarely attributed to it. This change is more often explained as its promoters depicted it: as a reform of defective law.[74] Defective law is by no means always swiftly reformed,[75] and we have seen that divorce was not in fact as difficult to obtain, expensive, cumbersome, slow as it was claimed to be by the 1853 Commission and in the Parliamentary Debates leading to the Act. Other equally or more likely explanations abound. For example reformers like Lord Campbell and Lord Brougham favoured it. The tale of expense etc. may have been believed. Reduced damages and absconding adulterers had made inroads on the system. The reform was presented as purely procedural, and judicial reform was in the air.[76] English law was less liberal than Scottish, and unlike that of other Protestant countries. The Church of England, which lost its jurisdiction over matrimonial cases by the 1857 Act, was under attack in the 1850s. Securalisation of marriage was already under way: marriage in registry offices, introduced 20 years earlier, accounted for 5 per cent of marriages by 1857.[77] It is quite unclear that the traditional explanation of the 1857 Divorce Act in terms of the inequities etc. of the previous system is correct.

However, it would certainly be even more perverse to turn instead to the emancipation of women. Of all explanations, this seems the least probable. Women's rights were being mooted, but in the area of married women's property.[78] Women objected to the Divorce Bill, and its opponents made much of its unfairness towards them. One of the results of the Act was to enable women to procure more divorces than before. But, apart from anything else, the absolute number was infintesimal. Only one wife in 100,000, or one per 55,000 by 1900, obtained a divorce each year.[79] In any case *post hoc* is not *propter hoc*.

Equal if not greater problems afflict the idea that it is the rise in the rate in divorce, rather than the relaxation of the laws, which is caused by the emancipation of women. To substantiate any hypothesis along these lines it would be necessary to demonstrate some correlation between it, or one of its components, such as women working, and the divorce rate. The data presented in Chapter 5[80] show, inter alia, that the divorce rate has been rising since at least the mid-eighteenth century, and that, apart from some bumps and peaks, it has risen exponentially at only mildly varying rates of around 3–6 per cent per annum.[81]

It seems absurd to suggest that the emancipation of women, however exactly construed, has similarly increased by 3–6 per cent per annum. This is not only because few of its aspects are readily quantified, but also because it is difficult to credit that its increase matches the magnitude of increase in divorce in the past two and a half centuries — from under one a year in 1730 to 150,000 per annum in 1980. There is also a problem about why the two should be associated. The particular connecting mechanisms suggested are apt to vary according to which feature is being treated as 'the emancipation of women'.

Such alternative hypotheses as that the relaxation of the divorce laws and increase in the divorce rate are connected with the erosion of the singular unity of a married couple are only a little more promising. There are similar problems of correlation, as well as the stumbling block that divorce was already increasing for a century before one could very plausibly date other incursions on the unity of husband or wife, or for that matter, most aspects of the emancipation of women.

It is quite possible that there is no particular factor which correlates with and can be construed as the cause of the increasing ease and frequency of divorce in a society, such as England.

A different kind of explanation may be more apposite. For example, it may be the case that divorce is a phenomenon which has a tendency to increase and grow progressively easier to obtain unless there is something to prevent the process. The Church of England's hostility to divorce clearly acted as a breaking mechanism in England while it retained its powers, and there could have been others. Thus, it has been suggested that before 1857 some Lord Chancellors, opposed to divorce, reduced the rate of divorce by private Act of Parliament.[82]

A mechanism which has been used to explain exponential increases elsewhere is that the probability of the occurrence of some phenomenon, here divorce, increases with the number there already are: the more divorces there are in an individual's environment, the more likely it is that he or she will obtain one also, and similarly, *mutatis mutandis*, for relaxations in the law. If so, growth of divorce feeds on itself, and search for correlates which might be causing it would prove vain: if an explanation of this type is borne out by the facts, there is not perhaps properly speaking, a cause.[83]

Whether this style of explanation, or the particular suggestion about English divorce, is substantiated or not, it seems evident that the society's received explanation, viz. that the increase in divorce is due to the emancipation of women, is not the right one. The remarkably uncritical acceptance of this view, by experts as well as popularly, is as much a rationalisation within the society as the popular theory that incest is forbidden because it produces idiot children.

Notes

1. G.B.L. Arner *Consanguineous Marriage in the American Population* PhD Columbia 98pp. including bibliography, March 1908, p. 51.
2. A.H. Huth *The Marriage of Near Kin considered with respect to the laws of nations, the results of experience, and the teachings of biology* London 1875, 359 pp., second revised and enlarged edition 1887, 457 pp.; A. Huth *Index to Books & Papers on the Marriage of Near Kin* London 1879, pp. 25–46. 1887 bibliography published separately 1887.
3. J. Lush *Animal Breeding Plans* Iowa 1943, pp. 24–5. There are sporadic mentions of the popular theory in seventeenth- and eighteenth-century writings. For example, in *The Anatomy of Melancholy* (1621), Burton speaks briefly of 'Church and Commonwealth, human and divine laws' as avoiding hereditary diseases by 'forbidding such marriages as are in any whit allied': A.R. Burton *The*

Anatomy of Melancholy what is it etc Oxford 1621, sixth enlarged edition London 1652, reprinted Everyman 1936, Part 1, Section 2, Mem 1 Subs 6. In 1789 Noah Webster asserted that it is 'just az criminal for a man to marry hiz Cousin, az it iz to sow flax every year on the same ground; but when he does this, he must not complain, if he has an indifferent crop': B.N. Webster (Junior) 'Explanation of the Reezons why Marriage iz Prohibited between Natural Relations designed to determin the Proprity of Marrying a Wife's Sister' 1789, p. 324, no xxvi in N. Webster *A Collection of Essays and Fugitive Writings on Moral, Historical, Political and Literary Subjects* Boston 1790. In 1673, in a work called *The marriages of Cousins Germans, vindicated from Censures of Unlawfulness and Inexpediency*, Dugard described, and objected to the popular disapproval of the marriage of first cousins (legalised in 1540). He remarked that people say 'The children are weak, it may be; grow crooked, or, what is worse, do not prove well; presently, Sir, it shall be said what better could be expected?'. He himself disputed either that these ills or barrenness attended the marriages or that even if they did this would prove God's hostility to such marriages: S. Dugard *The marriages of Cousins Germans, vindicated from Censures of Unlawfulness and Inexpediency* 1673, p. 38ff. I have not found it possible to tell whether the ill effects to progeny were popularly supposed to follow unions of affinal as well as consanguineous relatives.

4. Home Office, Criminal Law Revision Committee *Working Paper on Sexual Offences* 1980 HMSO, p. 41 para 113.

5. See Chapter 1, Section 2.

6. *Hansard* 4th series vol 191 House of Commons 26 June 1908 col 284.

7. *Hansard* 4th series vol 197 House of Lords 2 December 1908 col 1411.

8. *Hansard* 4th series vol 191 House of Commons 26 June 1908 cols 278–90, vol 197 House of Lords 2 December 1908 cols 1408–12. V. Bailey and S. Blackburn 'The Punishment of Incest Act 1908. A case study in law creation' 1979 *Criminal Law Review* 708 attribute the impetus for the Act to two pressure groups, the National Vigilance Association and the NSPCC, both founded in the 1880s. Incest had been an offence in Scotland since 1567.

9. Criminal Law Revision Committee *Working Paper on Sexual Offences*, p. 41 para 113.

10. Bailey and Blackburn 'The Punishment of Incest Act 1908', note 51.

11. Ibid. p. 716. The point was taken up in S. Wolfram 'Eugenics and the Punishment of Incest Act 1908' [1983] *Criminal Law Review*, 308–16.

11A. G. Mendel *Experiments in Plant Hybridization* 1865–6. See e.g. T. Dobzhansky *Evolution, Genetics and Man* New York 1955, p. 25; W. George *Gregor Mendel and Heredity* London 1975, p. 46ff. Before Mendelian theory, it was believed that 'the heredity of a child was a solution . . . of equal parts of parental heredities' (Dobzhansky *Evolution, Genetics and Man* 1955, p. 24). According to Mendel's paper, heredity travels through a large number of discrete bodies, later named 'genes', bearing different characteristics of each parent. Some are dominant and others recessive. Only where there is a recessive gene from each parent in the child's genes will the recessive characteristic generally be visible. For details see e.g. Dobzhansky *Evolution, Genetics and Man* 1955, Chapter 2 et al.

12. Lush *Animal Breeding Plans*, p. 24.

13. *Who Was Who*: Alfred Henry Huth was the owner of some 4,000 acres at Forsbury Manor, near Hungerford, as well as Vice-President of the Bibliographical Society and inheritor of the celebrated Huth library.

14. Huth *The Marriage of Near Kin*, p. 353.

15. Ibid. p. 358.

16. Arner *Consanguineous Marriage in the American Population*, p. 39.

17. Ibid. p. 86.
18. See Chapter 2, Sections 2 and 3.
19. *Hansard* 3rd series cxiv, 964 (1851 Commons), cxxxviii, 267 (1855 Commons), cxcv, 1315 (1869 Commons), cci, 911 (1870 Lords), ccxiv, 1876 (1873 Commons), ccxxii, 475 (1875 Commons), cclxx, 794 (1882 Lords), 4th series cxxi, 1108 (1903 Commons).
20. See Chapter 2, Section 3.
21. *Hansard* 4th series vol 124, House of Commons 26 June 1903, cols 698–701. These amendments are not mentioned by Bailey and Blackburn nor in earlier studies of the Punishment of Incest Act e.g. J.E. Hall Williams, 'Incest in English Law' Appendix to H. Maish *Incest* 1973.
22. *Hansard* 4th series vol 124, House of Commons 26 June 1903, col 699.
23. See Chapter 2, Sections 1 and 3.
24. See Chapter 2, Sections 1 and 3; Chapter 5.
25. Matrimonial Causes Act 1923 13 & 14 Geo 5 c 19.
26. Deceased Brother's Widow's Marriage Act 11 & 12 Geo 5 c 24.
27. The Marriage (Prohibited Degrees of Relationship) Act 21 & 22 Geo 5 c 31.
28. Marriage Enabling Act, 8 & 9 Eliz 2 c 29.
29. See above Chapter 2, Section 3 for details. See also below pp. 144–5 for a caveat. The Archbishop of Canterbury's Group reporting in June 1984 *No Just Cause*, recommended, by a small majority, that the remaining affinal relatives should be permitted to marry, with the proviso in the case of step-parents and children that they should only be allowed to do so when the younger was 18 if he or she had never lived in the household of the older, or otherwise at 21, Chapter 12 pp. 91–5. See also minority recommendations pp. 109–10. On the other hand, in April 1984 the Criminal Law Revision Committee 15th Report *Sexual Offences* London 1984, HMSO Cmd 9213 proposed that sexual relations with step-children under 21 should become an offence, although adding: 'If changes are made to the general law concerning the capacity of step-parents and step-children to marry, they will have to be matched by an appropriate change in the criminal law at that time: it would be absurd for the law to produce the result that sexual intercourse between a man and a woman amounted to an offence but that they could lawfully marry each other' p. 70 para 8.31.
30. In 1980 the Criminal Law Revision Committee employed the term 'incest' to refer to sexual unions between uncles and nieces, aunts and nephews (see note 31 below), having apparently excluded these relatives elsewhere (paras 108–10). In 1984 it decided to extend the term to sexual intercourse between a parent and adopted child ('because . . . the law regards the adopted child as the child of the parents') p. 72, 8.39 but not to use the term 'incest' for its recommended new offence of sexual intercourse with step-children under 21. This is referred to as 'analogous to incest' p. 70, 8.31 but to be called 'unlawful sexual intercourse' p. 73, 8.44 (6). The term 'incest' has more than one technical use and indeed its 'correct' use has been a subject of dispute among social anthropologists. Principal contenders for the meaning of 'incest' include (a) sexual relations, or sometimes (b) only extra-marital sexual relations, forbidden on account of the relationship between the parties and (c) sexual unions within the 'nuclear family' (parents and children and siblings), whether these are forbidden or not. The divergence in many societies between prohibitions of marriage between relatives and prohibitions of extra-marital sexual relations between them has led some to wish to mark the distinction by calling the latter 'incest prohibitions' (usage (b)) and to use the yet more disputed term 'exogamy' for the former. ('Exogamy' or 'rule of exogamy' was coined in 1865 to refer to rules enforcing marriage outside the tribe and rapidly applied to rules relating to 'clans' or groups in general. By 1877 Morgan

was suggesting that it was so 'tainted' that the best disposition which could be made of it was to put it aside. However, it survived, usually retaining the meaning of prohibiting marriage within a group of some sort but now not uncommonly also applied to all prohibitions of marriage. See below Chapter 8, Section 2). For a detailed history of usage of the words 'incest' and 'exogamy' up to 1956 see S. Wolfram *The Explanation of Prohibitions and Preferences of Marriage between Kin* DPhil thesis Oxford University 1956, Chapter 3, pp. 87–150.

31. Criminal Law Revision Committee 1980, p. 44 para 120: 'We have received no evidence to suggest that incest between uncle and niece and aunt and nephew should become criminal offences. In the law of Scotland incest between [them] . . . is prohibited, and the Scottish Law Commission [Memorandum no 44 para 6.20] provisionally recommended that this should continue'. In 1981 the Scottish Law Commission *The Law of Incest in Scotland* Cmd 8422 endorsed this: Criminal Law Revision Committee 1984 para 8.24, p. 68. Sexual relations between affinal relations are also incest in Scotland: Criminal Law Revision Committee, p. 68 note 1.

32. Criminal Law Revision Committee 1984, 8.44 (5) p. 73. *The Times*, for instance, denounced the proposal in a leader headed 'An Ill-Advised Logic', suggesting that the Home Secretary should consult the public: 'The opinion of the expert . . . is not always to be preferred to Everyman's commonsense' *The Times* 14 April 1984, p. 9 cols a–c.

33. These put parents and children in the first degree, brothers and sisters in the second degree. Cf Chapter 1, Section 1; Chapter 2, Section 1.

34. Criminal Law Revision Committee 1984, Section 8.9, p. 65.

35. Criminal Law Revision Committee 1984, Section 8.9–8.10, pp. 65–6.

36. Criminal Law Revision Committee 1984, p. 65 note 1.

36A. Criminal Law Revision Committee 1984, p. 65, Section 8.10, quoting Policy Advisory Committee.

37. Criminal Law Revision Committee 1984, Section 8.10, p. 66.

38. Criminal Law Revision Committee 1984, para 8.31, p. 70.

38A. Criminal Law Revision Committee 1984, para 8.44 (5), p. 73.

39. See Chapter 7, Section 1.

40. Bailey and Blackburn 'The Punishment of Incest Act 1908', p. 715.

41. See Chapter 1 for detail and Wolfram 'Eugenics and the Punishment of Incest Act 1908', p. 314.

42. Arner *Consanguineous Marriage in the American Population*, p. 51.

43. Lush *Animal Breeding Plans*, pp. 24–5.

44. Mendelian theory differs from earlier theory in the precise fashion of intensification. It had been supposed that each parent's contribution was halved in each generation [cf above note 11A]. According to Mendelian theory only the dominant gene will show in the first generation, and in the second the dominant character will show in a proportion of 3:1. See e.g. Dobzhansky *Evolution, Genetics and Man*, pp. 29–42; George *Gregor Mendel and Heredity*, pp. 51ff, 71ff.

45. In 1980 the Criminal Law Revision Committee. p. 43, Section 120, re-marked that in mother–son incest 'one or both parties will often be found to be suffering from a degree of mental abnormality'.

46. The brief discussion on incest in B.M. Hoggett and D.S. Pearl *The Family, Law and Society* 1983, p. 16, cites the view taken from O. Aberle, U. Bronfenbronner, E. Hess, O. Miller, D. Schneider and I. Sopuhler 'The Incest Taboo and the mating patterns of animals' *American Anthropologist* 1963 that in a population 'the ratio of deleterious and lethal recessive genes to selectively advantageous genes is very high indeed. This results from the random character of mutations . . .'.

47. The doctrine is particularly associated with Quine's name, especially W.V. Quine *Word and Object* MIT 1960, Section 13, and is still common. See e.g. M. Hollis 'The Social Destruction of Reality' in M. Hollis and S. Lukes (eds) *Rationality and Relativism* Oxford 1982, p. 72. For objections, see S. Wolfram 'Facts and Theories; Saying and Believing' in J. Overing (ed.) *Reason and Morality* ASA Monograph no 24 Tavistock Publications, London 1985a.

48. See Chapter 5 for an account of English practices.

49. *Hansard* 1st series xiv, 331 Lords, 2 May 1809.

50. *Royal Commission on Marriage and Divorce* 1956, p. 8 paras 39, 42.

51. *Royal Commission* 1956 para 48.

52. Evershed Foreword to R.H. Graveson and F.R. Crane (eds) *A Century of Family Law* London 1957, p. x.

53. Ibid. p. xvi.

54. *The Times* 29 March 1984, p. 3 cols a–c. See Chapter 5, Section 2.

55. See e.g. *The Times* 26 November 1984, p. 3 col c.

56. *The Morning Post* 19 April 1911.

57. Lord Guthrie in *The Divorce Commission. The Majority and Minority Reports Summarised*, London 1912, p. v.

58. 12, 13 & 14 Geo 6 c 51.

59. L. Holcombe *Wives and Property. Reform of the Married Women's Property Law in Nineteenth-Century England* Toronto and Oxford 1983, p. 107.

60. Evershed Foreword, pp. ix, xi.

61. A.V. Dicey *Lectures on the Relation between Law and Public Opinion in England during the nineteenth century* second edition London 1914, lecture X, p. 347. Cited from reprint of 1930 (first edition 1905).

62. Lord Gorrell in *Royal Commission on Divorce and Matrimonial Causes* 1912–13 vol 3, pp. 545–7.

63. Hoggett and Pearl *The Family, Law and Society*, p. 142, citing the 1912 Commission (without giving the reference).

64. Holcombe *Wives and Property*, p. 107. See also p. 105ff; Hoggett and Pearl *The Family, Law and Society*, p. 142, who refer to 87,000 separation orders by magistrates 1897–1906.

65. *Royal Commission on Marriage and Divorce* 1956, p. 9 paras 45, 47.

66. Evershed Foreword, p. xi.

67. See above p. 149.

68. Dicey *Lectures*, reprinted 1930, lecture II, pp. 43–4.

69. See e.g. Holcombe *Wives and Property*, pp. 108–9 and above Chapter 4.

70. Holcombe *Wives and Property*, p. 90ff. It probably resulted in amendments improving property provisions for divorced wives, although it is not clear provision was better than in practices before 1857.

71. See above Chapter 5, Section 2; Chapter 6, Section 1.

72. See above Chapter 5, Section 2.

73. Evershed Foreword, pp. xi, xii, xiv is a good example of the shifts from one of these meanings to another.

74. See references in S. Wolfram 'Divorce in England 1700–1857' *Oxford Journal of Legal Studies* 1985, vol 5 no 2, pp. 156 note 4; also Appendix 5.1B. See also e.g. Holcombe *Wives and Property*, pp. 93–6. (Holcombe's account of the pre-1857 position is more than usually inaccurate; in particular proceedings in the ecclesiastical courts and for damages which were necessary preliminaries to a divorce Act are treated as if competing: the conclusion mentioned in note 76 must therefore be treated with caution.)

75. See Alan Watson's numerous examples to the contrary in A. Watson *Legal Transplants* Edinburgh 1974; *Society and Legal Change* Edinburgh 1977; *The Nature of Law* Edinburgh 1977, especially Chapters 6 and 7.

76. Holcombe *Wives and Property*, p. 103 refers to it as 'the first major step taken to eliminate conflicting jurisdictions and rival courts . . . it anticipated the great reform . . . of 1873' and claims that it was 'but a part of the wider movement for legal reform which had as its goals . . . to . . . modernise the country's judicial procedure'.

77. An Act for Marriages in England 1836 6 & 7 W 4 c 85. Figures for secular marriages are given in Marriages (England and Wales) 1857 106−1−Sess 2.

78. See above Chapter 6, Section 1.

79. Sixty women a year in a married population of 6 million, rising to 200 a year by 1900, when the married population was 11 million, obtained divorces.

80. Especially Table 5.1 and Appendix 5.2; and S. Wolfram 'Divorce in England'.

81. An exponential increase is where there is an equal percentage increase in each period of time. Since the absolute figures are greater in each period of time, the absolute increase created by the equal percentage increase is greater in each successive period. Thus, to take a numerically simple example, a 1 per cent increase from t_1 to t_2 when the absolute figure at t_1 is 150, yields 150 + 1.5 = 151.5 at t_2. A 1 per cent increase from t_1 to t_2 when the absolute figure is 150,000 at t_1 yields 150,000 + 1,500 = 151,500 at t_2; at t_3 the figure will then be 151,500 + 1,515 = 153,015, et seq.

82. S. Anderson 'Legislative Divorce — Law for the Aristocracy?' in G. Rubin and D. Sugarman (eds) *Law, Society and Economy. Essays in Legal History* 1984, pp. 424ff.

83. A cause is normally a separate sufficient, or sometimes, necessary, factor which can be thought of as producing the effect in whatever circumstances, as the impact of one billiard ball on another makes it move, the absence of some vitamin results in some particular disease, pressure groups impel legislation. However, if e.g. bacteria increase at an exponential rate due to a particular rate of reproduction, the number at time t_1 may be said to be the cause of the number at time t_2, and the rate of reproduction the cause of increasing numbers. Analogously, a certain number of divorces in one year might possibly be termed the 'cause' of the next year's figure. That the probability of any individual obtaining a divorce increases with the number of divorces in his or her environment might be cast as in some sense a 'cause' of increasing divorce rates. But if so, 'causes' of increasing rates of divorce must be sought more widely, and in different places than in this or that social condition or change.

8 Experts Past and Present

Experts have proffered explanations of various aspects of restrictions on sexual unions between relatives in England and elsewhere for centuries: Philo, Plutarch, St. Augustine, Maimonides, Jeremy Taylor, Grotius, Hume, Hutcheson, Montesquieu, Bentham, McLennan, Morgan, Tylor, Durkheim, Fraser, Freud, Malinowski, Radcliffe-Brown, Evans-Pritchard, Lévi-Strauss, to name but a few. This field of kinship has excited more interest and speculation than any other.

In the hands of social anthropologists in the past century the subject has grown to include apparently related customs, not found in England, such as preferences for marriage between certain relatives, notably so called cross-cousins (the children of siblings of opposite sex)[1] and practices loosely called the 'levirate' and 'sororate'.[2] Even if we limit ourselves to prohibitions, as I shall do here, there are usually several competing theories. There has rarely been a consensus, and the various questions posed cannot be said to have been resolved. If evidence is brought to bear on any particular theory, the theory invariably appears incorrect. But the theories have proved resilient in the face of counter-evidence. Not many have been abandoned, fewer still as a result of evidence brought against them. As the Archbishop of Canterbury's Group put it in 1984: 'The reasons for the widespread prohibition are still a matter of controversy among anthropologists.'[3]

The bulk of theorising has attributed a purpose or function to prohibitions of marriage or prohibitions of sexual relations between relatives. The exception is the body of literature arising after McLennan's *Primitive Marriage* in 1865, known as evolutionary theory, which sought to assign causes, generally to restrictions on marriage within clans, a common meaning given to 'exogamy'. Relatively late and famous works in this genre were Fraser's *Totemism and Exogamy* (1910) and Freud's *Totem und Tabu* (1913). Their sub-titles are revealing. Fraser's four-volume work was sub-titled *A Treatise on Certain Early Forms of Superstition and Society*, Freud's *Totem and Taboo: Some Points of*

Agreement between the Mental Lives of Savages and Neurotics. More recent anthropological work is closer to that of earlier experts, if less often centred on England.

1. Early Theories of 'Incest'

During the seventeenth and eighteenth centuries theories were put forward, and elaborated and disputed, against a biblical background. Some of these appeared in the controversy about legalising marriage with a deceased wife's sister in the nineteenth century. Some reappeared, shorn of their biblical associations, among social anthropologists when the influence of evolutionary theories had waned.

For convenience, the theories can be divided into three sorts: (1) those that attribute the prohibitions to some feature of the household, (2) those maintaining that sexual unions are forbidden between relatives to avoid conflict with or destruction of previously existing relationships (social roles theories), and (3) those which claim that relatives are forbidden to marry in order that alliances by marriage should be created between otherwise separate persons or groups (the 'Alliance Theory'). These theories are not always kept strictly apart. Sometimes two or more are deliberately conjoined. Sometimes they merge under ambiguous terminology.

There have been three principal theories of the first sort, that is, centred on the household. We can refer to them as theories 1A, 1B and 1C.

One of these (1A), conveniently called the 'Chastity Theory',[4] is generally attributed to Maimonides[5] and in more rudimentary form to Philo.[6] It was popular in England in the seventeenth, eighteenth and nineteenth centuries. It held that it was necessary to forbid marriage between persons in such intimate contact as members of the same household because otherwise they would engage in extra-marital intercourse. Thus in 1682: 'By permission of Marriage, in such degrees, Families are apt to be turn'd into Styes of unclean Beasts'[7] or a century later, in 1774: 'Let Hymen light his torch — let sensual love be once admitted — every house will become a brothel.'[8] In 1984 a television series drew attention to what was called 'child sex abuse' which included e.g.

mother–son incest.[9] But, apart from such slight revivals, the theory has lacked modern exponents.

In its heyday, the most serious ill effect of promiscuity in the home was supposed to be that it would lead, by habit and example, to extra-marital sexual relations of all kinds becoming common, at that time, unlike the present,[10] believed to be a disastrous state of affairs. 'The long and helpless infancy of Man' Hume wrote in 1751, 'requires the Combination of Parents for the Subsistence of their Young; and that Combination requires the Virtue of CHASTITY or Fidelity to the Marriage-bed'.[11]

Contemporary discussion of the theory highlighted two other points of interest today. One was the relevance of forbidding marriage between relatives to penalising extra-marital sexual relations between them. As the theory stood, it appeared that 'those severe *penalties* should only have been made against *Fornication* or *Adultery*, Committed with those with whom we most familiarly *converse*, but not against *marrying* of them . . .' (1653).[12] It was commonly urged in reply that 'if such loves could be cemented in marriage'[13] they would sure to grow more frequent.

The other point bears on all theories associating prohibitions of sexual unions with the household. This was that the relatives living in the same household in seventeenth- and eighteenth-century England (as in twentieth-century England) normally consisted of parents and children only, and contact between the other relatives forbidden to marry (viz. all those in or within the third degree of consanguinity and affinity) was no closer than between friends and neighbours. This point was made not only by critics of the theory but also by adherents of it. Thus John Fry in 1756:

> The preventing of Uncleanness . . . (as Families are now circumstantiated, Male and Female children being usually brought up together) may . . . be a *Good Reason* for the discountenancing of Marriage betwixt Brother and Sister. [But] . . . if you extend it *any further* than to *Brother* and *Sister*, you may as well extend it to *Neighbours, School-fellows*, and *all other Persons* that use to converse freely together (1756).[14]

When we read today of the 'potentially disruptive effects of erotic interest within a close family living together'[15] reference is generally to a different effect — the emergence of sexual rivalry. The theory that restrictions on sexual unions between relatives curb jealousies in the family (theory 1B) received its fullest elaboration at the hands of twentieth-century anthropologists, notably Malinowski, but it was of nineteenth-century English origin. 'If some insurmountable barrier were not erected between near relations fated to live together in the closest intimacy,' Jeremy Bentham wrote in 1802, frequent contact might

> kindle a fatal passion. The family — that retreat wherein repose should be found . . . would itself become a prey to all the turbulance of rivalry, all the fires of love. Pangs of jealousy would banish confidence; the tenderest sentiments of the heart would be destroyed; eternal hate, or bitter feelings of revenge, of which the bare idea makes one tremble, would fill their place . . .[16]

Opponents of legalising marriage with a deceased wife's sister commonly urged in somewhat similar terms that it would lead to rivalries between sisters.[17]

The third theory (theory 1C) associating marriage prohibitions with the household was of later origin. It was the work of one man only, the anthropologist Westermarck, who originally proposed it in 1891.[18] He held that sexual relations are forbidden between members of the same household because most people have an innate aversion to them, founded on the biological disadvantages of such unions. Few accepted his views. None but Westermarck developed it. Its position was rather that of a target to later writers. I shall return to the claims of correlation between 'close living together and the prohibited degrees of marriage',[19] developed by Westermarck, in Section 2.

It was a commonplace in the seventeenth and eighteenth centuries that a man could not marry his mother because his mother was his natural superior and his wife his natural inferior: 'The duty and reverence of a Mother' as Jeremy Taylor put it in 1660 'cannot be paid to her by him who is her Husband'.[20] This reason for forbidding marriage between a man and his mother extended satisfactorily to aunts. But, it was objected, 'the *father's marrying* the daughter or neece, those of the *descending* line, to whom he *owes* no *reverence* is the same foul *Incest*' (1653).[21] Taylor asserted that the consideration did also have 'some proportion between a Father and Daughter, as being undecent that she from whom should claim the rights of a wife, to whom she owes the duty of a father'.[22] Fry, ever modern, saw similar objection to marriage with 'all that are appointed Guardians' (1756).[23]

The idea that marriage between certain relatives would upset the status relations between them merges readily with the more general theory that marriage and/or sexual relations between relatives confuses social roles, and is, or should be, forbidden for that reason.

Various confusions of social roles, apart from purely status ones, have been brought forward to explain or justify the prohibition of unions between various relatives. Thus Alleyne in the eighteenth century:

> once admit the daughter to the arms of her father, — let the son once ascend the mother's couch, — parental authority and filial piety will be confounded and lost in the luxurious warmth of conjugal attraction . . . (1774).[24]

Or Malinowski in the twentieth century:

> Emotions of reverence, dependence, respect . . . must give the leading tone to the boy's relation to his mother . . . Any approach . . . with sensual or erotic temptations would involve the disruption of the relationship . . . [and] a type of behaviour ['possessive, dominant, passionate'][25] completely incompatible with submission, dependence, reverence.[26]

Like the Rivalry Theory (theory 1B), with which it is not uncommonly combined, the Social Roles Theory (theory 2) has often been used primarily to account for prohibitions affecting close relatives. But attempts have also been made to extend it to cover more distant ones. For instance, Bentham in 1802 held that 'the danger of upsetting the . . . relations . . . between those who ought to command and those who ought to obey'[27] was a good reason for forbidding a man to marry not only his descendants, aunt, niece etc. but also step-relations, such as his father's widow or wife's descendants, and in-laws like his uncle's widow. In the twentieth century, Radcliffe-Brown and others widened and elaborated the theory to explain prohibitions of unions between other relatives in other societies.

The third common theory, which I refer to as the Alliance Theory, that kin are forbidden to marry so that ties are created between otherwise separate persons or groups, is commonly attributed to Plutarch[28] and St. Augustine.[29] It was a popular theory in the seventeenth and eighteenth centuries among adherents of the Parity of Reason interpretation of Leviticus. Introduced into anthropology by Tylor in 1889,[30] it became, in Lévi-Strauss's hands, perhaps the most fashionable of current theories.

St. Augustine believed the marriage of close kin to be undesirable when it confused social roles, but also whenever it reduced the total number of a person's relatives. The marriage of a brother and sister is now damnable, he said:

> . . . for there was just care had of charity, that they to whom concord was most usefull might be combined together in divers bonds of kindred and affinity: not that one should have many in one, but that every peculiar should be bestowed abroad . . .[31]

If, to take one example, a brother and sister marry, then their father and father-in-law will be the same person, so will their mother and mother-in-law, and similarly their children's father and uncle, and mother and aunt. And, according to St. Augustine, relationships which should unite nine people would be confined to three.[32] The enumeration is doubtful but the point is clear. If people already related marry, they and their children will have fewer relatives than if each marries someone unrelated.

In the seventeenth and eighteenth centuries, the Alliance Theory was sometimes used to suggest that first cousins, who had been allowed to marry in England since 1540, ought not to do so:

> . . . The reason is this. It is for the Interest of Mankind, that Friendships should be spread as far as may be, and that the Concerns and Interests of many men should be as much as may be, perplexed and entangled into one another, that so the same common Hopes, and Fears, and Ends and Desires, may produce an Harmony in Affection, and a common Bond of Unity and Peace . . . (1682).[33]

The Alliance Theory was also used to defend the status quo, for instance by Hutcheson (1755), who maintained that if close kin marriages were allowed they would be frequent, and

> by this means the sacred bonds of affection would be too much confined, each family would be a little system by itself, detached from others

whereas now

> multitudes of families are beautifully interwoven with each other in affection and interest.[34]

The Chastity, Rivalry and Social Roles theories had difficulty in accounting for the full range of English Prohibited Degrees. The Alliance Theory had the reverse problem that 'it proved too much'. As Alleyne put it:

> [it] would carry the prohibition an immense way, and would in a short time be the means of there being *no* competent degrees at all — by prohibiting any two people, standing in any degree of relationship, however distant, to encrease their charity to each other by a more intimate endearment — it therefore proves too much (1774).[35]

Or in Fry's words:

> . . . if the forementioned Reason of extending Friendships, etc. proved any thing, it would prove too much; for it would prove that we ought to marry none but Strangers, which is much more than is intended to be proved by it. That Argument, therefore, which proves too much, is generally allowed to be good for nothing (1756).[36]

In other words, the theory necessarily justifies prohibiting marriage between *any* relatives or indeed anyone in previous contact.

The only defence which seems to have been made to these attacks was St. Augustine's own comment that:

> . . . The ancient fathers had a religious care to keepe the kindred within such limits, lest it should spread unto nothing:

binding of it backe againe into it selfe when it was a little diffused, and calling it still to a new combination in it selfe.[37]

So put the theory is somewhat less absurd: it is where *effective* kinship ties are re-duplicated that marriage is, or should be, forbidden.

In so far as these various theories were tested in the seventeenth and eighteenth centuries, it was principally to see whether they accorded with the set of prohibitions believed to be set out in Leviticus. However, there were four different interpretations of Leviticus. Two gave definite, albeit different, sets of rules: the Parity of Reason interpretation, yielding the existing English Prohibited Degrees, and the literal interpretation, whereby just the relatives explicitly mentioned in Leviticus 18 and 20 were intended to be forbidden.[38] The other two — that the prohibitions were tailored to the society of the Ancient Jews, and that they were not prohibitions of unions between relatives at all (but a prohibition of extra-marital intercourse) — left their upholders free to advocate virtually any set of prohibitions. The theories were therefore not necessarily employed to explain existing English rules, or any other particular prohibitions of unions between relatives. They might instead be used to advocate changes. Many authors tried to combine theories, basing prohibitions between different relatives on different disadvantages of their union. Forbidding parents and children to marry might be justified in one way (e.g. to avoid upsetting status relations), forbidding brothers and sisters to do so in another (e.g. to prevent promiscuity). But in the event of discrepancy between prohibitions and theory, it could be, and often was, the prohibitions (or reading of them in Leviticus), rather than the theory, which was held to be at fault.

When the controversy about legalising marriage with a deceased wife's sister arose in the nineteenth century, the relatively general theorising of the previous centuries ceased. Attention centred on the pros and cons of allowing a man to marry his dead wife's sister. Among the cons were that sisters would become rivals for their husband's affections, that the relations between a man and his wife's sister would be altered for the worse by the possibility of marriage between them, that after his wife's death, her sister would no longer be able to live in his house as she could when no marriage was possible between them. Most of the theories, indeed all but the Chastity Theory, were revived by twentieth-century anthropologists.

2. Anthropologists and 'Exogamy'

With the publication of McLennan's *Primitive Marriage* in 1865, a new phase began in theories about marriage prohibitions. This was focused on other societies, especially 'primitive' ones, and, initially, on prohibitions of marriage (or sexual intercourse) between members of the same, generally unilinear, group.[39] For about 50 years, anthropologists sought to discover the primeval origins of prohibitions on unions between relatives and produced a variety of theories, since discarded as 'conjectural history'.

In *Primitive Marriage* (1865) McLennan coined the word 'exogamy' to refer to the principle 'which *prohibited marriage within the tribe*',[40] the 'rule forbidding marriage within the tribe or group of kindred'[41] and declaring the 'union of persons of the same blood to be incest'.[42] McLennan's 'tribes' were groups of people believing themselves to be related and perpetually at war with other similar groups. It was McLennan's belief that the custom of 'exogamy' (i.e. marrying outside the 'tribe') developed from a state of affairs in which a man could gain a wife only through 'marriage by capture', that is, by forceful capture from another tribe.[42A]

McLennan's 'tribes' were not necessarily unilinear. However, at the same period that he introduced the term 'exogamy', and put forward his theory of its origins, several anthropologists, including Tylor[43] and Morgan[44] drew attention to the rule, frequently found among primitive peoples, whereby an extensive range of unilinear relatives are forbidden to marry. In 1868 Morgan re-defined a 'tribe' as a 'group of consanguinei, with descent limited either to the male or the female line' and added that 'No man can marry a woman of his own tribe, whether descent is in the male or female line'.[45] This definition of a 'tribe' was fairly generally accepted in the early 1870s.[46]

In 1877 Morgan attacked McLennan's theory of the origins of 'exogamy' and his definition of the term.[47] In particular, he pointed out that the groups of kin within which people are forbidden to marry cannot be identified with groups at war with each other. 'Tribes' in the sense of exogamous kin groups are in fact always found to be living on peaceful terms with others of their kind with whom they intermarry. So far as 'tribes' *qua* hostile groups are concerned, the rule is generally not that members of one must marry members of another, but, on the contrary, that they must not. Tribes at war are generally 'endogamous' i.e. people must marry inside them. This attack was effective. McLennan's theory was discarded, and 'exogamous' ceased to be an attribute of 'tribes'.

Morgan's attack on McLennan included complaints about the confused use of 'exogamy' and 'endogamy': they had, he concluded, been 'so thoroughly tainted by the manner of their use in "Primitive Marriage", that the best disposition which can now be made of them is to lay them aside'.[48] In the course of his criticisms, Morgan attributed to McLennan the use of 'exogamy' and 'endogamy' to 'imply respectively, an obligation to "marry out," and an obligation to "marry in," a particular group of persons'.[49] Thereby he introduced a new sense, which the terms have retained ever since.

For some time after this, 'exogamy' generally referred (a) to the prohibition of marriage between unilinear relatives and (b) to the enforcement of marriage outside social groups of some kind. These groups were no longer 'tribes'. For several decades the chief characteristic ascribed to 'exogamous' groups, or 'clans', was 'totemism', whereby the killing or eating of the particular animal associated with the group was tabooed. 'Where totemism exists in full force', Frazer was writing in 1892 and 1899,

> a man may not marry a woman of the same totem as himself . . . where this rule of exogamy (i.e., marrying out of the clan) exists, we necessarily have two or more totem clans existing side by side.[50]

Durkheim (1897) and Freud (1913) were among those who produced theories based on the view that the groups of unilinear kin within which people were forbidden to marry in primitive societies were 'totemic'. Freud's *Totem and Taboo* (1913) exemplifies the style of theory, if not perhaps at its most convincing. According to Freud, men originally lived in hordes with a dominant male who monopolised the women and drove away his sons:

> One day, however, the sons came together and united to overwhelm, kill and devour their father, who had been their

enemy but also their ideal. After the deed they were unable to take over their heritage since they stood in one another's way. Under the influence of failure and regret they learned to come to an agreement among themselves, they banded themselves into a clan of brothers by the help of the ordinances of totemism, which aimed at preventing a repetition of such a deed, and they jointly undertook to forego the possession of the women on whose account they had killed their father. They were then driven to finding strange women, and this was the origin of the exogamy which is so closely bound up with totemism.[51]

Freud was not, of course, himself a professional anthropologist, and even he later referred to this tale as a 'vision' rather than a hypothesis.[52] But the ideas from which he had culled its ingredients can be found in many anthropological works of the late nineteenth and early twentieth century. Durkheim expressed a widely accepted opinion when he wrote in 1897:

> In order to gain a proper understanding of a practice or institution, a moral or legal rule, one must go back as nearly as possible to its first beginnings.[53]

Durkheim attributed the 'lack of success' in discovering 'why the majority of societies have forbidden incest, and even classed it among the most immoral of their practices' to a search for 'its cause in the *present* circumstances of the life of individuals or societies' (my italics). 'No satisfactory solution of the problem can be found along these lines', Durkheim maintained:

> because the beliefs and ways of life which seem most relevant to explaining and justifying our horror of incest are not themselves self-explanatory or self-justifying; their own causes and the needs which they satisfy lie in the past. So instead . . . we shall first take ourselves to the beginnings of this evolution, that is, to the most primitive form in which the prohibition of incest is to be found in history. This is the rule of exogamy. When we have described and accounted for this, we shall be in a better position to understand our own existing ideas and attitudes.[54]

There had already been rumblings against the procedure. 'Many learned men' Starcke wrote in 1889[55] 'are too disposed to seek for the explanation of a given custom in conditions of former times'. In his opinion, this was an error:

> . . . appeal to early times can only be effective when it has been shown to be impossible to discover the cause of such customs in the conditions under which they still continue. If this main principle is not accepted, we shall be led astray by every idle delusion. If we are able to trace the cause of a custom in existing circumstances, we must abide by that cause, and nothing but a definite historical account of the prior existence of the custom can induce us to seek for another explanation.[56]

In the hands of Radcliffe-Brown this was to become a blistering attack which totally discredited 'evolutionary' theories and 'conjectural history' among anthropologists. 'Throughout the nineteenth century' Radcliffe-Brown explained in 1936,

> . . . anthropologists seemed to feel that any theories they might have about the nature of society and of social institutions must be put into some sort of historical form . . . whenever it was desired to explain the existence of some particular custom or institution in a certain society the reason was not sought in the society itself but in some hypothetical pre-existing condition. Exogamy was explained as having resulted from a state of society in which the only way of obtaining a wife was by capturing a woman of another tribe . . .[57]

He continued

> One might think that the fallacious character of these hypotheses would be obvious to any intelligent person . . . the hypothesis is such that it cannot be verified . . . its verification would depend on obtaining knowledge about the past which is forever unobtainable . . . [it] does not explain the facts . . . Even if I can know . . . that a particular social institution or custom or belief arose in a certain way two or ten or a hundred centuries ago this affords no explanation of why it still exists . . .

It seems clear that if intelligent men . . . can accept and seek explanations of this kind it can only be because they are influenced by some very powerful prejudice or illusion. We can call it the 'Illusion of Historical Explanation'. By this . . . I mean . . . the nineteenth century belief that any explanation of social phenomena must . . . explain existing conditions by reference to some known or conjectured past . . .[58]

By this date (1936), belief in the connection between 'totemism' and 'exogamy' had worn thin. 'Totemism' received its death blow at the hands of Lévi-Strauss in 1962,[59] but it had already been realised that it was not a clear-cut institution. Thus while the *Encyclopedia Britannica* of 1929[60] still devoted a great deal of space to totemism and its association with exogamy, it referred to loose definitions and wide variations in the relations of groups to their 'totem' animals or plants. It also spoke of totemism without exogamy (in Australia) or indeed coupled with endogamy (in Africa and elsewhere),[61] of exogamy without totemism, of primitive peoples without either totemism or exogamy,[62] of the impasse in the search for historical explanations, such that 'many anthropologists have renounced [it] . . . and confine themselves to the search for functional explanations'.[63]

'Exogamy' had also altered. Lang (1903),[64] Hobhouse (1906),[65] Westermarck (1921 onwards)[66] no longer limited it to prohibitions of unions between unilinear relatives or members of clans. Usage became even more confused than in Morgan's day. The term might still be restricted to prohibitions between unilinear relatives[67] but it might also be applied indiscriminately to all prohibitions of sexual unions between any kin (including affines and adoptive relatives).[68] Other specialised uses developed. Thus Fortes (1936 and 1937)[69] and Evans-Pritchard (1949)[70] employed 'exogamy' to distinguish prohibitions of marriage from restrictions on extra-marital intercourse between relatives, which they called 'incest prohibitions'. Another group, including Malinowski (1927),[71] B.Z. Seligman (1950),[72] Murdock (1949),[73] Parsons (1954)[74] used 'exogamy' to mark off prohibitions on unions outside the 'nuclear family' (parents and children and siblings) from what they called 'the prohibition of incest', i.e. the supposedly universal prohibition of marriage and sexual intercourse within the nuclear family. Some, such as Fox (1967)[75] contrived to conjoin these usages by treating the 'incest prohibition' as the rule forbidding all sexual intercourse and thus marriage, within the nuclear family, and using 'exogamy' to refer to all (other) rules forbidding marriage. The only common denominator was that, as Westermarck put it in 1921 'Exogamous rules . . . forbid members of a particular group to marry any other member of it'.[76] Not surprisingly, 'exogamy' may be used to mean just 'marrying outside the group'[77] or outside a specified group,[78] as in 'Among the Bongo Bongo clans are exogamous'.

Most of the theories held by theologians, lawyers, and moral philosophers in seventeenth- and eighteenth-century England had re-emerged in social anthropology by the inter-war period or soon after. Malinowski, B.Z. Seligman, Murdock promoted the Rivalry Theory, and also the Social Roles Theory.[79] Radcliffe-Brown, Firth, Fortes embraced and developed versions of the Social Roles Theory, sometimes extending it to preferential marriage.[80] Lowie, Fortune, White, Lévi-Strauss resurrected and greatly elaborated the Alliance Theory,[81] introduced into anthropology by Tylor in the much quoted passage (1889):

> Among tribes of low culture there is but one means known of keeping up permanent alliance, and that means is intermarriage. Exogamy, enabling a growing tribe to keep itself compact by constant unions between its spreading clans, enables it to overmarch any number of small intermarrying groups, isolated and helpless. Again and again in the world's history, savage tribes must have had plainly before their minds the simple practical alternative between marrying-out and being killed out. Even far on in culture, the political value of intermarriage remains.[82]

The new experts had little or no knowledge of their predecessors' efforts, and often trod old ground. Not infrequently formulations of theories differed principally in style. Thus the Rivalry Theory as expounded by Malinowski in his expert opinion to the Church of England (1940):

> The main sociological reason for marriage taboos and prohibited degrees is the elimination of sex from relations of the family type. A group leading a joint life with intimacy of daily concerns, with the need of an organised authority and unselfish devotion, cannot tolerate within its framework the

possibilities of sexual approaches, for these act as a competitive and disruptive force incompatible with the even tenor and stability of the family.[83]

Or the same theory from the pen of the American anthropologist Murdock in 1949:

Conflict within the family is a source of weakness, as is abundantly demonstrated by the current sociological literature on family disorganisation. No form of conflict is more disruptive than sexual competition and jealousy. The reduction of sexual rivalry between parents and children and between siblings consolidates the family as a cooperative social group, promotes the efficiency of its societal services, and thus strengthens the society as a whole.[84]

If promiscuity was no longer supposed to destroy the family or society, conflicts of roles were. Thus Malinowski in 1927:

Incest would mean an upsetting of age distinctions, the mixing up of generations, the disorganization of sentiments and a violent exchange of roles at a time when the family is the most important educational medium. No society could exist under such conditions.[85]

Closer inspection reveals two important differences between old and new. Early non-anthropological experts had been largely concerned with the rules of their own society. However, from the start anthropologists had focused on other societies. They continued to do so. This was coupled with an emphasis on groups, not present in the previous English-orientated versions of the same theories. Thus in statements of the Alliance Theory:

In many [primitive societies] the consanguine group, small or extended, of unilateral or of bilateral descent lives sundered from other similar groups except for the interrelationships that attend intermarriage (1932).[86]

Or from another American, White, in 1948:

Marriages came to be contracts first between families, later between even larger groups. The individual lost much of his initiative in courtship and choice of mates, for it was now a group affair. Among many primitive peoples a youth may not even be acquainted with his bride before marriage . . . To be sure, there are tribes where one can become acquainted or even intimate with his spouse before marriage, but the group character of the contract is there nevertheless.[87]

In 1949, Lévi-Strauss gave new life to the Alliance Theory in his global work *Les Structures élémentaires de la Parenté*.[88] In a famous study in the 1920s, the French anthropologist Mauss had brought to the fore the phenomenon of exchanges of, often identical, gifts, in theory voluntary, in practice subject to numerous conventions and constraints.[89] Lévi-Strauss promoted the theory that marriage too was an exchange — of women between groups of men:

The g ɔbal relation of exchange constituting marriage . . . is establi ɲed between two groups of men, and women feature in it as one of the objects of exchange.[90]

Marriage prohibitions, according to Lévi-Strauss, were a means of forcing groups of men to give away their own women in exchange for women from other groups of men. Most of his attention, and that of his followers, was focused on the preferential marriage between cross-cousins so common in other societies. Lévi-Strauss treated this as a means of perpetuating alliances between the same groups over generations, and he founded a number of hypotheses on a distinction between the 'direct' exchange occurring with symmetrical or patrilateral cross-cousin marriage and the 'indirect' exchange of matrilateral cross-cousin marriage.[91] So far as marriage prohibitions were concerned, the Alliance Theory gained adherents, together with the thought that it is between groups, and by the mechanism of gift-giving, that marriages forge alliances. By forcing men of one group to exchange women with those others, groups which, especially in primitive societies, would otherwise be isolated, are brought into friendly relations.

It might be expected that the continuing interest in restrictions on unions between relatives, the greatly increased data from other societies, and the objectives of social anthropology, viz. an understanding of societies, would have encouraged testing of these various theories, rejection of those at variance with the facts, and search for new hypotheses if the old are found wanting.

The theories have continued to be debated but empirical testing has played only a minor role. Data from other societies support none of these theories. On the contrary they are singularly unfavourable to all of them. We need look no further than England to find grave empirical problems. Indeed many were already brought to light in the seventeenth and eighteenth centuries. However, anthropologists' discussions have centred so largely on other societies, that it is worth turning briefly to the lessons that can be learnt from them.

It will be recalled that Westermarck claimed a correlation between 'close living together and the prohibited degrees of marriage'.[92] The claim was made in 1891 and supported by what he called an 'abundance of ethnographic facts'.[93] His facts, like those of many after him, were culled haphazardly from every quarter of the globe, and he asserted, among other things, that

> Generally speaking, the prohibited degrees are extended much farther among savage and barbarous peoples than in civilised societies. As a rule, the former, if they have not remained in the most primitive social condition of man, live, not in separate families, but in large households or communities, all the members of which dwell in very close contact with each other.[94]

Much later, in 1940, Malinowski was to make similar observations to the Church of England with respect to English history, advising it that the diminished size of the household and reduced intimacy of relatives in England, together with the increased contact between unrelated people of opposite sex, made it less necessary to forbid marriage between affines than it had been in the past.[95]

There are serious difficulties in the way of thorough testing. The theories themselves are bedevilled by vague formulations and riddled with defensive subsidiary hypotheses. Nor is the empirical side easy to handle. Knowledge is not sufficiently advanced for the kind of procedure adopted by Murdock in *Social Structure* (1949) to prove rewarding. Taking '250 sample societies', he applied statistical tests and claimed to find high coefficients of association between relevant factors. But what he counted as one society, and thus his enumerations, were arbitrary, his classifications forced, his data almost certainly incomplete and doubtful, as well as presented in an uncheckable form — without sources or detail. Re-testing with a smaller, more manageable sample failed to corroborate his results.[96]

Detailed study of a single society would be more searching than miscellaneous examples or questionable statistical methods. A compromise I adopted in a study of marriage rules in the 1950s was to investigate some 15 'societies', about which fieldwork had supplied relatively ample data. I set the empirical claims made or implied in each theory, and the major subsidiary hypotheses used to defend them, one by one, against the relevant data. Since the same 15 societies were used throughout there is no reason to believe that there was any bias whether for one theory or against another.[97]

The results were interesting but not encouraging to the style of theory still put forward.

All the societies investigated were 'primitive': various African (Southern Bantu) tribes, together with some others depicted in well known monographs (the Bemba, Dobu, Tikopia, Trobriands). Nine, or possibly ten, of them had the extensive (unilinear) prohibitions supposed to typify primitive societies.[98] The other five or six did not. Some of these forbade first cousin marriage. Others allowed or even preferred it. One group of tribes (the Tswana) forbade marriage only in the direct line (blood and in-law) and between siblings. Evidently the 'prohibited degrees' are not regularly 'extended much further among savage and barbarous peoples than in civilised societies'.

The censuses available for villages in a few of the tribes in question revealed that in some the percentage of households containing relatives allowed to marry one another could be as high as 30 per cent. It did however appear that marriage was not possible within the smaller units of which the households were made up and that the households permitting marriage were of unusual composition. With some slight qualification, one might therefore, so far as this evidence goes, accept the point that societies generally forbid marriage between those customarily living in the same household. However, this is as much as there is to be said in favour of any of the theories being considered.

With one possible exception (the Dobu) none of these societies forbade marriage in any other residential grouping than the household or between all the unilinearly related people living close at hand. Nor was marriage forbidden only between those in territorial proximity. There was no co-variation between the genealogical (or unilinear) composition of the household and the range of marriage prohibitions (or unilinear ones). If anything, there was a negative correlation, societies with more extensive households having less extensive restrictions on marriage, those with less extensive households more extensive restrictions.

'Groups' within which marriage was forbidden were equally not identifiable with any other social group. In one society (the Hera) there were social groups within which marriage was forbidden, but these were not the most important social groups in the society. Similar social groups were reported in societies with totally different marriage rules, which did not prevent marriage within the groups in question. All the societies examined had social groups whose members were intimate but permitted to marry and/or which did not include the whole range of relatives forbidden to marry. Members of exogamous clans were no more intimate than members of clans which were not exogamous. There appears to be no relation whatever between a society's social groups and the relatives between whom it forbids marriage.

Obviously such facts are inimical to the Rivalry Theory and tell against the Alliance Theory. A further problem for anthropological versions of the Alliance Theory, with their emphasis on groups, is that the 'groups' within which marriage was forbidden could not be identified with groups which would be isolated but for marriage ties nor were exogamous groups of the same composition as groups arranging or involved in marriages. In many of the societies in my sample a marriage did not even seem to create links between groups. It resulted only in relationships between one spouse and the kin of the other. In none of them was there evidence that all the groups of the society were linked by marriage.

St. Augustine's version of the Alliance Theory and the Social Roles Theory, which has several variants,[99] are no better supported. Marriage prohibitions could not be considered as rules preventing the re-duplication of existing kinship ties. Marriage might be forbidden where the relationships it would create would bind only people not already bound by effective kinship ties. It was commonly permitted or even preferred where it would lead to re-duplications of ties, between the parties themselves or between others brought into relationship by marriage. Again, prohibitions of marriage between relatives do not appear identifiable with rules preventing marriage between persons whose proper social relations are of particular kinds. Not all relatives forbidden to marry stood in any particular status relations, much less ones which would conflict with the status relations of husband and wife. On the other hand, marriage was frequently forbidden where there would be no such conflict. There did not appear to be any (other) behaviour typical of relatives forbidden to marry or distinct from that between those permitted to marry. Marriages in fact forbidden would not always have led to 'incompatible' requirements of behaviour between the same people. Marriages which were preferred often did so in the sense that the proper behaviour required between those becoming related through them differed from behaviour required in virtue of previous kinship ties.

These negative findings, which can be amplified, and are doubtless repeated elsewhere,[100] are in no way surprising. The only wonder is that theories so blatantly false should have been held with such tenacity, even passion,[101] by the experts of a *soi-disant* scientific society.

Notes

1. That is between a man and his mother's brother's daughter, 'matrilateral cross-cousin marriage', and, less commonly, between a man and his father's sister's daughter, 'patrilateral cross-cousin marriage'.
2. The 'levirate' is the custom whereby a man takes his brother's widow to wife, the 'sororate' that whereby he takes his dead wife's sister. The union may or may not be obligatory in one or another circumstance (e.g. if there are no children). It may be a continuation of the previous marriage, the children ranking as the dead man's or woman's, or not.
3. Archbishop of Canterbury's Group 1984 *No Just Cause* 1984 Appendix VI: 3, p. 133.
4. For more detailed discussion of this and other theories see S. Wolfram 'The Explanation of Prohibitions and Preferences of Marriage between Kin' DPhil thesis Oxford 1956, 705 pp., Chapter 4, p. 150 et seq.
5. M. Maimonides *c.* 1183 *The Reasons of the Laws of Moses from the 'More Nevochim' of Maimonides* (J. Townley, translator) London 1827, Chapter 24.
6. Philo 1st century AD 'Περί των ἐν μερει διαταγμάτων' *The Special laws* Book 3 Section 4 (e.g. Loeb (ed.) 1927, vols vii–viii).
7. Anonymous *Mr Emmerton's Marriage with Mrs. Bridget Hyde Considered* 1682, p. 47.

8. J. Alleyne *The Legal Degrees of Marriage Stated and Considered, in a Series of Letters to a Friend* 1774, p. 10.

9. 'Twenty Twenty Vision: Child Sex Abuse' Channel 4, 1, 8, 15 December 1984.

10. See Chapter 6, Section 2.

11. D. Hume *An Enquiry Concerning the Principles of Morals* 1751 Section iv, p. 66.

12. H. Hammond *A Letter of Resolution to Six Quaeries of Present Use in the Church of England* 1653, p. 55.

13. H. Grotius *De Jure Belli ac Pacis* 1646, Book 2 Chapter 5 Section 13.3.

14. J. Fry *The Case of Marriages between Near Kindred, Particularly Considered, with respect to the Doctrine of Scripture, the law of Nature, and the laws of England* London 1756, p. 73 (second enlarged edition 1773). Fry was the author of the unusual interpretation of Leviticus 18 and 20 whereby what was prohibited was not marriage between the relatives listed or instanced, but promiscuity (cf Chapter 2).

15. Archbishop of Canterbury's Group 1984 *No Just Cause*, p. 133.

16. J. Bentham *Principles of the Civil Code*, first published in French as *Principes du Code Civil* 1802. First English translation in J. Bowring *The Works of Jeremey Bentham* Edinburgh 1843. I quote from a translation by J.M. Atkinson *Bentham's Theory of Legislation* 1914.

17. Cf Chapter 2, Section 2.

18. E. Westermarck *The History of Human Marriage* London 1891 second edition 1894; third edition 1901; fifth enlarged edition 3 vols 1921).

19. Westermarck *The History of Human Marriage* Chapter 15.

20. J. Taylor *Doctor Dubitantium* 1660 Book 2 Chapter 3 rule 3 Section 19 (vol i, p. 293).

21. Hammond *A Letter of Resolution*, p. 45.

22. Taylor *Doctor Dubitantium*.

23. Fry *The Case of Marriages between Near Kindred*, p. 67. Cf The Archbishop of Canterbury's Group 1984 *No Just Cause*, Appendix VI which refers to the 'need to protect young children from sexual exploitation by those in authority over them', p. 133.

24. Alleyne *The Legal Degrees of Marriage*, p. 9.

25. B. Malinowski 'A Sociological Analysis of the Rationale of the Prohibited Degrees in Marriage', Church of England Commission *Kindred and Affinity as Impediments to Marriage* 1940 Appendix 3, p. 102.

26. B. Malinowski *Sex and Repression in Savage Society* 1927, p. 250.

27. Bentham *Principles of the Civil Code*, Chapter 29 Section i (1914 translation).

28. Plutarch AD *c.* 96 αἴτια ʽΡωμαϊκα (*The Roman Questions*) no 108.

29. St. Augustine *De Civitate Dei contra Paganos* 417−26 (*The City of God*) Book 15, Chapter 16.

30. E.B. Tylor 'On a Method of investigating the Development of Institutions; Applied to the laws of Marriage and Descent' *Journal of the Royal Anthropological Institute* xviii, 1889, p. 267.

31. St. Augustine *De Civitate Dei contra Paganos*. Quotation is from J. Healey's translation of 1620. The original reads: 'Habita est enim ratio rectissima caritatis, ut homines, quibus esset utilis adque honesta concordia, diversarum necessitutinum vincilis necterentur, nec unus in uno multas haberet, sed singulae spargerentur in singulos . . .'

32. The slightly curious arithmetic, and the oddity of using it at all, is clearer when we bear in mind that Latin kinship terms differ substantially from English. For example, in Latin a wife's father and mother ('socer' and 'socrus') are sharply

distinguished from a mother's husband and father's wife ('vitricus' and 'noverca'), mother's brother ('avunculus') is a different relative from father's brother, father's sister ('amita') is distinguished from mother's sister.

33. J. Turner *A Letter of Resolution to a Friend concerning the marriage Cousin Germans* 1682, p. 7.

34. F. Hutcheson *A System of Moral Philosophy* 1755, Book 3 Chapter 1 Section x (vol ii, p. 172).

35. Alleyne *The Legal Degrees of Marriage*, p. 55.

36. Fry *The Case of Marriages between Near Kindred*, p. 75.

37. St. Augustine *De Civitate Dei contra Paganos*.

38. See above Chapter 2, Sections 1 and 2.

39. By a unilinear group is meant a set of persons related through males only (patrilineal) or through females only (matrilineal). Early terms for unilinear rules of descent were 'father-right' and 'mother-right' and there was much complex discussion about which came first. ('Mother-right' generally won because it seemed possible to be ignorant of physical paternity but not of maternity.)

40. J.F. McLennan *Primitive Marriage. An Inquiry into the Origin of the Form of Capture in Marriage Ceremonies* Edinburgh 1865, p. 53; repeated in J.F. McLennan *Studies in Ancient History, Comprising a Reprint of Primitive Marriage* London 1876, p. 41 and *Studies in Ancient History* (published posthumously) London 1886, p. 27. The italics are McLennan's.

41. McLennan *Primitive Marriage*, p. 93; *Studies in Ancient History* 1876, p. 74; *Studies in Ancient History* 1886, p. 50.

42. McLennan 1865 *Primitive Marriage*, p. 48 note; repeated *Studies in Ancient History* 1876, p. 37 note; *Studies in Ancient History* 1886, p. 25 note 1.

42A. This was supposed to be due to a shortage of women resulting from female infanticide.

43. E.B. Tylor *Researches in the Early History of Mankind and the Development of Civilisation* London 1865, pp. 277–85.

44. L.H. Morgan 'A Conjectural Solution of the Origin of the Classificatory System of Relationship' *Proceedings of the American Academy of Arts and Sciences*, vii, Boston 1868, p. 469.

45. Morgan 'A Conjectural Solution'.

46. See e.g. J. Lubbock *The Origin of Civilisation and the Primitive Condition of Man. Mental and Social Condition of Savages* London 1870, p. 92; (ditto later editions of 1870, 1875, 1882, 1889, 1902, 1912); J. Lubbock 'On the development of relationships' *Journal of the Royal Anthropological Institute* i London 1870, p. 6; A. Giraud-Teulon *Les Origines de la Famille. Questions sur les antecedents des societies patriarcales* Geneva and Paris 1874, pp. 105, 107ff, 113–14.

47. L.H. Morgan *Ancient Society or Researches in the Lines of Human Progress from Savagery, through Barbarism to Civilisation* New York 1877, p. 509ff.

48. Morgan 'A Conjectural Solution', p. 515.

49. Ibid. p. 511.

50. J.G. Frazer in The Anthropological Institute *Notes and Queries on Anthropology* second edition, London 1892, p. 160; and British Association for the Advancement of Science *Notes and Queries on Anthropology* third edition London 1899, p. 160.

51. Quoted from the relatively concise version in Freud's revised autobiography, published as *An Autobiographical Study* London 1935 (translated by J. Strachey), pp. 124–5. The original is to be found in *Imago* i and ii Vienna 1912-13, published in Vienna 1913 as *Totem und Tabu*; English translation by J. Strachey *Totem and Taboo* London 1950, pp. 141–6 (first translated by A.A. Brill New York 1918).

52. Freud *An Autobiographical Study*, p. 124.

53. E. Durkheim 'La Prohibition de l'inceste et ses origines' *L'Année Sociologique* i, Paris 1897, p. 1 (my translation). (English translations by E. Sagarin 'Incest: The Nature and Origin of the Incest Taboo' 1963; A. Ellis 'The Origin and Development of the Incest Taboo' 1964.)

54. Durkheim 'La Prohibition de l'inceste', pp. 1–2 (my translation).

55. C.N. Starcke *The Primitive Family in its origin and development* London 1889, p. 18, re-issued in the same format R. Needham (ed.) Chicago 1976.

56. Ibid. pp. 18–19.

57. A.R. Radcliffe-Brown *The Development of Social Anthropology*, lecture given in the University of Chicago 1936 (typescript presented by Radcliffe-Brown to Institute of Social Anthropology, Oxford), pp. 11–12.

58. Ibid. pp. 11–12.

59. C. Lévi-Strauss *Le Totemisme Aujourd'hui* Paris 1962, translated into English by R. Needham as *Totemism* Boston 1963, London 1964.

60. *Encyclopedia Britannica* 1929 fourteenth edition, 'Totemism' by W.E.A. (= W.E. Armstrong) vol 22, pp. 315–82.

61. Ibid. p. 315.

62. Ibid. p. 317.

63. Ibid. p. 318.

64. A. Lang *Social Origins* London 1903, p. 12.

65. L.T. Hobhouse *Morals in Evolution. A Study of Comparative Ethics* London 1906 (2 vols) vol 1, p. 143ff.

66. E. Westermarck *The History of Human Marriage* fifth enlarged edition, London 1921 (3 vols) vol 2, p. 82, and later works: E. Westermarck *A Short History of Human Marriage* 1926, p. 66; *Marriage* 1929, p. 20; 'Recent Theories of Exogamy' *Sociological Review* 1934 xxvi, p. 22 (reprinted *Three Essays on Sex and Marriage* London 1934, p. 127).

67. E.E. Evans-Pritchard *Kinship and Marriage among the Nuer* 1951 Chapter 2. The chapter is called 'Marriage Prohibitions and Incest' and closely resembles E.E. Evans-Pritchard 'Nuer rules of exogamy and incest' in M. Fortes (ed.) *Social Structure* 1949 except for the substitution throughout of 'marriage prohibitions' for 'rules of exogamy' for all non-unilinear marriage prohibitions.

68. E.g. Westermarck *A Short History of Human Marriage*, p. 108.

69. M. Fortes 'Kinship, Incest and Exogamy of the Northern Territories of the Gold Coast' in L.H.D. Buxton (ed.) *Custom is King. Essays presented to R.R. Marrett* London 1936, p. 250ff; M. Fortes *Marriage Law among the Tallensi* 1937, p. 2.

70. Evans-Pritchard 'Nuer rules of exogamy and incest'. Evans-Pritchard altered his usage in 1951, to restrict 'exogamy' to prohibitions relating to unilinear relatives. See above note 67.

71. E.g. Malinowski *Sex and Repression in Savage Society*, p. 195. Malinowski sometimes reverted to applying 'exogamy' only to unilinear prohibitions e.g. ibid. p. 243; B. Malinowski 'Parenthood — the Basis of Social Structure' in V.F. Calverton and S.D. Schmalhausen (eds) *The New Generation* London 1930, p. 153.

72. E.g. B.Z. Seligman 'The Problem of incest and exogamy: a restatement' *American Anthropologist* 1950 vol 52, p. 315.

73. E.g. G.P. Murdock *Social Structure* New York 1949, pp. 299, 301.

74. T. Parsons 'The Incest Taboo in relation to Social Structure and the Specialisation of the Child' *British Journal of Sociology* London 1954, v, p. 108.

75. R. Fox *Kinship and Marriage. An Anthropological Perspective* London 1967, e.g. p. 55.

76. Westermarck *The History of Human Marriage*, vol. 2, p. 82.

77. E.g. L. Mair *Marriage* London 1971, p. 23.

78. E.g. B.M. Hoggett and D.S. Pearl *The Family, Law and Society* London 1983, p. 14. The usage is currently even more common for 'endogamy' (marrying in) as in 'class endogamy'. See e.g. L. Stone *The Family, Sex and Marriage in England 1500–1800* abbreviated and revised edition Penguin 1979, pp. 50–1, 72; R.A. Houlbrooke *The English Family 1450–1700* London 1984, pp. 51, 71, 75.

79. Malinowski *Sex and Repression in Savage Society*; B. Malinowski 'Kinship' *Encyclopedia Britannica* 1929 vol 13, p. 407; Malinowski 'Parenthood'; Malinowski 'A Sociological Analysis'; B.Z. Seligman: e.g. 'Bilateral Descent and the Formation of Marriage Classes' *Journal of the Royal Anthropological Institute* vol 57, 1927; 'Asymmetry in Descent with Special Reference to Pentecost' *Journal of the Royal Anthropological Institute* vol 58, 1928; 'Incest and Descent: their Influence on Social Organisation' *Journal of the Royal Anthropological Institute* vol 59, 1929; 'The Incest Barrier: its Role in Social Organisation' *British Journal of Psychology* (general section) vol 22 1932; 'The Incest Taboo as a Social Regulation' *Sociological Review* vol 27, 1935; B.Z. Seligman 'The Problem of Incest and Exogamy'; Murdock *Social Structure*.

80. A.R. Radcliffe-Brown in A.R. Radcliffe-Brown and D. Forde (eds) *African Systems of Kinship and Marriage* London 1950: Introduction, especially pp. 60–72; R. Firth *We the Tikopia. A Sociological Study of Kinship in Primitive Polynesia* London 1936, pp. 336–43; Fortes 'Kinship, Incest and Exogamy', pp. 250–4.

81. R.H. Lowie 'Marriage' *Encyclopedia of the Social Sciences* New York, 1933 vol 10, p. 147; R.F. Fortune 'Incest' *Encyclopedia of the Social Sciences* New York 1932 vol 7, pp. 620–2; L.A. White 'The Definition and Prohibition of Incest' *American Anthroplogist* 1, 1948, pp. 423–33; C. Lévi-Strauss *Les Structures élémentaires de la Parenté* Paris 1949, revised 1967 and translated into English by J.H. Bell, J.R. von Sturmer and R. Needham as *The Elementary Structures of Kinship* London 1969. Also e.g Murdock *Social Structure*, p. 296ff.

82. Tylor 1889 'On a Method of investigating the Development of Institutions', p. 267.

83. Malinowski 'A Sociological Analysis', p. 105.

84. Murdock *Social Structure*, p. 295.

85. Malinowski *Sex and Repression in Savage Society*, p. 251.

86. Fortune 'Incest', p. 620.

87. White 'The Definition and Prohibition of Incest', p. 425.

88. Lévi-Strauss *Les Structures élémentaires de la Parenté*.

89. M. Mauss 'Essai sur le don. Forme et raison de l'échange dans les sociétés archaiques' *L'Année Sociologique* second series vol 1, 1923–4. Reprinted in M. Mauss *Sociologie et Anthropologie* Paris 1950, second edition 1966; translated into English by I. Cunnison as *The Gift. Forms and Functions of Exchange in Archaic Societies* London 1954.

90. Lévi-Strauss *Les Structures élémentaires de la Parenté*, p. 148 (my translation). The French reads 'La relation globale d'échange qui constitue le mariage . . . s'établit entre deux groupes d'hommes, et la femme y figure comme un des objets de l'échange . . .'

91. For exposition and discussion see Wolfram 'The Explanation of Prohibitions', especially Chapter 6 Sections ii and iii, pp. 372–418 and Chapter 8 Section iii, pp. 496–529; and e.g. Fox *Kinship and Marriage* passim. If men marry both their mother's brother's daughters and father's sister's daughters (symmetrical cross-cousin marriage), their unilinear groups will exchange women in each generation. If they marry their father's sister's daughters (patrilateral cross-cousin marriage) women pass in opposite directions in each generation and thus in the same one in alternate generations. Marriage with a mother's brother's daughter

(matrilateral cross-cousin marrige) leads to women passing in the same direction in each generation. The literature is extensive and technical. Among Lévi-Strauss' hypotheses was that direct exchange occurs in 'disharmonic' systems, i.e. in which residence and descent are in different lines (e.g. a man lives with his father but traces descent matrilineally), 'indirect' exchange in 'harmonic' systems i.e. where residence and descent are in the same line.

92. See above Chapter 8, Section 1.

93. Westermarck 1891, 1894, 1901 *The History of Human Marriage*, p. 321.

94. Ibid. p. 321.

95. Malinowski 'A Sociological Analysis'. See S. Wolfram 'Le mariage entre alliés dans l'Angleterre contemporaine' *L'Homme* 1, 1961, pp. 67−8.

96. See Wolfram 'The Explanation of Prohibitions', e.g. pp. 234−50. Where Murdock claimed the high coefficient of association of +.94 between (in this instance) using a kinship term applied to mother, sister and daughter for a first cousin and being forbidden to marry that cousin, my sample yielded at best the rather low figure of +.43 with a host of caveats.

97. See Wolfram 'The Explanation of Prohibitions' passim. The societies in question appeared under the following names (in alphabetical order): Basuto, Bemba, Dobu, Hera, Lovedu, Pedi, Pondo, Swazi, Thonga, Tikopia, Trobriands, Tswana, Venda, Xosa, Zulu. Most are Southern Bantu tribes, with a few additions to assist diversity. Details of selection appear in the Introduction. Appendix 1, pp. 598−636 contains information about the marriage prohibitions and preferences of these societies, with sources. For empirical data on theories mentioned here see especially Part 2 Chapter 4 'Marriage Prohibitions and the Family' Sections iv−vii and appendices to Chapter 4, pp. 195−276, Chapter 5 'The Social Roles Theory', pp. 276−364, Chapter 6 'The Alliance Theory' especially Sections iii and iv, pp. 379−418. Empirical findings are summarised in Chapter 9 Section i, pp. 546−57. See Wolfram 'Le mariage entre alliés dans l'Angleterre contemporaine', pp. 66−8 for a few of the empirical observations telling against certain theories.

98. For the sake of brevity I confine the following comments to prohibitions of marriage. Details of severity of prohibitions of marriage, as well as the often slight data on treatment of sexual intercourse in these societies can be found in Wolfram 'The Explanation of Prohibitions', Chapter 3 Section ii, pp. 96−114 and Appendix 1, pp. 598−636.

99. Some take into account not only the relationships of the immediate parties to a marriage but also those of others who become related (or related in a different fashion) through a marriage.

100. The above is a summary of material set out at length in Wolfram 'The Explanation of Prohibitions' passim.

101. An anecdote helps illustrate this point. In 1956 I presented a harmless enough paper on the subject to a crowded room at Nuffield College, Oxford, at which I was then a graduate student. The audience contained only one anthropologist who took such exception to my claims that the seminar became a brawl.

9 Fact and Theory

When Radcliffe-Brown was inveighing against conjectural history at Chicago in the 1930s, he made the point that

> if intelligent men . . . can accept and seek explanations of this kind it can only be because they are influenced by some very powerful prejudice or illusion.[1]

He called the particular illusion that of Historical Explanation.

The decline of 'Functionalism' as a mode of explanation in Social Anthroplogy was the result not so much of theoretical considerations as of empirical ones. Like the search for primeval origins, the search for useful purposes, or 'functions', had already been largely discarded in practice some decades before new creeds were generalised or popularised. By the late 1930s, when Radcliffe-Brown was assisting at the last rites of conjectural history, and while theories of, for example, prohibitions of 'incest' and 'exogamy' in terms of their function were issuing from every pen, 'functionalism' was already being superseded. As Pocock put it in 1961:

> a new approach was developing out of the increased emphasis on field-work and it may be characterized as a shift from function to meaning. This shift and the attendant theoretical development are associated primarily with the works . . . of Evans-Pritchard . . . In [his] . . . first book *Witchcraft, Oracles and Magic among the Azande*, . . . 1937, there is no explicit expression of theoretical divergence, but in fact one hears little of the function of institutions . . . The concern is rather to show first what the Azande do and what they believe about their actions, and then to relate beliefs and actions to each other in such a manner that, given certain premises, they are seen to constitute a logical system . . .[2]

Lévi-Strauss's *Les structures élémentaires de la Parenté* (1949) viz. 'The elementary structures of kinship' already bore the name and

186

examined the 'structures' of kinship, but it also contained strong functionalist and indeed evolutionary-style strands. Its immediate influence was confined to social anthropology and it was to be many years before it was translated into English — in revised form (1969).[3] Within anthropology, it led to 'structural' studies of such un-English and un-Western institutions as matrilateral cross-cousin marriage,[4] as well as to wide acceptance of the Alliance Theory of marriage prohibitions, which is nothing if not functionalist.[5]

The popularisation of 'structuralism' took place only in the later 1960s and probably owed most to another work of Lévi-Strauss *La Pensée Sauvage* (1962), published in English as *The Savage Mind* in 1966.[6] By this time, there was already a new shift, away from the 'models' of kinship structures, so fatally easy to fashion, to Evans-Pritchard's point of departure: indigenous thoughts and concepts.

In *Anthropologie Structurale* in 1958 (translated into English as *Structural Anthropology* in 1963)[7] Lévi-Strauss commented that 'home-made' conscious models should be respected for two reasons:

> First they may be good, or at least may offer a point of access to the structure; each culture has its theoreticians, whose work merits as much attention as does that of the ethnologist's colleagues. Next, even if these models are tendentious or inexact, the tendency and the kind of error which they reveal are an integral part of the facts to be studied; and perhaps they may be counted amongst the most significant of these . . .[8]

Lévi-Strauss added that Durkheim and Mauss

> . . . well understood that the conscious representations of the indigenous people were always worth more attention than the theories issuing — equally as conscious representations — from the observer's society.[9]

Explanations of prohibitions of unions between relatives in terms of a useful purpose which they serve, such as the Rivalry Theory, Social Roles Theory or the Alliance Theory, promoted by Lévi-Strauss among others, appear clearly contradicted by data from so-called primitive societies. And it is because 'functionalist' theories so often failed to fit the facts that social anthropologists gradually abandoned the quest for explanations of rules of conduct in terms of useful purposes they serve. But in the case of prohibitions of unions between relatives such explanations lingered on both inside and outside social anthropology. Contrary evidence from other societies was either ignored or explained away. So was the fact that they do not accord with prohibitions in England, the society to which many adherents of the theories belong.

Some of the problems encountered by these theories had already been explored by indigenous writers in the seventeenth, eighteenth and nineteenth centuries. Lawyers, theologians and other experts of the period had pointed out against the Chastity, Rivalry and Social Roles Theories that relatives forbidden to marry or have sexual intercourse in England extended beyond those living together or in intimacy or whose social relations were incompatible with the marriage tie, and objected to the Alliance Theory that it would carry the prohibitions 'an immense way' and 'proves too much'.[10]

The versions of these theories revived by twentieth-century anthropologists, with their emphasis on groups, faced another problem. Prohibitions of the English kind cannot be seen as rules of 'group' exogamy because the relatives forbidden to marry, whether now or in the past, cannot form discrete groups as sets of unilinear relatives may do. Patrilineal relatives, such as a man and his father and father's father, his sons and sons' sons, his own and these relatives' brothers and brothers' children, may form a group separate from other similar groups and perhaps distinguished by name (as with English family names which pass in the male line). A man and his relatives in or within the third degree of consanguinity (his parents, grandparents, children, grandchildren, siblings, parents' siblings, siblings' children) are differently situated. His son, for instance, is a consanguineous relative to his son's mother and her parents, siblings etc., while he himself is not. He is in the third degree of consanguinity to his brother's children, but his son is in the fourth degree. *Mutatis mutandis* similar features hold for English affinal relatives: a son's affines are no relations of his father, a brother's affines no relations of his sister, and so on.

In 1940, when he tendered his advice to the Church of England, Malinowski appeared oblivious of this difficulty in the way of regarding English marriage prohibitions as preventing marriage within groups.[11] By the later 1960s it was sufficiently well appreciated for an anthropologist like Fox to try to grapple with the problem. His efforts are a good illustration of the twisting and turning to which those under the influence of what Radcliffe-Brown called 'some very powerful prejudice or illusion' may be driven.

'The perspective I have chosen' Fox wrote in the preface to *Kinship and Marriage. An Anthropological Perspective* (1967) 'is that of the analysis of kinship *groups*'.[12] It was also that of Lévi-Strauss' elementary structures of kinship. Bravely or rashly, Fox included a chapter called 'Cognatic descent and Ego-centred groups',[13] 'uphill struggle'[14] though he found it. Here he explained with some care that 'by their very nature cognatic lineages are bound to overlap in membership',[15] that 'theoretically it is possible under such a system for everybody to be a member of every group in the society!',[16] and that

such a system is radically different from the unilineal . . . Cognatic descent groups . . . cannot really serve the same kind of function as unilineal descent groups. They cannot, to take a simple example, ever be residential groups.[17]

Loth to exclude them from the realm of groups, Fox distinguished them by such terms as 'cognatic descent groups' or 'kindreds'.[18] But he was obliged to acknowledge that 'such a group cannot perform the same functions',[19] even that:

It is perhaps wrong to call this a group at all, but rather should we call it a 'category' of persons . . . it only comes to life, as it were, when the purpose for which it exists arises — like headhunting . . . or the regulation of marriage. (In the latter case it need not exist as a group at all.)[20]

Such admissions did not prevent Fox from saying, in chapter 8, that 'our own complex system' nevertheless has 'rules of exogamy'.[21] At first he added 'but no rules of alliance'. However, a few pages later, he suggested that:

While it is hard to compare our society with primitive societies . . . we can easily look at it as a variant on the alliance theme and ask how women (and men for that matter) are distributed round the system through marriage, and what the directions and intensities of these flows are . . . it may give us new insights into the dynamics of our own society.[22]

Possibly. Still it seems clear that the Alliance Theory, like the other theories we have considered fails to fit the facts of English society, as of others, in any straightforward fashion.

By 1984 English anthropologists concerned with English marriage prohibitions might be more ready to allow that 'The reasons for this widespread prohibition are still a matter of controversy among anthropologists', but that they were not wholly liberated from the 'Functionalist Illusion' in this area was evident in the characteristic addition:

> Some suggested explanations (among others) are the potentially disruptive effects of erotic interest within a close family living together . . . and the need to protect young children from sexual exploitation by those in authority over them . . .[23]

In the passage from *Structural Anthropology* quoted above, Lévi-Strauss made the point that 'each culture has its own theoreticians' and that the 'tendency and the kind of error which they reveal is an integral part of the facts to be studied'. That he contrasted each culture's theoreticians with 'the ethnologist's colleagues' suggests that he did not have social anthropologists themselves in mind as theoreticians of their own culture nor perhaps their tendencies and errors as ethnographic facts requiring study. Still, there seems no reason to exclude them.

I mentioned earlier that there is a tendency to assign causes to rules and practices which are not favoured while those which are favoured are commonly assigned a useful purpose. The marriage rules and other rules or practices of primitive societies were not initially seen as rational, and during the period that they were not, historical explanation predominated. The growth of functional modes of explanation was probably as much the result of increased respect for the rules and practices of other societies as of disillusionment with 'conjectural history'.

The notion of rules of conduct or practices serving a useful purpose is closely bound up with the view that they are rational. The prototype of rational action is that it is performed in the belief that it will secure some end which can be seen as desirable. The adoption of a rule which seems to serve no desirable end seems irrational, and irrational acts are commonly viewed as the result of causes of one kind or another. However, an act may *seem* irrational which is in fact quite rational. Once we understand, for instance, that Trobriand Islanders regard the father as a relative by marriage, their promotion of the view that the father has no part in the procreation of children appears rational in a way that it would not otherwise do. The exchange of identical goods may appear absurd since it serves no economic purpose, until we observe that, like our own exchanges of Christmas cards or meals, it fosters good will.

The reluctance to attribute irrationality increases as we come nearer home, in space or time, unless indeed the present state of affairs appears undesirable. That people are on the whole rational, and in control of the rules of their society, is not an unreasonable supposition. There is nothing intrinsically improbable about the assumption made by proponents of functionalist theories in anthropology that rules and customs, such as restrictions on the marriage of particular relatives or the custom of going into mourning do or did serve a useful purpose and that their existence and form, change or disappearance will be found to depend on the circumstances which give them their utility. However, if theories framed on this basis regularly fail to explain the facts, then it does not appear rational to persist in promoting them, provided, that is, that the objective is better understanding of the facts, as opposed to, for example, bringing about a piece of legislation.

It is not only, nor even primarily, actions which are assessed as rational or otherwise. Philosophers often give priority to beliefs or assertions (or an amalgam of these) over acts. Thus for example Taylor in 1982:

> We call someone irrational who affirms both *p* and not-*p*. *By extension* [my italics], someone who acts flagrantly in violation of his own interest, or of his own avowed objectives, can be considered irrational.[24]

Elsewhere[25] I have drawn a sharp distinction between what it may be rational to say and what it may be rational to believe. Saying or writing something is a species of action and, if assessed for 'rationality', this must be in terms of whether it is a good or the best means of securing a desired objective. It may be rational for someone not to voice his beliefs or even to say or write something he does not believe, about which he has perhaps formed no opinion or which he positively disbelieves. Several examples have arisen in the course of considering English kinship. For instance the silence about eugenic factors in the Parliamentary debates leading to the 1908 Incest Act was probably due not to absence of beliefs about the biological ill effects of incest but to the injudiciousness of airing them. On the other hand, the reasons most often stated in favour of all sorts of different pieces of legislation about kinship in England (that it brings England into line with Scotland, opens to the poor what is open to the rich, makes no real change) are those apparently effective to bring forward but almost as certainly not the principal nor even genuine reasons for promoting the measures in question.

The rationality of beliefs is another matter. Beliefs are not acts. They do not have purposes. The rationality or otherwise of believing that something is the case depends on whether the available evidence does or does not suggest that it is so. The evidence may be of many different kinds, ranging from assurances by trusted sources to seeing with one's own eyes. Evidence may be so strong as to amount to proof, or it may be slight or conflicting, or otherwise indecisive.

I have suggested that the evidence against some common beliefs held about kinship, popularly or by experts, is fairly decisive, and moreover that those holding the beliefs do not do so rationally but on the basis of evidently inadequate evidence or in defiance of other facts which they know or believe. Examples included the English popular belief that incest is forbidden to prevent idiot children, that the increase in divorce in England is due to the emancipation of women and, in Chapter 8 the various theories competing to explain restrictions on sexual unions between relatives.

Earlier in this chapter I mentioned that the common failure of functionalist theories led anthropologists to turn in other directions. In the case of a belief so general as that rules of conduct or practices follow the prototype of rational, controlled action and serve useful purposes, the evidence against this belief can scarcely be decisive. But it can of course be suggestive, and in other

ways than merely repeated failure to find the connections between particular rules or practices and specific useful purposes.

Among the facts which were almost certainly influential in
making anthropologists 'shift', as Pocock put it, from 'function to
meaning' was an increasing concern with certain types of belief
which are not readily assessable for truth or falsity, or rationality
and irrationality, or not so assessable at all.

Beliefs of great generality, such as that God guides the world,
every event has a cause or all men are rational, may be highly
influential but are sufficiently difficult to evaluate to have been
treated at one time, by the Logical Positivists, as wholly untestable, and hence 'metaphysical' (nonsense). Among them are such
beliefs as the Azande view, made famous by Evans-Pritchard and
quoted, with varying degrees of accuracy ever since, viz. that
many events which we regard as chance happenings are caused by
witchcraft.[26] At the same period that metaphysical theories were
being castigated for their untestable nature by philosophers,
anthropologists were finding in their variation from one society to
another a possible source of explanation of differences in the
customs and practices of societies. Ayer's best-selling manifesto
of Logical Positivism, *Language, Truth and Logic*, denouncing
metaphysics in his own society, was published in 1936,[27] the year
before Evans-Pritchard's *Witchcraft, Oracles and Magic among
the Azande* (1937) which brought into prominence the different
metaphysical beliefs of other societies.

There is also another species of belief which is more genuinely
untestable than the metaphysical beliefs to which attention was
drawn in the late 1930s. We might distinguish them as beliefs of
classification or category beliefs, and characterise them, roughly,
as beliefs about which things are the 'same' and which 'different'.

The fact that different societies classify differently was a pre-
occupation of the *Année Sociologique* School of French anthropologists early in the century,[28] and the idea that a people should
be studied through its own categories was sporadically applied to
kinship in such dicta as 'Every kinship system . . . is a little
system of classificatory thought'.[29] But it was only in the 1950s
and 1960s that this approach began to predominate. When Lévi-
Strauss spoke of ' "home-made" conscious models' in 1958 he
was referring not so much to theories about aspects of kinship
which might be prevalent in a society as to their own descriptions of their categories and the relations between them. 'To

understand a people's thought one has to think in their symbols' Evans-Pritchard wrote in 1951, in emphasising the need for an anthropologist to begin by learning the language of the society he is studying:

> Also, in learning the language one learns the culture and the social system which are conceptualized in the language. Every kind of social relationship, every belief, every technological process — in fact everything in the social life of the natives — is expressed in words as well as in action, and when one has fully understood the meaning of all the words of their language in all their situations of references one has finished one's study of the society.[30]

In the introduction to his translation of Durkheim and Mauss's *Primitive Classification* in 1963, Needham spoke of 'what may be considered the prime and fundamental concern of social anthropology, viz., classification':

> When the ethnographer visits a strange people he carries with him . . . concepts [from his own society] . . . But gradually he learns to see the world as it is constituted for the people themselves, to assimilate their distinctive categories.[31]

One of the most potent forces in the shift from 'function' to 'meaning' was that functionalist explanations tended to ignore and cut across the categories and systematisations of the societies whose rules and customs were being explained. A society may well of course also have common or learned theories to explain its rules and practices, as in England the prohibition of incest is popularly ascribed to the biological ill effects of in-breeding or the increase in divorce to the emancipation of women, and the learned have devised other explanations. And these are as much ethnographic facts to be considered as classifications and systematisations. However, many anthropologists came to think that a society's categories had more influence on its rules and practices than its theories.

Notes

1. A.R. Radcliffe-Brown *The Development of Social Anthropology*, lecture given in the University of Chicago 1936 (typescript presented by Radcliffe-Brown to Institute of Social Anthropology, Oxford), pp. 11–12.

2. D.F. Pocock *Social Anthropology* London and New York 1961, pp. 72–3.

3. See above Chapter 8, Section 2. The original edition of 1949 was not translated. There was a revised edition in 1967. English version of revised edition by J.M. Bell, J.R. von Sturmer and R. Needham *The Elementary Structures of Kinship* London 1969.

4. See particularly E.R. Leach 'The structural implications of matrilateral cross-cousin marriage' *JRAI* vol 81 London 1951; revised in E.R. Leach *Rethinking Anthropology* first edition 1961, revised paperback edition 1966 Chapter 3, pp. 54–106.

5. See above Chapter 8, Section 2.

6. C. Lévi-Strauss *La Pensée Sauvage* Paris 1962. English translation [by S. Wolfram] *The Savage Mind* London and Chicago 1966.

7. C. Lévi-Strauss *Anthropologie Structurale* Paris 1958. English translation *Structural Anthropology* by C. Jacobson and B.G. Schoepf New York 1963, London 1968.

8. Lévi-Strauss *Anthropologie Structurale*, p. 306; the translation is Pocock's in Pocock *Social Anthrpology*, p. 87.

9. Lévi-Strauss *Anthropologie Structurale*.

10. See above Chapter 8, pp. 167ff and Section 2.

11. B. Malinowski 'A Sociological Analysis of the Rationale of the Prohibited Degrees in Marriage', Church of England Commission *Kindred and Affinity as Impediments to Marriage* 1940, pp. 101–6. See above e.g. Chapter 8, pp. 174–5, 177.

12. R. Fox *Kinship and Marriage. An Anthropological Perspective* London 1967, p. 11.

13. Ibid. Chapter 6.

14. Ibid. p. 175.

15. Ibid. p. 147.

16. Ibid. p. 149.

17. Ibid. pp. 149–50. These problems had already been pointed out in inter alia S. Wolfram 'The explanation of prohibitions and preferences of marriage between kin' DPhil thesis, Oxford University, 1956 with reference to English-style rules, especially Chapter 3 Sections iv–vi, pp. 123ff and applied to Malinowski 'A Sociological Analysis', S. Wolfram 'Le mariage entre alliés dans l'Angleterre contemporaine' *L'Homme* 1, 1961, pp. 67–8 and note 88; and were more generally explored in S. Wolfram 'Basic Differences of Thought' in R. Horton and R. Finnegan (eds) *Modes of Thought* London 1973, pp. 371ff.

18. Fox *Kinship and Marriage*, e.g. pp. 160, 161, 166.

19. Ibid. p. 166.

20. Ibid. p. 167.

21. Ibid. p. 223.

22. Ibid. pp. 238–9.

23. Church of England: Archbishop of Canterbury's Group *No Just Cause. The Law of Affinity in England & Wales: Some suggestions for change* London 1984, Appendix VI, p. 133.

24. C. Taylor 'Rationality' in M. Hollis and S. Lukes (eds) *Rationality and Relativism* Oxford 1982, p. 87.

25. S. Wolfram 'Facts and Theories: Saying and Believing' in J. Overing (ed) *Reason and Morality* ASA monograph no 24 London 1985a.

26. See E.E. Evans-Pritchard *Social Anthropology* London 1951, pp. 98–102

for a brief summary of the Azandes's 'system of thought'.

27. A.J. Ayer *Language, Truth and Logic* London 1936.

28. See especially E. Durkheim and M. Mauss *De quelques formes primitives de classification* Paris 1903 (*Année Sociologique* 1901–2), translated into English by R. Needham as *Primitive Classification* London 1963.

29. A.L. Kroeber 'Kinship and History' *American Anthropologist* vol 38 1936, p. 339.

30. Evans-Pritchard *Social Anthropology* pp. 79–80.

31. Needham in Durkheim and Mauss *De quelques formes primitives de classification*, p. viii.

10 Indigenous Structuring

In a late novel of Trollope's, *John Caldigate* (1879), the hero is imprisoned for bigamy: he is (wrongly) supposed to have married one Euphemia Smith in Australia before his (happy) marriage to the heroine, Hester, née Bolton. Trollope's characters argue about the effect of the sentence. Some say that the 'verdict itself dissolves the marriage', others that 'the verdict could have no such power'.[1] In the same novel, as the case is pending, Hester talks to her elder brother, a barrister:

> 'Father and son, or even mother and daughter, are not like husbands and wives, are they?'
>
> 'No; they are not,' said the barrister, not quite knowing how to answer so very self-evident a proposition, but understanding accurately the line of thought which had rendered it necessary for the poor creature to reassert at every moment the bond by which she would fain be bound to the father of her child.[2]

Many English people do not know with precision what validates or invalidates a marriage, which relatives they may not marry, how far 'incest' extends, what are the laws of inheritance, the effects on property of a divorce. There are few who would not regard it as too self-evident for ordinary mention that husbands and wives are closer than parents and children or what this means. In normal circumstances, people do not tell each other, nor often even think about, what they all take for granted. In discussing what I am calling the 'indigenous structuring' of English kinship I am largely concerned with beliefs about kinship matters which seem self-evident in this way within the society.

There has by now been a good deal of discussion of the view that 'the conceptual scheme governs and defines practices'[3] and of the form and place of what in 1976 Leach called, as broadly, 'the structures of ideas current in a society'.[4] In most cases, the claim is that if we understand the relevant scheme or structure, we shall, in some sense, also understand a variety of acts, rules and practices. This style of approach was already being applied to kinship in the 1950s, notably in Dumont's studies of Indian concepts of 'affinity'.[5]

It has not hitherto been very prominent in studies of English kinship, although if we go back, for instance, to English legal works of the nineteenth century or before, the framework of English beliefs of classification about kinship is lucidly enough laid out. Thus, husband and wife are 'as one'. There are two kinds of relatives: 'consanguineous' and 'affinal'. Consanguineous relationship is traced through parents. Affinal relationship is the relation between someone and his or her spouse's consanguineous relatives. Affinal relationship mirrors consanguineous relationship. Closeness of relationship goes by degree in a specified fashion. Kinship does not extend beyond 'consanguineous' and 'affinal' relations. Thus, while a married couple is similarly related to the kin on both sides, the consanguineous relatives of one spouse are not related to those of the other.

In the course of Part 1 I tried to animate this skeleton, by showing, for example, how these beliefs about kinship led, logically and probably in practice, from Leviticus to the English Prohibited Degrees of Consanguinity and Affinity, and were applied in mourning for the dead, or how a number of the changes which have taken place can be viewed as the gradual whittling away of the implications of the unity of husband and wife, while other related features, such as a preference for marriage between equals or the kinship terminology, have remained much the same over the centuries, and often go unnoticed.

In 1976, in his book called *Culture and Communication*, and sub-titled *An Introduction to the use of Structuralist Analysis in Social Anthropology*, Leach remarked that in their field research 'structuralists':

> attach particular importance . . . to informants' statements about what ought to be the case. Where there is a discrepancy between verbal statements and observed behaviour, . . . [they] tend to maintain that the social reality 'exists' in the verbal statements, rather than in what actually happens.[6]

He illustrated the justification for the 'structuralist' position by analogy. According to this approach:

the 'structure' of a system of social ideas bears the same sort of relationship to what actually happens as does a musical score to the performance. The score is, in a sense, the 'cause' of what happens, but we cannot work backwards and reliably infer the score from direct observation of any single performer's behaviour. In the musical case, the score originates 'in the mind' of the composer. By analogy, [there is a tendency] . . . to write of cultural systems being composed by a kind of collectivity — 'the human mind' . . .[7]

At least two problems obtrude themselves. The first is by what means the 'conceptual scheme' or 'structure of ideas' in a society is to be discovered. The other is how, if at all, conceptual schemes or structures of ideas may explain 'what happens'.

The limitations and pitfalls of 'observing behaviour' have often been pointed out. In particular, it is commonly argued by both anthropologists and philosophers, that we cannot give a correct description of the simplest action without knowing what the person performing it thinks he is doing. It is necessary, in Pocock's phrase, 'to find out . . . the meaning which people themselves attach to what they do'.[8] Just 'observing behaviour' can lead to gross errors. Someone might for, example, suppose, that he had discovered:

some dangerous sect of anarchists in the suburbs of an English city that deliberately exploited the Christian Sunday in order to endanger their neighbours' fences, and obscure visibility for traffic, by lighting large (possibly sacrificial) fires at the bottoms of their gardens.[9]

The most obvious method of avoiding mistakes like this is resort to verbal enquiry.

However, the unreliability of verbal statements has also had much attention. Thus Hare's influential book *The Language of Morals* (1952) opened with the words:

If we were to ask of a person 'What are his moral principles?' the way in which we could be most sure of a true answer would be by studying what he *did*. He might . . . profess in his conversation all sorts of principles, which in his actions he completely disregarded . . .[10]

In the last chapter I made the less extreme point that we cannot equate beliefs and assertions. Speaking and writing are species of action and commonly performed for a purpose. The purpose may be to communicate something believed to be true. But there are many other purposes of assertions: to persuade, impress, humour, insult, bewilder, be polite, avert a quarrel, display superiority, crack a joke, sell a horse, fool the spy, etc. etc. Assertions made for such purposes may well not be accompanied by belief that what is said is true. It would be a simple minded ethnographer who treated all verbal statements as expressions of belief, or for that matter, supposed he would be told everything that everybody believed.[11]

These and other difficulties have led some philosophers, notably Quine in *Word and Object* (1960) and elsewhere, to aver, not always on the soundest grounds, that neither verbal nor nonverbal behaviour ever suffices to establish so much as the meaning of words in a language or the content of an assertion, much less what is believed or what is being done.[12] Even if we do not follow philosophers into the more remote regions of scepticism, there clearly are many problems and complications about what is said and (other) behaviour as evidence of what is believed and about discovering the 'conceptual scheme' or 'structure of ideas' in a society.

Contra Leach, it is doubtful whether many 'structural' anthropologists seriously subscribe to so obviously foolish a view as that 'social reality "exists" in verbal statements rather than in what happens'.[13] However, they are especially concerned with the categories, beliefs and ideologies of societies, and they do generally consider that (well sifted) verbal statements are important to discovering them. The reasons for emphasis on verbal statements are not far to seek.

If it is difficult to construe individual acts and to find out that someone is burning rubbish, and not performing an esoteric rite, merely by watching him, or that in donning black clothes someone is going into mourning, it is very much more troublesome to uncover a whole scheme of mourning, the ins and outs of a preference for marrying equals, the norms of weddings, rules of residence, sexual mores of a society without resort to what people in the society say on such subjects. Vast quantities of data on behaviour would be necessary to perceive a pattern. The pattern that exists might be, and in structuralist eyes, often is, a matter of rules, conventions, etc. If so, such data as village censuses, lists of wedding 'guests', observation of who was wearing black (or whatever) when, apart from being procured inter alia by the medium of the spoken or written word, will be a roundabout and often inadequate means of research. Perceived behaviour is not likely to reveal a pattern so clear as to be indisputably correct. Apart from anything else, exceptions to and breaches of conventions, rules, proprieties are likely to muddy the water. The position could often be easily enough explained by the native. Two slightly different examples should serve to illustrate the point.

I have mentioned the English belief that a woman should not marry a man 'inferior' to herself: the husband should not be poorer, lower in rank or status, less educated, nor even younger or shorter in stature than his wife. Observation would almost certainly reveal that women do marry men inferior to themselves in one way or another. It is less sure that it would also reveal that such unions are not looked on with favour. The evidence is there. Fiction depicts some such wives as being cast off by their families, some such husbands as scoundrels. In practice, there will be jokes, or (generally discreet) adverse comment (it is not a love match, the man is mercenary, the woman anxious to secure a husband), or perhaps concealment of the peccant aspect as when wedding photographs made Prince Charles appear taller than his bride.[14] As natives know, there are no views about the proper relative girth of husband and wife (other than a general preference for the slender figure). A very complex computer-aided study would be necessary to display this simple and locally well-known fact.

Thanks to detailed (verbal) orders published in the *London Gazette*, it is possible, if laborious, to discover for how long the English court went into mourning, and for whom, in the nineteenth century. With the help of genealogies and other records, we can further glean the information that the court went into mourning at the deaths of relatives of the Sovereign and of some heads of some foreign states. But other such intricacies, such as that the norm was twelve weeks at the death of a husband or wife of the Sovereign, six weeks for a relative in the first degree, and so on, could probably not be reliably established without sight of the 'score', viz. the rules, which, in this case, were, fortunately, written down and preserved.[14A]

Investigators of English kinship in the relatively recent past, are not generally in the position of the alien ethnographer. They are commonly English-speaking. Often they are natives, and well acquainted with pertinent categories, conventions, norms, beliefs etc. The problem of discerning putative patterns, and of establishing their correctness, is less acute than it is in the situation more usual for the anthropologist, where unknown conceptual schemes and categories of ideas have to be painstakingly unearthed and the evidence of both words and acts carefully pieced together to avoid serious error. The danger in the case of English kinship is rather overlooking the familiar and obvious.

In likening the ' "structure" of a system of social ideas' to a musical score, Leach spoke of the score as 'in a sense the "cause" of what happens'. The question of how the structures of ideas or conceptual scheme of a society 'causes', or explains, what happens is important, among other things, to defining the difference between this mode of explanation and others.

At least in our society, the most common forms of explanation of human behaviour are by specifying either a cause of what happens or alternatively a purpose. On the causal model, what happens is usually thought of as governed by outside, perhaps uncontrollable, forces, or at least as the effect of other happenings, as when the not entirely fortunate growth of English divorce is attributed to the emancipation of women, the increase in extra-marital unions to improved contraception or primitive 'exogamy' to the Uprising of Sons against Fathers. In assigning purposes to rules, conventions and practices of societies, what happens is, by contrast, explained on the pattern of purposive rational action. Thus proscriptions on incest have a eugenic purpose, enforced 'marrying-out' creates alliances, formalised mourning comforts the bereaved.

Neither model fits explanations of societies' rules and practices in terms of their conceptual schemes. Indigenous classifications and associated beliefs are not outside forces. They also differ in kind and role from beliefs invoked in purposive explanation. When we say that someone did X because he believed it would bring about a certain end Y, this could be re-phrased 'he did X in order to bring about Y'. The belief that X brings about Y may be correct or incorrect, well- or ill-founded, and the act correspondingly rational or irrational. When it is suggested that mourning was longer in England for a spouse than for a parent because a spouse was believed to be closer, the 'because' clause cannot be re-phrased as an 'in order to' one. Again, the belief that a spouse is closer than a parent is neither true nor false, well- or ill-founded but merely a part of the categorisation of relatives in the society. In the approach adopted by 'structuralist'[15] anthropologists, the relation between a society's categories and 'what happens' is often handled on the model of the relation between its categories and words in the language. It is suggested that rules and customs mark socially made assimilations and distinctions in much the same way as these are marked on the linguistic plane by the use of the same or different words.

One inference commonly drawn is that in the same way that it is arbitrary which words mark off two different categories, so it is arbitrary which rules or customs do so. Thus Leach in 1976:

Any 'bit' of cultural information which is conveyed by the binary contrast X/Y (e.g. white/black) could as easily be conveyed by the binary contrast Y/X (black/white) and since all metaphoric associations are in the last analysis arbitrary, it is always likely that any particular significant contrast which occurs in one ethnographic context will turn up in reversed form in some other.[16]

Leach added that sometimes 'reversals may themselves be significant':

Local custom is quite often organised not simply on the basis that 'we, the X people, do things differently from them, the Y people' but on the principle 'our X customs are correct; those lousy Y people just across the valley . . . do everything back to front!'
   The question of whether a particular tribal community burn or bury their dead, or whether their houses are round or rectangular may sometimes have no functional explanation other than that the people concerned want to show themselves different from and superior to their neighbours . . . The more similar the general cultural patterning of the two communities, the more critical will be the significance which is attached to such minor points of reversal. English-speaking Americans and Englishmen should be able to think of dozens of relevant examples. What you should do with your knife and fork . . .

not only differs according to whether you are in England, France or the United States, it is 'bad manners' if you get it wrong![17]

If we apply this style of approach to kinship customs, some previously intractable problems dissolve. For example, it no longer seems so surprising that English (or other) prohibitions of marriage and sexual intercourse between relatives serve none of the particular purposes they have been thought to do, or that rules of mourning in nineteenth-century England did not follow the pattern one would expect if their object were to assist the bereaved. A not improbable hypothesis is that they serve no more tangible a purpose than marking off relatives from non-relatives. Relatives are unmarriageable. They were mourned for at death, according to the degree of relationship. The categories of 'relatives' are also marked off (and internally distinguished) by the use of kinship terms and, for instance, as properly participating in weddings (if along with 'friends'). In this connection it is worth recalling that the 'cognatic' nature of English kinship, or more generally, the non-transitive nature of the concept of 'being related by kinship to' in England, places restrictions on the kind of customs which could set 'relatives' apart from 'non-relatives'. In societies where kin are conceived of as unilinear relatives, the category may be distinguished by such requirements as that they should live in proximity, bear a common name or adopt distinctive observances, such as having a 'totem' animal.[18] The nearest England gets to groups of kin is in the 'nuclear family'. But it should be noted that as children correctly leave home at adulthood, or, previously with daughters, at marriage, the 'nuclear family' cannot be identified with a category of relatives — parents and children. The 'nuclear family' is a married couple and children who have not yet left home.

Many categories are very deep-seated, and customs associated with them often attract strong sentiment. It is not always readily accepted that neither categories nor customs can, strictly speaking, be regarded as 'rational'. There is nothing either rational or irrational about associating e.g. unmarriageability with relatives nor about the particular categories of kinship operating in a particular society. It might well be argued in England that someone *is* similarly related to both parents since everyone receives half their genes (previously blood and characteristics) from each parent. That being similarly related to both parents is a matter of deeply entrenched local categories, and not how things 'really' are is easily demonstrated. This feature of English kinship long pre-dated any detailed knowledge of genetics. 'Kinship' neither need be nor by any means always is based on what could be considered biological facts or factors.

If a variety of social practices, including many associated with kinship, are primarily ways of marking categories, it is easy to understand why study of them should have progressed so slowly by comparison with the study of, for instance, physical phenomena, viz. because the favoured modes of explanation in the society are inapplicable to this range of phenomena.

The analogy between words and customs, to which anthropologists have now turned, is sometimes pressed beyond the view that customs, like words, may primarily delimit categories. It is suggested, as by Leach in *Culture and Communication* (1976), or by Lévi-Strauss in *La Pensée Sauvage* (1962), that customs 'convey messages' or 'communicate information'. But the nature of the 'messages' or 'information' is obscure, and it is possible to consider societies' customs, practices, etc as marking categories, as words also do, without making suppositions of this kind. Why should we suppose that the customs, conventions or laws which appear to mark categories have any particular purpose beyond just that of marking categories?

I have several times drawn attention to the recurrence in political settings of the same arguments to promote widely different and sometimes radical changes in English kinship. Examples are that the measure in question will help bring England into line with Scotland, that it opens to the poor what is open to the rich, that it is not really a change, or, sometimes, that it equalises the sexes. The arguments are evidently persuasive. Often they have a taint of deceit.

If what is proposed cannot in fact be justified by its desirable social consequences nor shown to be unwarranted by bad social consequences, then the most persuasive type of argument for or against it is what can be distinguished as 'category-based' argument. A good argument of this kind for a change is that it does not run contrary to but reinforces socially accepted categories. Thus the 'unity' of husband and wife is an approved assimilation which ought to be preserved. Everyone is also supposed to be equal in the eyes of the law: the law properly makes no distinction between rich and poor, or men and women. Again, England and Scotland are one nation. Accordingly if, for example, altering the divorce law can be shown not to impair the unity of husband and wife, as it might well seem to, but, on the contrary, rather to remove inequities between rich and poor or men and women, and/or a local variation in the law, then it will appear not to weaken but to strengthen approved categories. Category-based argument is often apposite and bona fide. But it is also readily abused.

Notes

1. A. Trollope *John Caldigate* London 1879, Chapters 44, 45, 56, 58 et al.
2. Ibid. Chapter 31.
3. C. Lévi-Strauss *La Pensée Sauvage* Paris 1962, p. 173. English translation [by S. Wolfram] *The Savage Mind* London and Chicago 1966, p. 130.
4. E. Leach *Culture and Communication. The Logic by which Symbols are connected. An Introduction to the use of Structural Analysis in Social Anthropology* Cambridge 1976, p. 4.
5. L. Dumont 'The Dravidian Kinship Terminology as an Expression of Marriage' *Man* vol 53, 1953; L. Dumont *Hierarchie et Alliance* 1954.
6. Leach *Culture and Communication*, p. 5.
7. Ibid. p. 5.
8. D.F. Pocock *Social Anthropology* London and New York 1961, p. 85.
9. Ibid. p. 85.
10. R. Hare *The Language of Morals* Oxford 1952, p. 1.
11. Philosophers like Quine who identify beliefs and their verbal expression very closely also often qualify 'asserting' by 'sincerely'. Cf S. Wolfram 'Facts and Theories: Saying and Believing' in J. Overing (ed.) *Reason and Morality* ASA Monograph 24 London 1985a, p. 79ff; and above Chapter 9.
12. These views are especially associated with W.V. Quine *Word and Object* 1960 and other works, and feature in much philosophical literature as 'the indeterminacy of translation', 'the referential opacity of belief contexts' etc. Cf Wolfram 'Facts and Theories', p. 79ff; and S. Wolfram 'Quine, Statements and "Necessarily True" ' *Philosophical Quarterly* 1975 for elaboration of the claim that Quine's sceptical conclusions rest on unsound arguments.
13. Leach *Culture and Communication*, p. 5.
14. He is in fact slightly shorter, and stood on something for the photographs.
14A. See e.g. R. Davey *A History of Mourning* London [1889] p. 103.
15. 'Cognitive' anthropology is sometimes separated from 'structural' anthropology to distinguish investigation of indigenous systems of thought from model building. This is not invariable and I have included it as a species of 'structural' anthropology.
16. Leach *Culture and Communication*, p. 63.
17. Ibid. pp. 63−4.
18. See above Chapter 9; and S. Wolfram 'Basic differences of thought' in R. Horton and R. Finnegan (eds) *Modes of Thought* London 1973, pp. 373ff.

11 The Future

New techniques in the production of babies led to the setting up in 1982 of a Royal Commission to examine 'social, ethical and legal implications'. In 1984 a report was issued, called the *Report of the Committee of Inquiry into Human Fertilisation and Embryology* and known as the 'Warnock Report'.[1] Swiftly followed by the first 'surrogate' baby in England, 'Baby Cotton',[2] it caused a considerable stir.

Production of a baby requires a sperm and ovum to meet, so that the sperm 'fertilises' the ovum, and also requires 'incubation' of the embryo so created. Incubation still has to take place in a woman's uterus, but sexual intercourse is no longer needed for a sperm to fertilise an ovum. The new techniques include being able to remove ova from women, as well as sperms from men, to store them, to bring them together outside a uterus, and to implant ova, either fertilised or ready to fertilise, in a uterus. The techniques are at slightly different stages of development. Sperms are readily extracted, stored, and inserted. Ova are more difficult to extract, store and implant, but the difficulties are likely to be overcome in the near future.[3]

The Warnock Committee applied itself, among other things, to various new possibilities that arise in parenthood.

Sperms taken from the husband may fertilise the wife's ovum outside the uterus, or *in-vitro*, as well as in it, or *in-vivo*. Where the child is incubated by the wife, the process is readily likened to fertilisation of the wife by the husband by sexual intercourse. The Committee 'found no moral objection to *in-vitro* fertilisation itself'.[4]

However, the possibility of freezing and storing sperms, ova and fertilised embryos leads to several novelties. First, a married couple may have a child, certainly after the death of the husband, and, barring the problem of the incubating uterus, possibly after the death of the wife. Secondly, there can be embryos created from the sperm of a husband and ovum of a wife, or sperms and ova of their creation, which are not in the possession of the husband and wife. The Warnock Committee proposed that there should be legislation so that (it should remain the case that) only children *in utero* at the time of a man's death may succeed to and inherit from him.[5] It considered that it should be permissible for sperms, ova and embryos to be preserved for future use so that someone now fertile who might cease to be so could later have children.[6] Hitherto, relative age of siblings has been determined by order of birth. The Warnock Committee proposed that this should continue, in spite of the new alternative of determining which is the elder by order of conception.[7]

By English law, the husband of a woman bearing a child is presumed to be its natural father unless it is proved that he is not, in which case the child is illegitimate. Custody of an illegitimate child falls to the mother, although the natural father, if known, has some rights and duties. The Warnock Committee recommended that where a man who is not her husband donates a sperm to a woman (as opposed to having sexual intercourse with her), he should have no tie with the female recipient or with the ensuing child.[8] Similarly, if a woman donates an ovum to another woman, she should thereby gain no rights and incur no duties.[9] It further proposed that where 'foreign' sperm or ovum or both have been donated, the woman bearing the child and her husband should, with certain qualifications, be deemed the child's mother and father.[10] The cases closely resemble those of adoptive children, already assimilated to 'blood' children of the adoptive parents.

Even when children could only be produced by what are rapidly coming to be called 'natural' means, i.e. 'sexual intercourse', a woman could have a child by a man other than her husband. If the husband condoned it, there was no problem. Similarly, a man could impregnate a woman by intercourse and persuade her to transfer the child to himself and his wife.[11] The new techniques, apart from allowing impregnation to take place without intercourse, also make it possible for the wife's ovum to be transferred to another woman, so that an embryo created from the wife's ovum and husband's sperm may be incubated by a woman other than the wife. One such child has been born in Australia. If the Warnock Committee's suggestion that 'donors' of ova and sperms to a uterus should have no tie with the child born were put into effect, such a child would *ipso facto* be the child of the incubating woman and her husband. It would never be the child of the woman providing the ovum or the man

supplying the sperm. The Warnock Committee wished addition-
ally to make it criminal to arrange 'surrogacy', i.e. that a woman
incubate a baby, whether from her own ovum or another's, with
the promise to transfer the baby to commissioning parents. It also
held that there should be legislation to render any contract with
an incubating woman to hand over the baby invalid i.e. such that
it would not be upheld in a court of law.[12]

The first birth of a 'surrogate' baby, from the ovum of the
carrying woman and sperm of the commissioning man, in
England in January 1985, received wide publicity, and the
Government introduced legislation to ban commercial surrogacy.[13] Contrary to the spirit of the Warnock Report, and
impending legislation, the commissioning couple received custody
of the child, with the aid of the law courts. However, the claim
that this should not in general be allowed to occur was reiterated.
The grounds are of interest.

According to Mary Warnock 'the centre of the moral objection
to surrogacy' is

> a deep and widely held belief that the relation of a child to the
> woman who carries it and gives birth to it is different from
> the relation of that child to its father . . . The surrogate
> mother is closer to the child, both in space and time, than the
> donor of sperm, who may indeed never know whether a child
> is born or not as a result of his donation. The mother cannot
> but know . . . [14]

We have seen that in the English kinship system someone is
normally related in the same way, and equally closely to, both
parents. The suggested identity of treatment of sperms and ova,
supplying 'genetic' parenthood, conforms to this pattern. And it
would perhaps be surprising if the objection to 'surrogacy' rested
purely on a distinction between the relation of a child 'to the
woman . . . who gives birth to it' and that 'to its father'.[15]

The media concentrated on a different aspect of Baby Cotton,
viz. the payment of money to the incubating woman. Warnock
also continues:

> The moral repugnance stems from the thought of a woman
> deliberately becoming pregnant for money . . . and from the
> thought of other people . . . offering her money to do this, for

their own ends . . . [People] feel very differently if what they
think of is surrogacy undertaken between sisters or friends . . .
what is really felt to be wrong is surrogacy for money . . . as
. . . a service to be paid for like any other.[16]

The Surrogacy Arrangements Act of 1985 made the arranging of
surrogacy for money an offence.

English law has recognised two possibilities as to who is the
father of the child. Normally the father is the husband of a
woman giving birth to a child. However, if she has no husband or
it is proved that the child could not have been produced from the
sperm of her husband, the 'father' of the child is distinct from a
woman's husband. According to a nineteenth-century legal
authority in cases where rapid re-marriage by a widow produces
the possibility that either the first or the second husband could be
the 'father' of the child, it could choose between them when
adult.[17]

Until one woman could supply the ovum from which a child is
conceived and another incubate and give birth to the child, there
was only one possible 'real' mother, namely, the woman giving
birth to it, who also supplies the ovum. There are now two
possibilities, viz. the 'genetic' mother and the 'incubating'
mother. As the law stands, the woman giving birth is the mother
but the Warnock Committee considered that, although the
woman giving birth should *ipso facto* be the mother, laws should
be changed so that a genetic mother could adopt the child.[18] The
objection to 'surrogacy' does not seem to lie in the belief that the
'genetic' mother should have no rights to a child unless she has
also incubated it. The rights, like those of a 'genetic' father who
is not the husband of the woman giving birth to a child, would be
merely secondary. But it is not the case that the woman giving
birth is thought of as unequivocally 'the mother' in the case
where the ovum was not hers. As the Warnock Report put it:
'There are inevitably going to be instances where the stark issue
arises of who is the mother.'[19]

The nearest parallel to the woman incubating a child from an
ovum not her own, is a man whose wife gives birth to a baby
from the sperm of a different man. Clearly the parallel is not
exact. However to find the basis of the 'moral objection' to
surrogacy we need to turn away from kinship categories to those
which are associated with customs relating to money.

When the Press captions a baby 'Born to be Sold' in England, the transaction certainly appears wrong. Human beings are not commercial goods. They belong to a different category. Animals may be bought and sold, but not human beings. Man is marked off from any other sort of thing by a variety of customs, among them, in current English thinking, that they may not be bought and sold. Babies are certainly human beings. Ova, sperms and embryos are more doubtful, and the Warnock Committee was very much less sure that these should not be trafficked for money.[20]

The Agency arranging the contract for 'Baby Cotton' put the transaction in a different category by speaking of the agreed money payment (£6,500) to the incubating woman as 'compensation' to her, not as payment for a baby. The services of human beings, unlike human beings themselves, are frequently paid for. However, some acts are thought of as not properly performed for money. Among these is sexual intercourse. A 'woman deliberately becoming pregnant for money' seems to come into this category. So does 'renting out' her uterus.

As the debate developed, so did familiar arguments. The Warnock Report invariably refers to 'donors' of sperms, ova and embryos. A 'donor' is normally giving away a gift, and not receiving money payment. The Warnock Committee represented supplies of ova as a by-product from 'donors who are giving an egg while undergoing some other treatment'. There are 'relatively minor surgical risks',[21] and no money appears to pass. It is a kind of anonymous gift to assist research or other women who are infertile. Sperms, which are supplied by masturbating men, for research or use in artificial insemination are paid for, although the sum is small. By 1984–5, the *Oxford University Gazette* was carrying the frequent advertisment:

Help Wanted Semen donors urgently required for important biomedical research and treatment programme . . . Payment £5 per donation.[22]

Why then should women not be paid a suitable sum for the more onerous service of 'incubating' a child for a woman who cannot do so? Yet the Law Society demanded that it should become a criminal offence for a woman to offer, for reward of any kind, to bear a child for another, for a man or woman to offer such a reward, and for a person to act as an agent or intermediary in such a transaction.[23]

The subject has been debated under the aegis of 'treatment' or 'therapy' for the infertile, although it does not 'cure' them but rather consists of someone else supplying what they cannot. Thus it has been suggested that if donating sperms and ova for those who are 'infertile', in the sense of being unable to produce these, is an acceptable form of therapy, the 'donating' of a uterus should be treated in the same fashion. Why should women who are infertile through inability to incubate a baby not be allowed appropriate 'treatment', just as infertile men are?

The sticking point is most commonly the money. Among other things, the expense being substantial, something would be available to the rich which is not available to the poor. (Or should the National Health Service, and taxpayers, foot the bill?) In reply it is generally argued that to make it a crime for a commercial agency to arrange surrogacy, and/or a crime to solicit a woman to act as a surrogate and/or for a woman to take this role, is to drive it underground and thus not subject to satisfactory control. A minority of the Warnock Committee recommended that surrogacy should be permitted as a 'treatment for childlessness' by a system of a central authority with power to license non-profit-making agencies, like those arranging adoption.[24]

The issue could be of short duration if, for example, means were found of replacing the organs in a woman preventing successful incubation with more satisfactory ones, by transplantation or otherwise, or alternatively of incubating an embryo artificially, that is, without the use of a live woman. In the meantime, the most likely train of events appears to be a good deal of category-based argument. Two points are especially worth noting.

One is that in the Warnock Report and in the Law Society's current proposals, the new situations arising from developments of techniques in the production of babies are brought under existing kinship categories wherever possible. So, for instance, the Warnock Report's suggestion that the number of children who may be 'fathered' by donations from a single donor should be limited to ten,[25] and similarly for women donors of ova,[26] inter alia 'because of the remote possibility of incest'.[27] The Law Society went further. According to *The Times* in February 1985, it was calling:

> for the criminal law to be extended to make it an offence knowingly and wilfully to fertilise by whatever means the egg of a woman in a legally prohibited relationship with the donor.[28]

An even clearer example of assimilating new with old is supplied by the Warnock Committee's proposal that a child should not succeed to nor inherit from its genetic father unless already *in utero* at the time of the father's death.[29] There are societies in which a marriage is not terminated by the death of a spouse. A man may have a right, even a duty, to take over his dead brother's wife in order that children may be born who rank as the legitimate issue of the dead man. Or a woman may bear children for her dead sister or other female relative, the children being for all purposes the dead woman's. In England a marriage has always come to an end with the death of husband or wife. Marriage is (only) until 'death us do part'. The Warnock Committee did not want this situation altered, supplying as its reason that

> It is obviously essential that there should be some finality for those adminstering estates of deceased persons since, in such cases posthumous fertilisation could cause real problems of inheritance and succession. Account would have to be taken of issue who might be born years after the death.[30]

In England inherited ranks are transmitted by kinship rules but property, apart from that which is entailed, may be left 'by will', that is, as the dead person directed before his death. Legatees are not normally confined to those already living. They may include, for instance, issue of the testator's issue, not yet born or conceived. It was not clear whether the Warnock Committee wished to prevent willing of property to issue of the testator's not *in utero* at the time of the testator's death. The point was not discussed. But it seems improbable that such a restriction on disposition of property after death would seem just.

The technical possibility of choosing the sex of a baby raised another problem. It might initially be used 'solely for the purpose of avoiding hereditary sex-linked disorders', and there seemed no objection to offering a choice to 'couples who have good medical reasons for choosing the sex of their child'.[31] But, the Committee continued,

> if an efficient and easy method of ensuring the conception of a child of a particular sex became available, it is likely that some couples would wish to make use of it for purely social reasons.[32]

It made no recommendations, other than that 'do-it-yourself' sex selection kits should be controlled to ensure safety etc. However it expressed unease because of the inequality of women which might result:

> It is often suggested that a majority of couples would choose that their first child was male, and if this happened, it could have important social implications, since there is considerable evidence that the firstborn sibling may enjoy certain advantages over younger siblings. It would have particular implications for the role of women in society, although some would argue that these effects would today be less damaging than they might have been a hundred years ago.[33]

An obvious explanation of the fact that kinship structures appear to alter relatively little over time is that change can often be accommodated in existing categories. These categories are generally taken for granted, as if they were facts of nature. Hence, the choices made by a society faced with new alternatives are most commonly so far as possible within their confines.

New possibilities which can be fitted directly into existing categories thus present few problems. The difficulties begin when this is not so, if, for instance, effecting an apparently appropriate assimilation of something to one category would require alteration in another. Thus 'treating an infertile woman' by 'baby-buying' or 'uterus-renting' contravenes the English treatment of human beings and of sexual style services as not properly passing for money. On the other hand, if ova or embryos may only be incubated by others 'for love', this confines the 'treatment' to the random set of those fortunate enough to have willing relatives or friends, and this offends against 'justice'.

Issues of this kind are often called 'moral' issues, and the difficulty of resolving them is attributed to this status. At one time, moral philosophers believed 'moral issues' to be in general irresolvable. Hare's *The Language of Morals* (1952) represented a point of view common at the period whereby there is no general test of moral right and wrong. This was succeeded by a revival of the radically opposed view, known loosely as 'utilitarianism', that *moral* questions, and their solutions, must rest on considerations of harm and happiness, and that many apparently irresolvable issues are in fact subject to rational solutions if the consequences in terms of harm and happiness are properly set out.[34]

The Warnock Report highlights the difficulties of assimilating category-based considerations to 'moral' considerations, at least as these are currently regarded by (English) professional philosophers.[35] The discomfort engendered is conspicuous in the brief Foreword:

> In common usage, the word 'ethical' is not absolutely unambiguous . . . feelings . . . run very high . . . [and] are . . . very diverse; and moral indignation, or acute uneasiness, may often take the place of argument. But that moral conclusions cannot be separated from moral feelings does not entail that there is no such thing as moral reasoning . . . We have attempted . . . to *argue* . . . though we have necessarily been mindful of the truth that matters of ultimate value are not susceptible of proof.[36]

'A strict utilitarian', the passage continues, 'would suppose that . . . it would be possible to calculate benefits and their costs'. But even if it were, this 'could not provide a final or verifiable answer to the question whether it is *right* . . .' What the Committee discovered was that 'What is common is that people generally want *some principle or other* to govern the development and use of the new techniques':

> There must be *some* barriers . . . *some* limits fixed . . . The very existence of morality depends on it. A society which had no inhibiting limits, especially in the areas with which we have been concerned, questions of birth and death, of the setting up of families, and the valuing of human life, would be a society without moral scruples. *And this nobody wants.*[37]

The Committee added that 'the law itself . . . is the embodiment of a common moral position', and that in recommending legislation it was trying to suggest the 'minimum requirement for a tolerable society'. It concluded the introduction to its report and proposals with:

> Barriers, it is generally agreed, must be set up; but there will not be universal agreement about where these barriers should be placed. The question must ultimately be what kind of society can we praise and admire? In what sort of society can we live with our conscience clear?[38]

It would be excessive to claim that no set of categories, rules or customs produces more happiness or more harm than another. We have only to invoke Nazi society to see how evil a society can be. But in many cases the happiness and harm offered by alternatives appear evenly or uncertainly balanced. If an issue occurs at this level, which is important enough to be classed as 'moral', the chances are that there is a category-based problem. The history of English kinship suggests that, in the realm of kinship, 'barriers' that appear 'morally' right often lack utilitarian justification, and are rather part of a system of categories and associated rules and customs. Such systems differ from society to society, and, as Lévi-Strauss once pointed out, each of:

> tens of thousands of societies . . . has claimed that it contains the essence of all the meaning and dignity of which human society is capable and . . . its claim has in its own eyes rested on a moral certainty comparable to that which we can invoke in our own case.[39]

This is not intended to denigrate the English system of kinship, past or present. But it would clearly be foolish to suppose that the catgories and beliefs on which it is built enjoy a monopoly of either rationality or 'morality'.

Notes

1. *Report of the Committee of Inquiry into Human Fertilisation and Embryology* HMSO, Cmd 9314, London 1984 (Chairman M. Warnock), referred to as the 'Warnock Report'.

2. An American agency set up a contract between a married woman and a commissioning married couple. She agreed to bear a child by artificial insemination for a sum of money (£6,500), the child to go to the 'natural' father and his wife at birth. The baby, a girl, born in January 1985 was nicknamed 'Baby Cotton'.

3. Warnock Report 1984, p. 17ff, Chapter 4 et seq. Artificial insemination of a woman from the sperms of her husband or a 'donor' has been available under the Health Service since 1968 (ibid. p. 19, 4.7). By the time of the Warnock Report there had been 'some hundreds of births throughout the world' from an ovum removed from a woman to be fertilised *in-vitro* i.e. outside the uterus (ibid. 5.5 et seq, p. 31ff). While semen is readily stored, 'human eggs cannot be successfully used after freezing and thawing' (ibid. p. 35, 6.3); but 'freezing, storing and thawing eggs is likely to become feasible within a few years' (ibid. p. 36, 6.3). Embryos created by artificial insemination can also be removed for re-implanting (ibid. 7.1, p. 39) but the Warnock Committee considered that this carried too great a risk to the embryo-donor for safe use at the present time (ibid. 7.5, p. 40).

4. M. Warnock 'The surrogacy scandal' *The Listener* 24 January 1985, p. 3.

5. Warnock Report 1984, p. 55, 10.9; p. 57, 10.15 (Rec 61 and 64). Recommendations made in the course of the report are also gathered together and listed by number pp. 80—6. I cite these as 'Rec' with number.

6. Ibid. p. 54ff, 10.6 et seq.

7. Ibid. p. 57, 10.14 (Rec 63).

8. Ibid. p. 25, 4.22 (Rec 52).

9. Ibid. pp. 37—8, 6.8; p. 40, 7.6 (Rec 55).

10. Ibid. p. 26, 4.25; pp. 37—8, 6.8; p. 40, 7.6 (Recs 51, 54, 56).

11. A recent case of the latter sort received publicity in connection with Baby Cotton. The wife was shown on television in 1984 and 1985 as very grateful to 'Mary' who had carried her husband's child for her.

12. Warnock Report 1984, p. 47, 8.18—8.19 (Recs 57—9).

13. See e.g. *The Times* 5 February 5 1985, p. 1 cols f—g. A controversial private Bill by Enoch Powell, The Unborn Children (Protection) Bill, curtailing research on embryos almost to nil, was introduced early in 1985, before a Government Bill had been prepared, and passed a second reading in the House of Commons. On 25 April 1985 BBC 'Panorama' and ITV 'World in Action' carried programmes on this. The House of Commons debated the second reading of the Government's Surrogacy Arrangements Bill, limited to outlawing commercial surrogacy on 15 April 1985. (*Hansard* 1984—5 6th series vol 77 House of Commons 15 April cols 23—56, *The Times* 16 April 1985, p. 4 cols a—d.) The Bill became law in July 1985: Eliz II: Surrogacy Arrangments Act 1985 c 49. S. Wolfram 'Surrogacy in the U.K.' paper presented to the Society for Applied Anthropology at Reno USA 1986 [in press] gives further details.

14. Warnock 1985 'The surrogacy scandal', p. 3.

15. Ibid.

16. Ibid. p. 3.

17. J.T. Hammick *The Marriage Law of England* second revised edition 1887, p. 29 note (d).

18. Warnock Report 1984, p. 47, 8.20.

19. Ibid. p. 37, 6.8.

20. It recommended that 'there should be a gradual move towards a system where semen donors should be given only their expenses' (ibid. p. 28, 4.27) but considered purchase or sale of sperms, ova or embryos should not be wholly prohibited but rather be allowed to take place under license only (ibid. p. 19, 13.3).

21. Ibid. p. 36, 6.6.

22. Quoted from *Oxford University Gazette* 31 January 1985, p. 407.

23. *The Times* 4 February 1985, p. 3 col b–c.

24. Warnock Report 1984, W. Greengross and D. Davies 'Expression of Dissent: A. Surrogacy', pp. 87–9.

25. Ibid. pp. 26–7, 4.26 (Rec 23).

26. Ibid. p. 36, 6.6 (Rec 27).

27. Ibid. p. 26, 4.26.

28. *The Times* 4 February 1985, p. 3 cols b–c.

29. Warnock Report 1984, p. 55, 10.9 (Recs 61 and 64).

30. Ibid. p. 55, 10.9.

31. Ibid. p. 51, 9.11.

32. Ibid.

33. Ibid. p. 51, 9.11.

34. Cf S. Wolfram 'Anthropology and Morality' *Journal of the Anthropological Society of Oxford* (JASO) vol XIII no 3 1982, pp. 262–74 for fuller discussion.

35. The chairman, Dame Mary, now Baroness, Warnock, is a philosopher by profession.

36. Warnock Report 1984, Foreword, pp. 1–2, paras 1–4.

37. Ibid. Foreword, p. 2, para 5.

38. Ibid. Foreword, p. 3, para 8.

39. C. Lévi-Strauss *La Pensée Sauvage* Paris 1962 Chapter 9, p. 329. English translation [by S. Wolfram] *The Savage Mind* 1966, p. 249.

Bibliography

Books and Articles

O. Aberle, U. Bronfenbronner, E. Hess, O. Miller, D. Schneider and I. Sopuhler 'The Incest Taboo and the mating patterns of animals' *American Anthropologist* 1963

C.G. Addison *Wrongs and their Remedies* (third and subsequent editions *Addison on the Law of Torts*) first edition 1860

J.L. Adolphus and T.F. Ellis *Queen's Bench Reports* (new series) London 18 vols 1843–56

J. Alleyne *The Legal Degrees of Marriage Stated and Considered, in a Series of Letters to a Friend* 1774

R.T. Anderson *Changing Kinship in Europe* Kroeber Anthropological Society no 28, Berkeley, California 1963

S. Anderson 'Legislative Divorce — Law for the Aristocracy?' in G. Rubin and D. Sugarman (eds) *Law, Society and Economy. Essays in Legal History* 1984

Anonymous *Mr Emmerton's Marriage with Mrs. Bridget Hyde Considered* 1682

Anonymous [H.R. Reynolds] (A Barrister of the Middle Temple) *Considerations on the State of the Law regarding Marriage with a Deceased Wife's Sister* 1840

Anonymous *An Englishwoman's Letter to the Right Honourable Sir Robert Harry Inglis, bart. M.P. on the proposed Alteration of the Marriage Law* 1849

Anonymous [H.F. Bacon] Συγγένεια *A dispassionate Appeal to the Judgment of the Church of England on a Proposed Alteration of the Law of marriage* 1849

Anonymous *An Earnest Address on the proposed Alteration in the Law of Marriage* [c. 1850]

Anonymous (A Member of the University of Oxford) *Marriage with a Deceased Wife's Sister in a Social Point of View Inexpedient and Unnatural* 1858

Anonymous (B.A.W.) *The Woman's Question and the Man's Answer; or, Reflections on the Social Consequences of Legalizing Marriage with a Deceased Wife's Sister* 1859

Anonymous *Cassell's Handbook of Etiquette* London 1860

Anonymous (A Philosophical Inquirer) *The present state of the Marriage Law proved unscriptural and the proposed illogical* 1860

Anonymous *The Reply to Mr Commissioner Kerr's 'Question in Common Law'* 1864

Anonymous (A Graduate in Classical and Mathematical Honours, Cambridge, of BD Standing) *The Present State and the Proposed State of the Marriage Law, Theologically, Morally, Socially and Legally Considered* 1864a

Anonymous (An Anxious Observer) *Marriage with a Deceased Wife's Sister Forbidden by the Word of God* 1869

Anonymous (A Solicitor) *Observations on the Deceased Wife's Sister Question* 1872

Anonymous [Eliza Cheadle] *Manners of Good Society, Being a Book of Etiquette* London 1872

Anonymous (One who does not want to) *Should Englishmen be Permitted to Marry their Deceased Wives' Sisters?* 1883

Anonymous *Marriage with a Deceased Wife's sister forbidden to Christians* 1886
Anonymous (A Member of the Aristocracy) *Manners and Rules of Good Society*
　15th edition 1888, 26th edition 1902
Anthropological Institute *Notes and Queries on Anthropology* second edition,
　London 1892
L.H. Armstrong *Good Form. A Book of Everyday Etiquette* London 1889, p. 188
G.B.L. Arner *Consanguineous Marriage in the American Population* Columbia
　1908
Jane Austen *Sense and Sensibility* 1811
—— *Pride and Prejudice* 1813
—— *Mansfield Park* 1814
—— *Emma* 1816
A.J. Ayer *Language, Truth and Logic* London 1936
V. Bailey and S. Blackburn 'The Punishment of Incest Act 1908. A case study in
　law creation' [1979] *Criminal Law Review* 708
J. Bentham *Principles of the Civil Code*, first published in French as *Principes du
　Code Civil* 1802; first English translation in J. Bowring *The Works of Jeremey
　Bentham* Edinburgh 1843. I quote from a translation by J.M. Atkinson
　Bentham's Theory of Legislation 1914
R. Bickersteth etc. *Marriage with a Deceased Wife's Sister* 1851
T. Binney *The Men of Glasgow and the Women of Scotland* [n.d. probably *c.*
　1878]
British Association for the Advancement of Science *Notes and Queries on
　Anthropology* third edition London 1899
P.M. Bromley *Family Law* sixth edition 1981
Charlotte Brontë *Jane Eyre* 1847
H. Brougham *Speeches of Henry, Lord Brougham upon Questions relating to
　Public rights, Duties, and Interests; with Historical Introduction and a Critical
　Dissertation upon the eloquence of the Ancients* Edinburgh 1838 (4 vols)
A.R. Burton *The Anatomy of Melancholy what is it etc* Oxford 1621, sixth
　enlarged edition London 1652, reprinted Everyman 1936
L.H.D. Buxton (ed.) *Custom is King. Essays presented to R.R. Marrett* London
　1936
V.F. Calverton and S.D. Schmalhausen *The New Generation* London 1930
Cassell's Domestic Dictionary. An Encyclopedia for the Household London
　[1877—9]
D. Cecil *Melbourne* 1965 edition
F. Clifford *A History of Private Bill Legislation* London 1885
G. Craik *The Romance of the Peerage* London 1948
S.M. Cretney *Principles of Family Law* third edition 1979
W.C. Curteis *Reports of Cases Argued and Determined in the Ecclesiastical Courts
　at Doctor's Commons* London 3 vols (1840—4)
R. Davey *A History of Mourning* London [1889]
F.A. Dawson *May a Man marry his Deceased Wife's Sister?* 1859
D. Defoe *The Fortunes and Misfortunes of the famous Moll Flanders &c* 1722,
　Rinehart edition 1949 (printed from the third edition)
J.F. Denham *Marriage with a Deceased Wife's Sister not Forbidden by the law of
　Nature, not Dissuaded by Expediency, not Prohibited by the Scriptures* 1847
A.V. Dicey *Lectures on the Relation between Law and Public Opinion in England
　during the nineteenth century* second edition London 1914, lecture X, p. 347,
　cited from reprint of 1930 (first edition 1905)
Charles Dickens *David Copperfield* 1848—9
Dictionary of National Biography 'Caroline Norton'
T. Dobzhansky *Evolution, Genetics and Man* New York 1955

G.C.M. Douglas *The law of the Bible as to Prohibited Degrees of Marriage* 1858

S. Dugard *The marriages of Cousins Germans, vindicated from Censures of Unlawfulness and Inexpediency* 1673

H.H. Duke *The Question of Incest relatively to the Marriage of Sisters in Succession* 1882

L. Dumont 'The Dravidian Kinship Terminology as an Expression of Marriage' *Man* vol 53, 1953
—— *Hierarchie et Alliance* 1954
—— 'Hierarchy and Marriage Alliance in South Indian Kinship' Occasional papers *Journal of the Royal Anthropological Institute* 1957
—— *Une Sous-Caste de l'Inde du Sud. Organisation Sociale et Religion des Pramalai Kallar* Paris 1957

E. Durkheim 'La Prohibition de l'inceste et ses origines *L'Année Sociologique* i, Paris 1897 (English translations by: E. Sagarin *Incest: The Nature and Origin of the Incest Taboo* 1963; A. Ellis *The origin and development of the Incest Taboo* 1964)
—— and M. Mauss *De quelques formes primitives de classification* Paris 1902 (*Année Sociologique* 1901–2), translated into English by R. Needham as *Primitive Classification* London 1963

M. Edgworth *Helen. A Tale* London 1834

George Eliot *Adam Bede* 1859
—— *A Mill on the Floss* 1860
—— *Middlemarch* 1871–2

Encyclopedia Britannica 1929 vol 7: 'Duel'
—— 1929 vol 22: 'Totemism' by W.E.A. (= W.E. Armstrong)
—— 1967 vol 7: 'Divorce'

R.C.K. Ensor *England 1870–1914* Oxford 1936

E.E. Evans-Pritchard *Witchcraft, Oracles and magic among the Azande* Oxford 1937
—— 'Nuer rules of exogamy and incest' in M. Fortes (ed.) *Social Structure* 1949
—— *Kinship and Marriage among the Nuer* 1951
—— *Social Anthropology* London 1951

Evershed: Foreword to Graveson and Crane (eds) *A Century of Family Law* 1957

R. Firth *We the Tikopia. A Sociological Study of Kinship in Primitive Polynesia* London 1936

E.M. Forster *Mariannne Thornton* 1956

M. Fortes 'Kinship, Incest and Exogamy of the Northern Territories of the Gold Coast' in L.H.D. Buxton (ed.) *Custom is King. Essays presented to R.R. Marrett* London 1936
—— *Marriage Law among the Tallensi* 1937
—— (ed.) *Social Structure* 1949

R.F. Fortune 'Incest' *Encyclopedia of the Social Sciences* New York 1932 vol 7

T.C. Foster *A Review of the Law relating to Marriages within the Prohibited Degrees of Affinity and the Canons and Social Considerations by which the law is supposed to be justified* 1847

R. Fox *Kinship and Marriage. An anthropological perspective* London 1967

J.G. Frazer in The Anthropological Institute *Notes and Queries on Anthropology* second edition, London 1892 and British Association for the Advancement of Science *Notes and Queries on Anthropology* third edition, London 1899
—— *Totemism and Exogamy. A Treatise on Certain Early Forms of Superstition and Society* London 1910, 4 vols

S. Freud *An Autobiographical Study* London 1935 (translated by J. Strachey)
—— in *Imago* i and ii, Vienna 1912–13, published in Vienna 1913 as *Totem und Tabu*; English translation *Totem and Taboo: Some Points of Agreement*

between the Mental Lives of Savages and Neurotics by J. Strachey London 1950 (first translated by A.A. Brill New York 1918)

J. Fry *The Case of Marriages between Near Kindred, Particularly Considered, with respect to the Doctrine of Scripture, the law of Nature, and the laws of England* London 1756 (second enlarged edition 1773)

W. George *Gregor Mendel and Heredity* London 1975

A. Giraud-Teulon *Les Origines de la Famille. Questions sur les antecedents des societies patriarcales* Geneva and Paris 1874

J. Goody *The Development of the Family and Marriage in Europe* CUP 1983

G. Gorer *Death, Grief and Mourning in Contemporary Britain* London 1965

Gorrell in *Royal Commission on Divorce and Matrimonial Causes* 1912–13 vol 3

R.H. Graveson and F.R. Crane (eds) *A Century of Family Law* London 1957

W. Greengross and D. Davies 'Expression of Dissent: A. Surrogacy', Warnock Report 1984, pp. 87–9.

H. Grotius *De Jure Belli ac Pacis* 1646

Guthrie in *The Divorce Commission. The Majority and Minority Reports Summarised* London 1912

P. Hale *Marriage with a Deceased Wife's Sister repugnant to Christian feeling and contrary to Christian practice*

J.E. Hall Williams 'Incest in English Law' Appendix to H. Maish *Incest* 1973

J.T. Hammick *The Marriage Law of England* second revision and enlarged edition 1887

H. Hammond *A Letter of Resolution to Six Quaeries of Present Use in the Church of England* 1653

R. Hare *The Language of Morals* Oxford 1952

A.P. Herbert *Holy Deadlock* 1934

L.T. Hobhouse *Morals in Evolution. A Study of Comparative Ethics* London 1906, 2 vols

F. Hockin *Marriage with a Deceased Wife's Sister Forbidden by the Law of God* [1881]

B.M. Hoggett and D.S. Pearl *The Family, Law and Society*, London 1983

Vyvyan Holland *Son of Oscar Wilde* 1954, Penguin 1957

L. Holcombe *Wives and Property. Reform of the Married Women's Property Law in Nineteenth-Century England* Toronto and Oxford 1983

W.S. Holdsworth *A History of English Law* 1922

M. Hollis 'The Social Destruction of Reality' in M. Hollis and S. Lukes (eds) *Rationality and Relativism* Oxford 1982

R.A. Houlbrooke *The English Family 1450–1700* London 1984

G. Howard *A History of Matrimonial Institutions* Chicago 1904

D. Hume *An Enquiry Concerning the Principles of Morals* 1751

F. Hutcheson *A System of Moral Philosophy* 1755

A.H. Huth *The Marriage of Near Kin considered with respect to the laws of nations, the results of experience, and the teachings of biology* London 1875, second revised and enlarged edition 1887

—— *Index to Books & Papers on the Marriage of Near Kin* London 1879, pp. 25–46; 1887 Bibliography published separately

R.C. Jenkins *The Repeal of the prohibitions of marriage with a deceased wife's sister advocated, Doctrinally; Historically; Socially* 1883

Justinian *Institutes* AD 533, Book III, Title VI 'De gradibus cognationis' in *Imperatoris Iustiani Institutionem* J.B. Moyle (ed.), Oxford 1883, fifth edition 1912, translated by J.B. Moyle as 'Of the Degrees of Cognation' in *The Institutes of Justinian* Oxford 1883, fifth edition 1913

A.L. Kroeber 'Kinship and History' *American Anthropologist* vol 38 1936

A. Lang *Social Origins* London 1903

P. Laslett (ed.) *Household & Family in Past Time* CUP 1972
E.R. Leach 'The structural implications of matrilateral cross-cousin marriage' *Journal of the Royal Anthropological Institute* vol 81 London 1951, revised in E.R. Leach *Rethinking Anthropology* first edition 1961, revised paperback edition 1966 Chapter 3
—— 'Rethinking Anthropology' in E.R. Leach *Rethinking Anthropology* London 1961, revised edition London 1966
—— *Culture and Communication. The Logic by which Symbols are connected. An Introduction to the use of Structural Analysis in Social Anthropology* Cambridge 1976
J. Le Mesurier *A few Words on the Real Bearings of the Proposed Change in the Marriage Law from a Clergyman to his Parishioners* 1883
C. Lévi-Strauss *Les Structures élémentaires de la Parenté* Paris 1949, revised and translated into English by J.H. Bell, J.R. von Sturmer and R. Needham as *The Elementary Structures of Kinship* London 1969
—— *Anthropologie Structurale* Paris 1958; English translation by C. Jacobson and B.G. Schoepf *Structural Anthropology* New York 1963, London 1968
—— *La Pensée Sauvage* Paris 1962; English translation [by S. Wolfram] *The Savage Mind* London and Chicago 1966
—— *Le Totémisme Aujourd'hui* Paris 1962, translated into English by R. Needham as *Totemism* Boston 1963, London 1964
J. Locke *An Essay Concerning Human Understanding* 1690, revised editions 1694, 1695, 1700 and fifth edition published posthumously 1706; currently preferred edition P.H. Nidditch (ed.) Oxford 1975, based on the fourth edition
R.H. Lowie 'Marriage' *Encyclopedia of the Social Sciences* New York 1933, vol 10
J. Lubbock *The Origin of Civilisation and the Primitive Condition of Man. Mental and Social Condition of Savages* London 1870; further editions 1870, 1875, 1882, 1889, 1902, 1912
—— 'On the development of relationships' *Journal of the Royal Anthropological Institute* i, London 1870
J. Lush *Animal Breeding Plans* Iowa 1943
Mrs Massey Lyon *Etiquette. A Guide to Public and Social Life* London 1927
J. Macrae *The Scriptural Law of Marriage with reference to the Prohibited Degrees* 1861
M. Maimonides *c.* 1183 *The Reasons of the Laws of Moses from the 'More Nevochim' of Maimonides* translated by J. Townley, London 1827
L. Mair *Marriage* London 1971
H. Maish *Incest* 1973
B. Malinowski 'Baloma; the Spirits of the Dead in the Trobriand Islands' *Journal of the Royal Anthropological Institute* London 1916; reprinted in B. Malinowski *Magic, Science and Religion and other Essays* Illinois 1948
—— *Sex and Repression in Savage Society* 1927
—— 'Kinship' *Encyclopedia Britannica* 1929 vol 13
—— *The Sexual Life of Savages in North-Western Melanesia. An ethnographic account of Courtship, Marriage, and Family Life among the Natives of the Trobriand Islands, British New Guinea* London 1929
—— 'Parenthood — the Basis of Social Structure' in V.F. Calverton and S.D. Schmalhausen *The New Generation* London 1930
—— 'A sociological analysis of the rationale of the Prohibited Degrees of Marriage' Appendix 3 in Church of England Commission *Kindred and Affinity* (1940)
P. Maranda *French Kinship: Structure and History* The Hague & Paris 1974
Marriage Law Defence Association (A Sister and a Widow) no 5
Marriage Law Defence Association no 8 *Remarks on Dr.McCaul's Plea from Lev.*

xviii, 18, for Marrying a Deceased Wife's Sister
Marriage Law Defence Union no 4
Marriage Law Defence Union no 8
Marriage Law Defence Union no 12
Marriage Law Defence Union no 15
Marriage Law Defence Union no 26
Marriage Law Defence Union no 30
Marriage Law Defence Union no 34
Marriage Law Defence Union no.39
Marriage Law Defence Union no 43
Marriage Law Defence Union nos 22 and 45
Marriage Law Defence Union no 53
M. Mauss 'Essai sur le don. Forme et raison de l'échange dans les societes archaiques' *L'Année Sociologique* second series vol 1, 1923–4. Reprinted in M. Mauss *Sociologie et Anthropologies* Paris 1950; translated into English by I. Cunnison as *The Gift. Forms and Functions of Exchange in Archaic Societies* London 1954
A. McCaul *The Ancient Interpretation of Leviticus xviii, 18, as received in the Church for more than 1500 years, a sufficient apology for holding that, according to the Word of God, marriage with a deceased wife's sister is lawful* 1859
J.F. McLennan *Primitive Marriage. An Inquiry into the Origin of the Form of Capture in Marriage Ceremonies* Edinburgh 1865
—— *Studies in Ancient History, Comprising a Reprint of Primitive Marriage* London 1876
—— *Studies in Ancient History* (published posthumously) London 1886
J.F. MacQueen *A Practical Treatise on the Appellate Jurisdiction of the House of Lords and Privy Council together with the Practice on Parliamentary Divorce* London 1842
G. Mendel *Experiments in Plant Hybridization* 1865–6
M. Mensor *The Question Solved: or, Inquiry into the law of Marriage with a Deceased Wife's Sister* [c. 1885]
J.S. Mill *The Subjection of Women* 1869
Montesquieu *De l'esprit des loix ou de rapport que les loix doivent avec la constitution de chaque gouvernement, les moeurs, le climat, la religion, le commerce & c* Geneva 1748
L.H. Morgan 'A Conjectural Solution of the Origin of the Classificatory System of Relationship' *Proceedings of the American Academy of Arts and Sciences* vii Boston 1868
—— *Ancient Society or Researches in the Lines of Human Progress from Savagery, through Barbarism to Civilisation* New York 1877
H.N. Mozley 'The Property disabilities of a married woman and other legal effects of Marriage' in J.E. Butler (ed.) *Women's Work and Women's Culture* London 1869, pp. 186–246
G.P. Murdock *Social Structure* New York 1949
H.N. Oxenham *The Deceased Wife's Sister Bill considered in its Social and Religious Aspects* 1885
T. Parsons 'The Incest Taboo in relation to Social Structure and the Specialisation of the Child' *British Journal of Sociology* London 1954 v
J.F. Phelps *The Divine Authority of the 'Table of Prohibited Degrees'* 1883
Philadelphus [F. Pott] *Marriage with a Deceased Wife's Sister* 1885
J. Phillimore *Reports of Cases Argued and Determined in the Ecclesiastical Courts at Doctor's Commons; & in the High Court of Delegates* London 3 vols 1818–27

Philo 1st century AD Περί των ἐν μερει διαταγμάτων *The Special laws*
Plutarch *c.* 96 AD δίτια 'Ρωμαϊχα (*The Roman Questions*)
D.F. Pocock *Social Anthropology* London and New York 1961
W.V. Quine *Word and Object* MIT 1960
A.R. Radcliffe-Brown *The Development of Social Anthropology*, lecture given in
the University of Chicago 1936 (typescript presented by Radcliffe-Brown to
Institute of Social Anthropology, Oxford)
—— in A.R. Radcliffe-Brown and D. Forde (eds) *African Systems of Kinship
and Marriage* London 1950
S. Richardson *Pamela, or Virtue Rewarded* 1740
C. Rover *Women's Suffrage and Party Politics in Britain 1866–1914* Toronto and
London 1967
St. Augustine *De Civitate Dei contra Paganos* (*The City of God*); quotation is
from J. Healey's translation of 1620
W. Salkeld *Reports of Cases Adjudged in the Court of the King's Bench* London 3
vols 1795
J.J. Scarisbrick *Henry VIII* 1968, Penguin edition 1971
D.M. Schneider 'Kinship, Community, and Locality in American Culture' in J.A.
Lichtman and J. Challoner (eds) *Kinship and Community* Washington DC
1979
B.Z. Seligman 'Bilateral Descent and the Formation of Marriage Classes' *Journal
of the Royal Anthropological Institute* vol 57, 1927
—— 'Asymmetry in Descent with Special Reference to Pentecost' *Journal of the
Royal Anthropological Institute* vol 58, 1928
—— 'Incest and Descent: their Influence on Social Organisation' *Journal of the
Royal Anthropological Institute* vol 59, 1929
—— 'The Incest Barrier: its Role in Social Organisation' *British Journal of
Psychology* (general section) vol 22, 1932
—— 'The Incest Taboo as a Social Regulation' *Sociological Review* vol 27, 1935
—— 'The Problem of incest and exogamy: a restatement' *American Anthropo-
logist* 1950 vol 52
W. Shakespeare *Hamlet* 1602
M.L. Shanley ' "One must ride behind". Married Women's Property & the
Divorce Act of 1857' *Victorian Studies* vol 25 1982
E. Shorter *The Making of the Modern Family* London 1976
H.W. Simpson 'An Argument to Prove that Marriage with a Deceased Wife's
Sister is forbidden by Scripture' 1860 in C.W. Holgate *A Memorial of H.W.
Simpson* 1902
C.N. Starcke *The Primitive Family in its origin and development* London 1889, re-
issued in same format, R. Needham (ed.) Chicago 1976
L. Stone *The Family, Sex and Marriage in England 1500–1800* London 1977,
revised edition 1979
O.M. Stone *Family Law. An Account of the Law of Domestic Relations in
England and Wales in the last quarter of the twentieth century with some
comparisons* London 1977
M.C.M. Swabey and T.H. Tristram *Reports of Cases decided in the Court of
Probate & in the Court of Divorce and Matrimonial Cases*, London 4 vols
1860–71
C. Taylor 'Rationality' in M. Hollis and S. Lukes (eds) *Rationality and Relativism*
Oxford 1982
J. Taylor *Ductor Dubitantium, or the Rule of Conscience in all her Generall
Measures; Serving as a Great Instrument for the Determination of Cases of
Conscience* London 1660 2 vols
William Makepeace Thackeray *Vanity Fair* 1847–8

J.F. Thrupp *The Christian inference from Leviticus xviii, 16, sufficient ground for holding that according to the Word of God Marriage with the Deceased wife's sister is unlawful. A letter to the Rev Dr. McCaul* 1859

L. Tolstoy *War and Peace* 1866

Anthony Trollope *Barchester Towers* 1858

—— *Doctor Thorne* 1858

—— *Framley Parsonage* 1861

—— *Can You Forgive Her?* 1864

—— *Miss Mackenzie* 1864

—— *The Small House at Allington* 1864

—— *The Claverings* 1867

—— *The Last Chronicle of Barset* 1867

—— *Phineas Finn* 1869

—— *The Vicar of Bullhampton* 1870

—— *Ralph the Heir* 1871

—— *The Prime Minister* 1875

—— *The Eustace Diamonds* 1876

—— *Is he Popenjoy?* 1878

—— *John Caldigate* 1879

—— *The Duke's Children* 1880

—— *Ayala's Angel* 1881

J. Turner *A Letter of Resolution to a Friend concerning the marriage Cousin Germans* 1682

E.B. Tylor *Researches in the Early History of Mankind and the Development of Civilisation* London 1865

—— 'On a Method of investigating the Development of Institutions; Applied to the laws of Marriage and Descent' *Journal of the Royal Anthropological Institute* xviii, 1889

E. Vaughan *Report & Arguments of that Learned Judge Sir John Vaughan Kt . . .* London 1677

M. Warnock 'The surrogacy scandal' *The Listener* 24 January 1985

A. Watson *Legal Transplants. An approach to comparative law* Edinburgh 1974

—— *The Nature of Law* Edinburgh 1977

—— *Society and Legal Change* Edinburgh 1977

B.N. Webster (Junior) *Explanation of the Reezons, why Marriage iz Prohibited between Natural Relations designed to determin the Proprity of Marrying a Wife's Sister* 1789, no xxvi in N. Webster *A Collection of Essays and Fugitive Writings on Moral, Historical, Political and Literary Subjects* Boston 1790

E. Westermarck *The History of Human Marriage* London 1891; second edition 1894; third edition 1901; fifth enlarged edition 3 vols 1921

—— *A Short History of Human Marriage* 1926

—— *Marriage* 1929

—— 'Recent Theories of Exogamy' *Sociological Review* 1934 xxvi

—— *Three Essays on Sex and Marriage* London 1934

L.A. White 'The Definition and Prohibition of Incest' *American Anthropologist* 1, 1948

Who Was Who: Alfred Henry Huth

S. Wolfram 'The explanation of prohibitions and preferences of marriage between kin' DPhil thesis, Oxford University 1956, 705 pp.

—— 'Le mariage entre alliés dans l'Angleterre contemporaine' *L'Homme* 1, 1961

—— 'Basic differences of thought' in R. Horton and R. Finnegan (eds) *Modes of Thought* London 1973

—— Review of P. Maranda *French Kinship: Structure and History* in *Man. Journal of the Royal Anthropological Institute* vol 10 London 1975

—— 'Quine, Statements and "Necessarily True" ' *Philosophical Quarterly* 1975
—— 'Drawing the marriage Lines' *The Guardian*, 24 June 1980
—— 'Anthropology and Morality' *Journal of the Anthropological Society of Oxford* (JASO) vol XIII no 3, 1982
—— 'Eugenics and the Punishment of Incest Act 1908' [1983] *Criminal Law Review*
—— 'Facts and Theories: Saying and Believing' in J. Overing (ed.) *Reason and Morality* ASA Monograph 24 London 1985a
—— 'Divorce in England 1700–1857' *Oxford Journal of Legal Studies* 1985 vol 5 no 2
—— 'Surrogacy in the UK' paper presented to the Society for Applied Anthropology at Reno, USA 1986 [in press]
W.P. Wood *A Vindication of the Law prohibiting Marriage with a Deceased Wife's Sister?*, 1861
T.D. Woolsey *Essay on Divorce and Divorce Legislation* New York 1869
C. Wordsworth *An Address on Marriage with a Deceased Wife's Sister*

Commissions

First Report of the Commissioners Appointed to Inquire into the State and Operation of the law of Marriage as Relating to the Prohibited Degrees of Affinity, and to Marriages Solemnised Abroad or in the British Colonies London 1848 Cmd 973, reprinted *British Parliamentary Papers* vol 1 Dublin 1969
First Report of the Commissioners appointed by her Majesty to enquire into the law of divorce & more particularly into the mode of obtaining divorces a vinculo 1853, reprinted in *British Parliamentary Papers* vol 1 1969
Divorce Acts 123 — Session 2, May–June 1857, reprinted in *British Parliamentary Papers* Irish University Press vol 3 1971
'Marriages (England and Wales)' 1857, 106–1 — Session 2
On Married Women's Property Bill, Special Report 17 July 1868, para 2, reprinted in *British Parliamentary Papers: Marriage and Divorce* vol 2, 1970, p. ix
The Divorce Commission. The Majority and Minority Reports Summarised London 1912
Royal Commission on Divorce & Matrimonial Causes HMSO Cmd 6478, 1912–13
Church of England Commission *Kindred and Affinity as Impediments to Marriage being the Report of a Commission appointed by his Grace the Archbishop of Canterbury* London 1940
Royal Commission on Marriage and Divorce HMSO Cmd 9678, 1956
Criminal Law Revision Committee, *Working Paper on Sexual Offences* London 1980 HMSO
HMSO *Social Trends* 11, 1981
Scottish Law Commission *The Law of Incest in Scotland* 1981 Cmd 8422
Criminal Law Revision Committee, 15th Report *Sexual Offences* London 1984 HMSO Cmd 9213
Church of England: Archbishop of Canterbury's Group *No Just Cause. The Law of Affinity in England & Wales: Some suggestions for change* London 1984
Report of the Committee of Inquiry into Human Fertilisation and Embryology HMSO, Cmd 9314, London 1984 (Chairman M. Warnock), referred to as the 'Warnock Report'

Private Acts of Parliament

Duke of Norfolk's Divorce Act 1700 11 & 12 Gul 3 *c 2*
Box's Divorce Act 1701 12 & 13 W 3 *c 18*
Jermyn's Divorce Act 1711 MS 9 Anne *c 30*
Cobb's Divorce Act 1729 2 Geo 2 *c 31*
Mrs Addison's Divorce Act 1801 41 Geo 3 *c 102* (incestuous adultery)
Rt. Hon Henry Wellesley's Divorce Act 1810 50 Geo 3 *c 1*
Lord Cloncurry's Divorce Act 1811 51 Geo 3 *c 73*
Earl of Rosebery's Divorce Act 1815 55 Geo 3 *c 104*
Lismore's Divorce Act 1826 7 Geo 4 *c 55*
Mrs Turton's Divorce Act 1 & 2 W 4 1830 *c 35* (incestuous adultery)
Mrs Battersby's Divorce Act 1840 3 & 4 Vic *c 48* (adultery and bigamy)
Cheape's Divorce Act 1844 7 & 8 Vic *c 47*
Hill's Divorce Act 1849 12 & 13 Vic *c 34*
Ashby's Divorce Act 1850 13 & 14 Vic *c 23*
Mrs Hall's Divorce Act 1850 13 & 14 Vic *c 25* (adultery and bigamy)
Chippindall's Divorce Act Gentleman 1850 13 & 14 Vic *c 22*
Hartley's Divorce Act 1850 13 & 14 Vic *c 19*
Heathcote's Divorce Act 1851 14 & 15 Vic *c 24*
Webster's Divorce Act 1851 14 & 15 Vic *c 25*
Talbot's Divorce Act 1856 19 & 20 Vic *c 16*
Campbell's Divorce Act 1857 20 & 21 Vic *c 10*
Edward Berry & Doris Eilleen Ward (Marriage Enabling) Act 1980 *c.1*
John Francis Dare & Gillian Lodel Dare (Marriage Enabling Act) 1982 *c 1*
Hugh Small & Norma Small (Marriage Enabling Act) 1982 *c 2*

Public Acts of Parliament

An Act concerning the King's Succession 1533 25 H 8 c 22 sec 3
An Act concerning Succession of the Crown 1536 28 H 8 c 7
A Provision for Dispensations &c 1536 28 H 8 c 16
Concerning Precontracting & Degrees of Consanguinity 1540 32 H 8 c 38
An Act Declaring the Queen's Highness to have been born in most Just and Holy
    Matrimony 1553 1 Mary 2 c 1 sec 8
An Act repealing all Articles and provisions made against the See Apostolick of
    Rome since the twentieth year of King Henry VIII 1554 1 & 2 P & M c 8
The Act of Supremacy 1558 1 Eliz I c 1
Marriage Act 1753 26 Geo 2 c 33
Ecclesiastical Courts Act 1813 53 Geo 3 c 127
The Marriage Act 1835 5 & 6 Wm 4 c 54 (known as Lord Lyndhurst's Act)
An Act for Marriages in England 1836 6 & 7 W c 85
The Matrimonial Causes Act 1857 20 & 21 Vict c 85
Municipal Franchose Act 1869 32 & 33 V c 55
Elementary Education Act 1870 33 & 34 V c 75
Married Women's Property Act 1870 33 & 34 V c 93
Judicature Act 1873 36 & 37 Vic c 66
Married Women's Property (Scotland) Act 1877 40 & 41 V c 29
Married Women's Property (Scotland) Act 1881 44 & 45 V c 21
The Married Women's Property Act 1882 45 & 46 V c 75
Local Government Act 1894 56 & 57 V c 73
Local Government Act (Scotland) 1895 57 & 58 V c 58

The Deceased Wife's Sister's Marriage Act 1907 Edw 7 c 47
The Punishment of Incest Act 1908 8 Edw 7 c 45
Representation of the People Act 1918 7 & 8 Geo 5 c 64
The Qualification of Women Act 1918 8 & 9 Geo 5 c 47
The Sex Disqualification (Removal) Act 1919 9 & 10 Geo 5 c 71
The Deceased Brother's Widow's Marriage Act 1921 11 & 12 Geo 5 c 24
The Matrimonial Causes Act 1923 13 & 14 Geo 5 c 19 (repealed and re-enacted
    1925)
Law of Property Act 1925 15 & 16 Geo 5 c 20
Representation of the People (Equal Franchise) Act 1928 18 & 19 Geo 5 c 12
The Marriage (Prohibited Degrees of Relationship) Act 1931 21 & 22 Geo 5 c 31
Law Reform (Married Womens and Tortfeasors) Act 1935 25 & 26 Geo 5 c 30
Matrimonial Causes Act 1937 I Ed 8 & Geo 6 c 57
Legal Aid & Advice Act 1949 12, 13 & 14 Geo 6 c 51
Marriage Act 1949 12, 13 & 14 Geo 6 c 76
Marriage Enabling Act 1960 8 & 9 Eliz 2 c 29
Matrimonial Homes Act 1967 c 75
Theft Act 1968 c 60 s 30
Divorce Reform Act 1969 Eliz II 1969 c 55
Law Reform (Miscellaneous Provisions) Act 1970 c 33
Matrimonial Proceedings and Property Act 1970 c 45
Finance Act 1971 c 68
Surrogacy Arrangements Act 1985 c 49

Court Cases

Hill v. Good 1677
Aughtie v. Aughtie 1810
Faremouth & others v. Watson 1811
Elliot & Sudjeon v. Gurr 1812
Blackmore & Thorpe v. Brider 1816
R. v. Sherwood & Ray 1837
R. v. Hall 1845
R. v. Chadwick 1847
R. v. St. Giles-in-the-Field 1847
Brook v. Brook, House of Lords 1861
Wing v. Taylor 1861
R. v. Harrald 1872 QED vol 7
R. v. Clarence 1888 QBD vol 22

Other Sources

BBC TV: 'The Pallisers'
Hansard
ITV, Channel 4: 'Twenty Twenty Vision: Child Sex Abuse' 1, 8, 15 December
    1984
London Gazette
Oxford University Gazette
The Times

Appendix: Chronological Table

This table is of course in no way exhaustive, and is intended only as a brief chronological guide to events relating to kinship and marriage in England.

1533–58	Acts of Parliament reducing Prohibited Degrees of Consanguinity and Affinity, and discontinuing dispensations
1540	Most grounds for annulling marriages removed
1560	Scotland introduces divorce for adultery and malicious desertion
1563	Archbishop Parker's Table of Levitical Degrees proposed
16th C	Institution of marriage settlements (property settled on wife) by her family or husband for her separate use
1603	Archbishop Parker's Table adopted into Canons of the Church of England (forbids marriage in or within the third degree of consanguinity and affinity)
1603	Bigamy becomes a crime (previously subject only to ecclesiastical courts)
(1640–60	Civil War and Cromwellian Protectorate)
1662	Book of Common Prayer includes Archbishop Parker's Table
1670	Lood Roos' divorce by private Act of Parliament
1692	Harris v. Hicks: marriages within Prohibited Degrees can be declared void only during lifetime of both parties
1700	Parliament decides that dissolving marriages to permit re-marriage comes within its jurisdiction: divorces are performed by Private Acts of Parliament (until 1857). Adultery (by wife) or adultery compounded by incest or bigamy (by husband) sole grounds
1753	Lord Hardwicke's Act regulates celebration of marriages, and institutes their registration
(1789)–1815	(French Revolution, followed by Napoleonic Wars)
1801	Mrs Addison's Divorce Act for incestuous adultery (first divorce granted to a woman)
1814–15	End of Napoleonic Wars: English can go to the Continent again
1835	Lord Lyndhurst's Act: Marriages within Prohibited Degrees, previously voidable, become void *ab initio*
1836	Marriage Act: marriages can be celebrated in Registry offices instead of only in Church and other accredited places of worship
1842	First Parliamentary Bill to legalise marriage with a deceased wife's sister
1845	Maule's Judgment in R. v. Hall (mocking divorce procedures)
1848	Royal Commission . . . [into] the Prohibited Degrees
1853	Royal Commission . . . into the law of Divorce
(1854–6	Crimean War)
1857	Matrimonial Causes Act transfers jurisdiction over divorces to courts (and adds desertion etc to offences compounding adultery for which wife can get divorce) Incest ceases to be under any jurisdiction

231

1858	Divorces increase from *c.* 3 per annum to *c.* 150 per annum
1861	Wing v. Taylor: according to common law, extra-marital relations do not create affinity
1861	Brook v. Brook: marriages within the Prohibited Degrees contracted abroad are void
mid-19th C	Mourning obligatory at death of spouse (2 years) and consanguineous and affinal relatives, longer the closer the relationship to the deceased (1 year first degree, six months second degree, 3 months third degree etc.), also by servants, and by Court and public at death of Sovereign (1 year Court, 3 months public), or close relatives of Sovereign
1870	Married Women's Property Act: earnings of married woman her own
1882	Married Women's Property Act: property brought into marriage by wife 'her separate property'
1880s	Mourning for relatives has begun to decrease (to about two-thirds of previous periods)
1888	R. v. Clarence: Husband not guilty of rape despite venereal disease unknown to wife
1900	Mendelian genetic theory becomes known
1900	There are *c.* 500 divorces per annum
1907	Deceased Wife's Sister's Marriage Act: legalises marriage with a deceased wife's sister; adultery with living wife's sister still 'incestuous'
1908	Punishment of Incest Act: sexual relations between close blood relatives becomes a crime
1910	Public mourning at death of Sovereign reduced from 12 weeks to 8 weeks
1911	Powers of House of Lords curtailed
(1914–18	World War I)
1918	Women (over 30 years) get the right to vote in Parliamentary elections, and to sit in Parliament
1921	Deceased Brother's Widow's Act: legalises marriage with a deceased brother's widow
1923	Wife can procure divorce for simple adultery ('incestuous adultery' ceases to be a category)
1931	Marriage (Prohibited Degrees of Relationship) Act legalises marriage between a man and his deceased wife's aunts and nieces, and nephews' and uncles' widows
1937	Matrimonial Causes Act makes desertion and cruelty independent grounds for divorce
(1940–5	World War II)
1940	Church of England Commission to bring Church into line with Statute Law on Prohibited Degrees
1960	Marriage Enabling Act: allows marriage with relatives of divorced spouse and divorced spouse of relative as if spouse were deceased
1969	Divorce Reform Act: 'Irretrievable breakdown' of marriage becomes grounds of divorce (i.e. divorce can take place by consent, no longer (only) for an offence by other spouse)
1978	General Marriage (Enabling) Bill: first Bill to try to legalise marriage between affinal relatives in direct line — unsuccessful
1978	First 'test-tube' baby born, in England
1980	Number of divorces reaches 150,000 per annum

1980	First private Act of Parliament allowing a marriage between affinal relatives in direct line
1980	Punishment of Incest Act under review by Criminal Law Revision Committee
1984	Church of England Commission recommends by small majority that affinal relatives in the direct line should be allowed to marry (except in cases of minors of household)
1984	Criminal Law Revision Committee recommends that sexual relations between brothers and sisters over 21 years should cease to be 'incest' (an offence)
1984	'Warnock Report' on human fertilisation and embryology
1985	Birth of 'Baby Cotton'
1985	Commercial Surrogacy Arrangements Act: makes arranging of surrogacy for money an offence

Index

Aberle 146, 158n46
abortion 121
actions 6, 186, 190−4, 197, 198−
  202, 211−14
  assertions 191−2, 200, 202
    inconsistent 191
  for money 211−14
  rational 190−3
Addison, C.G. 96n60
Addison (Mrs) 26, 28, 29, 46n22,
  79, 92n19, 127n68
Adolphus & Ellis 45n11
adoptive relative 143, 144, 156n3,
  157n30, 173, 208, 210
adultery 52−3, 79−82, 89, 118−
  19,121−2, 127n68, 127n73,
  163, 208
  attitudes to 52−3, 62n4, 87,
    119, 121−2, 127n73
  condoning 118−19, 127n68,
    208
  evidence 61n2, 82, 94n47,
    118−19
  grounds for divorce 52, 78−
    82, 118−19, 121−2
  hotel cases 89, 152
  incestuous 28, 29−30, 46n22,
    79, 118, 127n68, 142, 143
    definition 30
  men's 18
  penalties 52−3, 62n4, 86
  women's 18, 86−7, 121,
    127n73, 208
  see also criminal conversation,
    divorce, extra-marital
    sexual relations, sexual
    intercourse
affine, affinity 12, 13, 17, 20n13,
  27−8, 36−8, 39, 40−4, 46n22,
  51n98, 56, 64−6, 142, 144−5,
  156n3, 173, 188, 198

concept of 12, 13, 16, 20n13,
  27−8, 142, 145
  mourning 56
  see also relationship
age 67, 70, 75n11, 75n12, 201,
  208, 213
  husband and wife 70, 201
  inheritance 75n11, 213
  succession 75n11, 213
Alleyne 162, 165, 167, 181n8
alliance theory 162, 166−9, 174,
  175, 179−80, 187, 188, 189−
  90
  see also prohibitions of sexual
    unions between relatives
An Act Concerning the King's
  Succession 1533 23, 45n3
An Act Concerning Precon-
  tracting & Degrees of
  Consanguinity 1540 23, 77−8
An Act Concerning Succession of
  the Crown 1536 23, 26, 27,
  45n3
An Act Declaring the Queen's
  Highness to have been born in
  most Just and Holy Matrimony 1553 23
An Act repealing all Articles and
  provisions made against the
  See Apostolick of Rome since
  the 20th year of King Henry
  VIII 1554 23
An Act of Supremacy 1558 23
An Act for Marriages in England
  1836 23, 26, 27, 86, 116,
  125n56A, 125n57
Anderson, R.T. 74n1, 74n2
Anderson, S. 93n20, 93−4n34,
  94n39, 155, 161n82
animals 16, 158n46, 170, 173, 211
Année sociologique 193

235

annulment 77–8, 121
Anonymous 1682 161, 180n7
Anonymous [H.R.Reynolds]
   1840 47n37, 47n39, 48n61,
   49n70
Anonymous 1849 48n46
Anonymous [H.F.Bacon] 1849
   47n38, 49n70
Anonymous [*c.* 1850] 47n36
Anonymous (A Member of the
   University of Oxford) 1858 33,
   48n49
Anonymous (B.A.W.) 1859 33,
   48n46
Anonymous *Cassell's* 1860 54–5,
   62n7
Anonymous (A Philosophical
   Inquirer) 1860 50n79
Anonymous 1864 34, 48n59,
   50n50
Anonymous (A Graduate) 1864a
   48n61, 49n74, 49n79, 50n83
Anonymous (An Anxious
   Observer) 1869 49n67, 49n71
Anonymous (A Solicitor) 1872
   34, 48n59
Anonymous [Eliza Cheadle] 1872
   54–5, 62n7
Anonymous (One who does not
   want to) 1883 47n38
Anonymous 1886 49n78
Anonymous (A Member of the
   Aristocracy) 1888 57, 58,
   62n16, 63n18, 63n19
Archbishop of Canterbury 147
Archbishop of Canterbury's
   Group *see* Church of England
Archbishop Parker 26–7
   Archbishop Parker's Table *see*
   Parker's Table
Armstrong 57, 63n17
Arner 138, 141, 145, 155n1,
   156n16–17, 158n42
artificial insemination 211, 217n2,
   217n3, 218n20
Ashby 92–3n27, 94n47, 95n49
assertions 7, 191–2, 198–206
   see also actions, belief,
      political platforms

Aughtie v Aughtie 1810 29,45n19
aunts 31–3, 36, 144, 157n30,
   157n31, 165, 166
   & nephews 15, 36, 144,
      157n30, 157n31
Austen, Jane 52, 53, 65, 66, 71,
   72, 74n5, 74n6, 76n27, 116–17
Australia 208
Ayer 193
Azande 186, 193, 195n26

Bailey & Blackburn 51n106, 139,
   156n10, 157n21
Bakewell 138, 141, 145
bastardising 46n22, 119, 127n70
   see also divorce, illegitimate
Basuto 185n97
Battersby (Mrs) 92n20
Beaufort, Duke of 30
Bedford College 113
belief 3–4, 6–7, 11–18, 137–47,
   149–55, 159n47, 186–8,
   191–4, 197–206
   category 11–18, 193–4,
      202–3
   discovery of 201–2
   expert 147, 149–55
   illfounded 6, 137–47, 149–55,
      187–8, 192–3
   inconsistent 5, 6–7, 145–7,
      159n47
   metaphysical 193
   popular 19, 137–47, 149–55,
      155n3, 197
   rational 192, 202, 204
   religious 3, 7n9
   scientific 5, 7n9
   self-evident 4, 12, 197
   see also actions, categories,
      classification, rationality
Bemba 185n97
Bentham 161, 164, 165
bereaved 54, 58–9, 202
   see also mourning
Beresford Hope 33, 48n46
Berry & Ward (Marriage
   Enabling) Act 1980 41
Bickersteth etc 47n37

bigamy 78, 79, 90n8, 91n12, 118, 197
Bingham *see* Lismore
Binney 38, 49n79, 50n80
biological theory 137−47, 164
   see also genetic theory, incest, prohibitions of sexual unions between relatives
Blackmore & Thorpe v Brider 1816 29, 45n19
blood relation
   see consanguinity, relationship
Bolingbroke 95−6n60
Book of Common Prayer 26
Box 80
breach of promise 117−18, 126n64A, 126n66
Britten 92n27
Bromley 92n25, 99
Brontë 116
Brook v Brook 1861 29, 43, 46n24
brothers and sisters 11, 15, 17, 34, 36, 40, 43, 44, 55, 64−8, 82, 94n48, 95n50, 127n68, 138, 142, 143, 144, 163, 166, 168, 188
   half- 43, 65
   in-law 12, 17, 31−6, 40, 61n2, 64−7, 74n5, 82, 138, 142, 143, 168
   step- 65, 66
Brougham 83−4, 87, 92n25, 95n52, 95n53,95n55, 99, 109, 110, 153
Browning, E.B. 110
Burton 155n3
Buss, Miss 124n43
Buxton 87, 96n74

Cadogan *see* Wellesley
Cambridge 113, 124n44
Campbell, Jane *see* Addison (Mrs)
Campbell, Lord 79, 83
Campbell (1857) 95n49
carnal knowledge 28, 77
   see also sexual intercourse

Cassell's 58, 63n20
categories 4, 11−18, 26−7, 38−9, 58, 64−9, 142−3, 144, 146−7, 189, 193−4, 200, 202, 204−6, 210−16
   arguments 210−16
   kinship 12−18, 26−7, 38−9, 58, 144, 200−6
   money 209−10
   problems 210−16
Caton 92−3n27
causes 6, 11, 137, 143−5, 149−55, 160n83, 161, 171−3, 190, 191, 193, 199, 202
Cecil 94
change 3−5, 11, 17, 18, 21−30, 39−40, 41−4, 53, 57−8, 83, 85−7, 111−12, 113, 120, 122, 126n65, 147−55, 168, 198, 205−6, 212, 214
   mourning 53, 57−8
   no change 41, 85, 198, 212, 214
   prohibited degrees 21−30, 41−4
   unity of husband and wife 111−12, 122
   women 113
   see also divorce, political platforms, unity of husband and wife, women
Charles, Prince 117, 201
chastity theory 162−3, 167−9, 175, 188
   see also prohibitions of sexual unions beteen relatives
Cheape 94n39
Cheltenham Ladies' College 124n43
Chippendall 81, 84
Christianity 2, 16, 18, 38, 66, 74n2, 86, 96n65
Church of England 5, 7n9, 21, 26, 27, 29, 41−2, 47n35, 50n92, 78, 83, 86, 116, 119, 125n56A, 142−3, 153, 155, 188−90
Church of England *Report . . . Kindred and Affinity* 1940 7n9, 41, 188−9
Church of England *No Just Cause*

1984 7n9, 141–2, 161, 163,
181n15, 190
Churchill 39
clans 157n30, 161
classification 11–18, 19n2, 58,
64–9, 74n2, 193–4, 198, 199,
202–6
as one 16–18, 64–5, 68
assimilation 11, 15–16, 58,
64–9, 203
distinction 64–9, 203
see also belief, categories,
conceptual scheme
Clifford 94n48, 99
Cloncurry 94n41
Cobb 80
cognatic 2, 4, 7n8, 188–90,
195n17, 204
see also relationship
cognitive anthropology 206n15
see also structuralism
collateral 13, 67, 68
see also relationship
complimentary mourning 66,
74n6
see also mourning
conception 118–19, 120, 122,
126n64, 127n81, 207
see also reproduction
concepts see categories
conceptual scheme 199–202
conjectural history 169, 172, 186,
190
see also evolutionary theory
connections 66, 71, 74n6
consanguinity 12–13, 142–4
basis for marriage law 49n64,
142–3
treatment of 144
see also relationship
contraception 6, 120–1, 126n64,
202
conventions 114
see also customs
Cotton, baby 207, 209, 211,
217n2
court mourning 3, 56–7, 201–4
see also mourning
courts 28–9, 84, 107, 109–11,

113–14, 123n11A, 159n74,
160n76
common law 107, 109, 110–
11, 123n11A, 125n55
ecclesiastical 28–9, 123n11A
equity 109, 110–11, 123n11A
Judicature Act 1873 111
cousins 11, 15, 21, 34, 39, 55,
57, 64–5, 66, 68, 69, 126n66,
138, 139, 145, 155n3, 161,
166, 176, 178, 180n1, 184n91,
187
cross-cousins 161, 176, 180n1,
184n91, 187
marriage 21, 39, 138, 139, 145,
155n3, 161, 166, 178
mourning 55, 57
terminology 69
see also relationship
Craik 90–1n8
crêpe 55, 56, 58, 60, 61, 62n9,
63n30
Cretney 92n25
Crimean war 109
criminal conversation 79, 81–6,
91n16, 92n18, 93n28, 94n39,
96n62, 102
abolition 96n62
see also adultery, divorce
criminal conversation cases 82–4,
94n27, 94n41, 94n42, 94n46,
94n48, 95n49
Ashby 95n49
Bingham see Lismore
Bolingbroke 95–6n60
Campbell 95n49
Cloncurry 94n41
Dennis 82, 94n48
Exmouth see Pellew
Hartley 83–4, 85
King 94–5n48
Lismore 94n47, 95n46,
95–6n60
Pellew 95–6n60
Rosebery 83, 94n42
Turton 95n49
Wellesley 94n41
Criminal Law Review 139, 156n6,
156n11

Criminal Law Revision Committee 15, 20n11, 44, 51n110, 120,
138,139, 144−5, 146−7,
157n29, 157n30, 158n3
1980 Report 15, 20 n11, 44,
138, 139, 144−5, 157n30,
158n3
1984 Report 15, 20 n 11, 44,
51n110, 120, 144−5, 147,
157n29, 157n30
Cripps 95n55
Cromwell 52
cross-cousins 161, 176, 180n1,
184n91, 187
see also cousins, relationship
Curteis 45n18
customs 3, 6, 7, 52−61, 67, 78,
114, 116−18, 120−1, 137, 172,
190, 201−5
breaches 201
desirable 6, 137, 190, 202
marking categories 203−5
social 52−61, 70−4, 116−18,
120−1
marriage 70−4, 116−18
mourning 53−61
undesirable 6, 137, 190, 202

Dare & Dare (Marriage Enabling
Act) 1982 41, 51n100
daughters 15, 17, 35, 43, 44,
65−7, 68, 138, 164−5, 197
adoptive 44
in-law 65
step- 44, 142
Davey 201, 206n14A
Dawson 36, 49n67
Dawson, Mrs 92n20
De Vries 140
death duties 34, 75n11
see also inheritance
debts 18
deceased wife's sister 3, 7n9, 18,
21−3, 27, 30−40, 64, 141−2,
162, 164, 168−9
arguments 31−40
biblical 7n9, 35−9
principles 36−9
social 31−5, 36

Royal commission 1848 31
Scotland 31
Deceased Brother's Widow
Marriage Act 1921 40, 43, 143
Deceased Wife's Sister's
Marriage Act 1907 21−3, 30,
40, 43, 142, 143, 145, 147
Defoe 28, 29
degree reckoning 13−16, 21−6,
53, 144, 158n33, 197
modes
canon law 14−15, 22
civil law 14−15, 25−6, 64
other 15, 144
mourning 53, 54, 56−9, 64
prohibited degrees 21−6
see also mourning, prohibited
degrees, relationship
Denham 34, 48n58, 49n74
Dennis 82, 94n48, 95n50
Dicey 149, 151
Dickens 65, 71, 72, 75n13
Dictionary of National Biography
94n44
Dillon 94n47, 95n50
direct exchange 176
direct line 12, 41, 67−8, 143, 178
see also relationship
dispensations 21
divorce 2−3, 4, 6, 77−106, 137,
142, 143, 147−55, 197
attitude to 87, 89−90, 147−50
Catholic Church 77−8
Church of England 41, 77−8,
96n65, 153, 155
cost 80−4, 92n25, 93n28,
94n37, 94n39, 148−9, 153
courts 78−9, 160n74, 160n76
criminal conversation 79,
81−6, 91n16, 92n18, 93n28,
94n39, 96n62, 102
abolition 96n62
see also criminal conversation cases
damages 80, 81−2, 83−6,
94n39, 94n43, 94n48,
95−6n60, 102
decree nisi 120, 127n68
decree absolute 127n68

divorce—*cont.*
definition 78
ecclesiastical 78, 79, 90n80,
160n76
a mensa et thoro 78, 79, 81,
85−6, 90n8, 91n16,
92n27, 93n28, 94n37,
94n39, 118, 127n67
a vinculo matrimonii 78
explanations 6, 137, 147−55
deficiencies of previous law
149−50, 153
emancipation of women
137, 149, 150−4, 192,
194
exponential increase 155,
160n81, 160n83
grounds 78−82, 86−7
adultery 79−82, 86−7, 152
aggravations of adultery
28−30, 43, 46n22,
91n17, 148, 152
cruelty 79, 89, 152
desertion 79, 89, 148, 152
irretrievable breakdown 89
see also adultery, criminal
conversation, women
Henry VIII statutes 77−8
hotel cases 89, 152
impediments to 82, 94n48,
95n49, 95n50, 118, 127n68
India 94n39, 102
increase 77, 88−90, 147−55,
149−50
introduction 77−9
judicial separation 78, 86, 103
lament 77, 147−8
legislation
Matrimonial Causes Act
1857 3, 79, 85−8,
91n17, 95n62, 143, 147,
148, 151−2, 153, 154,
159n70
Matrimonial Causes Act
1923 43, 79, 89, 91n17,
148, 152
Matrimonial Causes Act
1937 43, 79, 89, 91n17
148, 152, 153

Divorce Reform Act 1969
89, 148, 152, 153
private Act of Parliament 28,
46n22, 81−2, 94n35,
98−102,
property 197
rates of 3, 79, 80, 87−9,
92n22, 92n24, 97n75, 98,
103−6, 147−8, 149−50,
152−3, 154, 160n79
inaccuracies about 80,
92n24, 99
relaxation of law 149−51
Royal Commissions
1853 79−80, 83, 85, 93n28,
99
1912 88, 97n76, 99, 103−6,
127n66A, 148−9
1956 88, 97n76, 99, 104−6,
148, 150−1
Scotland 2, 78, 85, 87, 147,
153, 206
social class 78−81, 85, 87−8,
92n25, 93n34, 95n60,
100−1, 148−9, 151
women 79, 86, 92n20, 152, 154
see also annulment, divorces
Divorce Acts, 123 − sess 2, May
− June, 1857 98
Divorce Reform Act 1969 89,
148, 152, 153
divorces
Addison (Mrs) 26, 28, 29,
46n22, 79, 92n19, 127n68
Ashby 92−3n27, 94n47, 95n49
Battersby, (Mrs) 92n20
Box 80
Britten 92n27
Campbell 95n49
Caton 92−3n27
Cheape 94n39
Chippendall 84
Cloncurry 94n41
Cobb 80
Cripps 95n55
Faussett 92−3n27
Hall (Mrs) 87, 92n20, 95n55
Hartley 83−4, 85
Heathcote 46n22, 127n70

divorces—*cont.*
Hill 94n47, 95n55
Humphreys 95n55
Jermyn 80, 93n32
Lismore 94n47
Macclesfield 79, 91n13
Mathyson 95n55
Norfolk 91n13, 94n48
Queen Caroline 95n53
Rich 90n8
Rosebery 29, 46n2, 52, 61n2,
82, 84, 94n42, 95n52
Talbot 94n47, 95n55
Tayleur 92–3n27
Turton (Mrs) 29, 46n22, 92n20
Waldy 95n55
Webster 82, 94n46
Wellesley 94n41
see also criminal conversation
cases, divorces *a mensa et
thoro*
divorces *a mensa et thoro*
Campbell 95n49
Dennis 94n48, 95n50
Dillon 94n47, 95n50
King 94–5n48
Lismore 95n47
Turton, Mrs 95n49
Dobu 178, 185n97
Dobzhansky 13, 20n6, 145,
158n44
Douglas 49n77–8
duels 118, 126n65, 126n66
Dugard 156n3
Duke 49n76
Dumont 12,19n4, 197–8
Durkheim 161, 170, 171, 187,
194, 196n28

ecclesiastical courts 28–9,
45n9A, 78, 142–3
see also courts
Ecclesiastical Courts Act 1813
42, 51n107
Edgworth 60
Edward VII 57
Edward VIII 73

Elementary Education Act 1870
113, 124n43A
Eliot, G. 53, 60, 120
Elliot & Sudjeon v Gurr 1812 29,
45n19
Encyclopedia Britannica 89, 99,
126n65, 173
endogamy 7n8, 170, 173, 184n78
engagement 117–18, 121, 126n66
Ensor 124n43
entailed estates 67, 71, 75n11,
121, 213
ethnocentricity 12
Evans-Pritchard 161, 173,
183n67, 183n70, 186, 187,
193–4, 195n26
Evershed 148, 149, 151,
159n73
evolutionary theory 161–2,
169–73, 186–7
exchange 176, 191
direct 176
indirect 176
excommunication 29, 42
Exmouth *see* Pellew
exogamy 7n8, 21, 157n30, 161,
169–74, 179, 183n67,
183n70–1, 186, 188, 202
definitions 161, 169–73,
183n67, 183n70–1, 188
experts 5, 43, 60, 93n34, 137, 141,
147, 149, 158n32, 161–80, 188
explanation 1, 6, 11, 21, 54,
58–9, 137, 143–5, 147–55,
160n83, 161–180, 186–93,
202–5
category 202–5
causal 6, 11, 137, 143–4, 145,
147–55, 160n83, 171–3,
190–1, 202
divorce 147–55, 192, 194
expert 21, 137, 147–55,
161–8, 192
functional 54, 58–9, 186–8,
190–4
historical 169–73, 186, 190
illfounded 6, 58–9, 137,
145–7, 147–55, 161,
177–80, 187–90

explanation—*cont.*
  popular 21, 137, 143, 145−6,
    147−55, 192
  prohibitions of sexual unions
    between relatives 6, 138−
    47, 161−80
  purposive 6, 11, 54, 58−9,
    137, 161−9, 174−80, 186,
    190, 202
  religious 137, 146, 168, 169
  scientific 137, 146−7, 180
  structural 202−5
  testing 168, 177−80
exponential increase 88−9,
  160n81
extra-marital sexual relations 3, 6,
  27−8, 31, 32, 42−3, 52−3, 71,
  117, 118−22, 125n56, 128n83,
  159n30, 162−3, 202
  affinity 27−8
  see also adultery, premarital
    sexual relations, sexual
    intercourse

Faremouth & others v Watson
  1811 29, 45n19
father-right 182n39
fathers 12, 59, 60, 64−5, 67, 68,
  72, 128n83, 130, 138, 165, 166,
  188, 197, 209, 210, 212, 213
  in-law 59, 64−5, 71, 72, 166
  step- 65, 166
Faussett 92−3n27
female infanticide 182n42
fiction 3, 39, 53, 54
fieldwork 1−2, 4, 178, 186
Finance Act 1971 112, 124n38
Firth 174
*First Report . . . into . . .
  Prohibited Degrees* 1848 31,
  32, 42−3
*First Report into the Law of
  Divorce* 1853 79−80, 83, 85,
  93n28, 99
fornication 129, 163
Forster, E.M. 40, 50n90
Fortes 173, 174
Fortune 174, 175, 184n86

Foster 47n38
Fox 2, 173, 189−90, 184n91
France 2, 7n2, 15, 61n2, 62n10A,
  90, 121, 122, 126n65, 127n71
Frazer 161, 170
Freud 161, 170−1, 182n51
friends 66, 130, 163, 204, 210, 214
Fry 163, 165, 167, 181n14
function 11, 54, 59, 186
  see also useful purpose
functionalism 186−8, 190−4
  see also explanation
funerals 58

genetic theory 13, 20n11, 120,
  139−41, 144, 156n11A,
  158n44, 158n46, 204−5, 209,
  213−14
Germany 7n3
George IV 83, 95n53
George, W. 158n44
gifts 176, 208−9, 211
Giraud−Teulon 169, 182n46
girth 201
Girton College 124n44
Gladstone 33, 86−8, 96n63
  wife's sister 33
  divorce 86−8
God 5, 11, 23, 35, 86, 129−32,
  145, 146, 155n3, 193
Goody 2, 74n1, 74n2
Gorer 54, 58
Gorrell 150, 159n62
granddaughter 35, 43, 68
grandmother 26, 35, 43, 65, 68
grandparents 26, 44, 55, 65, 68,
  188
  step- 42, 65
Graveson 89, 95n1, 99
grief 53−4, 55, 58−9, 62n9
  see also mourning
Grotius 161, 163, 181n13
groups 157n30, 169−71, 174−6,
  178−9, 188−90, 191, 195n17,
  204
guardians 116, 165
Guthrie 159n57

Haldane 41
Hale 49n78
Hall Williams 157n21
Hall (Mrs) 87, 92n20, 95n55
Hamlet 29, 45—6n20
Hammick 31, 47n33, 75n8,
    91n11—12, 108, 210, 217n17
Hammond 163, 181n12
Hare 199, 215
Harris v Hicks 29
Hartley 83—4, 85
headhunting 189
health 90, 148
Heathcote 46n22, 127n70
height 72—3
Henry VIII 21, 23, 28, 77,
    145
Herbert, A.P. 89
heredity 13, 38, 50n83, 120,
    138—47, 155n3 156n11A,
    158n44
    theories of 13, 38, 50n83,
        138—47, 155n3, 156n11A,
        158n44, 158n45—6
    see also genetic theory
Hill 94n47, 95n55
Hill v Good 1677 27, 45n10
historians 2, 4, 11
Hobhouse 173
Hockin 49n68
Hoggett & Pearl 92n25, 99, 150,
    158n46, 159n63, 159n64, 174,
    184n78
Holcombe 92n24, 92n25, 93n28,
    94n37, 99, 109—14, 123n11A,
    125n55, 148, 150, 159n74,
    160n76
Holdsworth 92n24, 99
Holland, V. 60
Hollis 159n47
Houlbrooke 75n14, 77, 90n3, 174,
    184n78
House of Commons 30, 40,
    46n28, 79, 87—8, 110
House of Lords 40, 50n88, 79, 83,
    87, 110, 123n11A, 152
    deceased wife's sister 40
    divorce 79, 83, 87, 152
    reform 40, 50n88

household 4, 32, 41, 42, 71—2, 77,
    157n29, 162—4, 168, 177,
    178—9
Howard 99
Hume 161, 163
Humphreys 95n55
husband and wife 15—18, 35,
    37—8, 54, 60—1, 64, 68, 72—4,
    86—7, 107, 112, 115—22,
    133—4, 164, 197, 207—8
    property 112
    see also marriage, married
        women's property, unity of
        husband and wife, women
Hutcheson 161, 167
Huth 47n34, 138, 139—40, 141,
    155n2, 156n13—15

illegitimacy 13, 27, 29, 46n22, 59,
    67, 121, 145, 208
in-breeding 54, 137—47, 155n3,
    164, 192, 194
    God's wrath 155n3
    see also genetic theory,
        heredity, incest
incest 3, 5, 15, 20n11, 29—30,
    42—4, 137—47, 155—8,
    161—80, 186, 192, 194, 197,
    212—13
    adoptive relatives 44, 143,
        157n30, 173
    affinity 142, 156n3 26—8,
        36—44, 51n98
    Church of England 26, 27,
        47n35, 50n92, 143
    concept of 43—4, 51n110, 142,
        143, 157n30, 158n31
    Criminal Law Revision
        Committee 20n11, 44,
        125n26, 138, 139, 144—5,
        147, 157n30, 157n29,
        158n31—2
    1980 20n11, 138, 139,
        156n4—9, 157n30,
        158n31, 158n45, 158n31
    1984 20n11, 125n26, 144,
        147, 157n29, 158n30,
        158n32, 173

incest—*cont.*
  definitions 138, 142–3, 157n30
  divine law 145–6, 155n3
  divorce 46n22, 143
  ecclesiastical courts 27, 28–9,
    42, 45n9A, 142–3
  genetic effects 5, 20n11, 54,
    137–47, 158n46, 156n11A,
    164
    see also genetic theory,
      heredity, in-breeding
  Henry VIII statutes 145
  in-breeding 137–47, 155n3
  incestuous adultery 28–30,
    43, 46n22, 118, 142,
    143
    definition 30
  Leviticus 168
  Matrimonial Causes Act 1857
    30, 42
  penalties 29–30, 42–3, 44
  Punishment of Incest Act 1908
    42–4, 51n106, 137–47, 192
  Scotland 3, 138–9, 156n8,
    158n31
    see also Scotland
  step-children 144–5, 157n29,
    157n30
  theories about 137–47, 161–
    80; *see* prohibition of sexual
    unions between relatives
    see also exogamy, incestuous
      adultery, incest
      prohibition, incest taboo,
      prohibited degrees,
      prohibition of sexual
      unions between relatives
incest prohibition 7n8, 137,
  157n30, 171, 173–4
incest taboo 44
incestuous adultery 28, 29–30,
  46n22, 118, 143
  definition 30
  see also adultery, divorce,
    incest
incubation 201, 208–9, 211–12
infertility 121, 212, 214
India 81, 94n39, 102, 198
indigenous structuring 11–18,

187, 193–4, 197–206
  see also categories, classifica-
    tion
industrial revolution 77
inheritance 17, 34, 67, 75n11,
  121, 208, 213
  death duties 34, 75n11
  will 75n11, 213
  in-law 34
  intestacy 34, 75n11
Ireland 7n1, 97n76
Italy 139

jealousy 33, 164, 174–5
Jenkins 50n79
Jermyn 80, 93n32
jilting 117–18, 126n65, 126n66
Judicature Act 1873 36 & 37 Vic
  c 66 110–11
judicial separation 78, 86, 103
justification 5, 137, 146
  religious 137, 146
  scientific 137, 146–7
  see also explanation
Justinian 20n8

Katherine of Aragon 28
kindreds 189
King 94–5n48
kinship terminology 4, 11, 17,
  64–9, 181n32, 185n96, 198,
  204
  aunt 66, 68
  brother 64–5, 68
  children 65, 67–8
  cousin 11, 64–5, 69
  father 64–5, 67, 68
  'great' & 'grand' 68–9
  in-law 17, 64–6, 74n2, 74n4,
    74n5
  maternal 66–7
  mother 64–5, 68
  nephew 66, 68
  niece 66, 68
  parent 64–5, 67–8
  paternal 66–7
  sibling 68
  sister 64–8

kinship terminology—*cont.*
  spouse 68
  step- 17, 64−6
  uncle 64−5, 66, 68
  see also relationship
kissing 117, 122, 126n63A
Kroeber 193, 196n29

Lady Margaret Hall 124n44
Lang 173
language 1, 11, 64−9, 193−4,
  200, 203, 205
Laslett 77, 90n2
Laud 90n8
Law of Property Act 1925 111
Law Reform (Misc. Provisions)
  Act 1970 126n64A
Law Reform (Married Womens
  and Tortfeasors) Act 1935 111
Law Society 211−12, 213
lawyers 3, 11, 137, 174, 188
Leach 16, 20n14, 187, 195n4, 197,
  198−9, 200, 202, 203−4, 205
Legal Aid Advice Act 1949 148,
  159n58
Le Mesurier 49n68
Lévi-Strauss 1, 161, 166, 173, 174,
  176, 184n90, 184n91, 186−7,
  190, 193, 195n3, 197, 206n3,
  205, 216
levirate 121, 161, 213, 180n2
Leviticus 23−4, 26−7, 35−6, 38,
  166, 168, 181n14, 198
  interpretations 26, 27, 168,
  181n14
Lismore 94n47, 95n46, 95−6n60
Local Government Act 1894 113,
  124n49
Local Government Act
  (Scotland) 1894/5 113
Locke 11, 19n2
logical positivism 193
London Gazette 3, 57, 201
Lord Chancellors 87, 96n73, 113,
  123n11A, 155
Lovedu 185n97
Lowie 174
Lubbock 169, 182n46

Lush 138, 145, 155n3, 158n43
Lyndhurst 28−9, 30, 31, 42n26,
  86, 96n68
Lyon, Mrs Massey 57, 62n14, 59,
  63n22

Macclesfield, Earl of 79, 91n13
Macrae 31, 49n71, 49n76
Maimonides 161, 162
maintenance orders 150
Mair 174, 184n77
Maish 157n20
Malinowski 1, 6, 7n10, 12, 19n3,
  41, 77, 128n81, 161, 164, 165,
  173, 174−5, 177, 183n71,
  188−9
Maranda 2, 7n2, 7n10, 15
marital breakdown 150
marriage 16−18, 37−9, 69−74,
  107−13, 115−34, 213
  age 70
  alliances beteen groups 16−17
  annulment 28, 77, 121
  ceremony 115−17, 125n56A
  Christian 16
  conditions of contracting
    115−18, 125n56A
  consent 78, 116
  consummation 78, 115, 117,
    118
  custody of children 18
  death 37, 213
  domicile 18
  equality in 38, 69−72, 75n14,
    198
  household 71−2, 77
  impediments 66, 78, 116, 118,
    129−30
  love 70, 133
  marrying up or down 69−76,
    76n27, 198, 201
  mercenary 70−1, 108−9,
    125n55
  mourning 56
  pregnancy *per alium* 127n66A
  procreation of children 120−1,
    129, 132

marriage—*cont.*
  property 18, 107–13, 115,
    125n55
    see also married women's
      property
  rank 18, 72–3, 75n14
  remarriage 37, 62n10
  romantic 70–1, 108
  secular 47n35, 86, 96n67, 116,
    125n57, 153
  settlements 108–9, 111
  sexual intercourse 18, 118–22,
    127n73A
  surname 18
  social class 69–72
  taxation 112
  unity of husband and wife
    16–18, 64
  voidability 28–30, 42–3, 49,
    78, 91n12, 116, 125n56A
  wedding 116–17, 120, 129–
    34, 200, 201, 204
    day 125n59
    dress 121
    guests 201
    night 117
    presents 116
    ring 130–1
    service 116, 119, 120,
      129–34
    trousseau 116
  wife's legal position 73–4,
    107–9, 110, 111–12
    see also married women's
      property, women
  see also divorce, engagement,
    husband and wife, unity of
    husband and wife
Marriage Act 1753 125n56A
Marriage Act 1949 125n56A
Marriage Enabling Act 1960 44,
  143
marriage enabling Acts 41
Marriage Law Defence Association 31, 38, 48n55, 48n56,
  48n63
Marriage Law Defence Union 31,
  36, 47n34, 48n49, 48n56,
  48n63, 49n65, 44n66B,

  44n66C, 49n68, 49n69,
  49n72, 49n77
Marriage (Prohibited Degrees of
  Relationship) Act 1931 40–1,
  44, 143
married women's property
  107–14, 151–4
  marriage settlements 108–9,
    111, 113–14
Married Women's Property Act
  1870 107, 108–10, 112, 147,
  151–4
Married Women's Property
  (Scotland) Act 1877 111
Married Women's Property
  (Scotland) Act 1881 111
Married Women's Property
  Act 1882 107, 108, 112,
  113–14
'Marriages (England and Wales)'
  1857 106 – 1 – Sess 2
  160n77
maternity 182n39, 208–10
matrilateral cross cousin 161, 176,
  180n1, 184n91, 187
matrilineal 4, 7n8, 11, 182n39,
  188
Matrimonial Causes Act 1857 30,
  42, 79, 85–7, 110, 143, 148,
  151–2, 153, 159n70
Matrimonial Causes Act 1923 43,
  79, 89, 91n17, 95n62, 143, 147,
  148, 152
Matrimonial Causes Act 1937 79,
  89, 91n17, 148, 152, 153
Matrimonial Homes Act 1967
  112, 124n40
Matrimonial Proceedings and
  Property Act 1970 112
Matthyson 95n55
Maule J. 83, 92n25
Mauss 176, 187, 194, 196n28
McCaul 50n79
McLennan 1, 21, 45n1, 161,
  169–70, 182n42A
MacQueen 94n48
medicine 139, 211, 212,
  214
Melbourne, Lord 82

Mendel 13, 139, 140, 156n11A
Mendelian theory 140, 158n44
see also genetic theory,
heredity
Mensor 37, 49n70, 49n76, 50n79,
50n80
metaphysics 193
see also beliefs
Mildmay *see* Rosebery
Mill, J.S. 73−4, 107, 108, 110,
113
Moffat, (Mrs) 92n20
money 209−16, 217n3, 218n20
Montesquieu 161
morality 33, 41, 52, 54,90, 171,
199, 209, 210, 215−16
Morgan, L.H. 157n30, 161, 169−
70, 173
mother-right 182n39
mothers 12, 32, 36, 43, 56, 64−5,
72, 158n45, 165, 166, 197, 209,
210
in-law 42, 56, 64−5, 71, 166
step- 32, 65, 165
mourning 2, 3, 4, 6, 17, 32−3,
53−63, 64, 66, 67, 74n6, 122,
191, 198, 200−4
affines 58
complimentary 66, 74n6
court 3, 56−7, 59, 62n12, 201
decline in 6, 34, 57−9
definition 53−4
degree reckoning 53
explanations 54, 58
grief 53−4, 55, 58−9
obligations 54−61
clothes 55, 60, 61, 62n9,
63n30
curtailment 55, 60−1
extension 59−60
men 55−6, 57n
seclusion 54, 56, 58, 61
marriage 32−3, 56, 61,
62n10A, 122
women 55−6, 57, 58
periods of 54−6, 62n12
public 3, 56,57,59, 62n12
relatives 2, 56−61
degrees 53, 54, 56−9,64

see also degree reckoning
illegitimate 59
legitimate 59
widows 60−1, 63n30
servants 56−7
sources on 54−5
Sovereign 56−7, 62n12
Mozley 107, 108−9, 123n3, 123n8
Municipal Franchise Act 1869
113, 124n47
Murdock 173, 174, 175, 177−8,
185n96

Nazi 216
nephew 66, 68, 144, 157n30,
158n31
grand- 75n13
Newnham College 124n44
niece 35, 66, 68, 120, 144, 157n30,
158n31, 164
Nightingale, Florence 109'
Norfolk, Dukes of (1700) 79,
91n13; (1811) 87, 94n48
North London Collegiate School
124n43
Norton 82
Norton, Caroline 94n44
nuclear family 94n44, 157n30,
173, 174, 204

Offences against the Person Act
1861 91n12, 120, 127n77
one flesh 16, 17, 35, 36, 37, 115,
133
one parent families 122
ostracism *see* social penalties
Oxenham 48n49
Oxford, Bishop of 90
Oxford University 113, 124n44
Oxford University Gazette 211

Paget *see* Wellesley
parents and children 15, 17, 27,
43, 54−5, 60, 64−5, 67, 68,
119, 157n29, 163, 168, 188, 197

parents and children—*cont.*
  adoptive 44, 157n30
  in-law 17, 42, 64–5, 143
  step- 42, 44, 51n110, 65, 143,
    144–5, 157n29
parity of reason 26–7, 166, 168
Parker's Table 25–30, 45n7, 64,
  145, 168
Parkinson 122
Parsons 173
paternity 1, 121, 182n39, 191,
  208, 210
  Trobriand denial of 12
patrilateral cross cousin 161, 176,
  180n1, 184n91
patrilineal 4, 7n8, 11, 182n39, 188
Pedi 185n97
peerage 80–1, 93n34
Pellew 95–6n60
penalties 29–30, 52, 53, 61, 78,
  89–90, 90n8, 91n12, 119–22,
  125n56, 128n83, 138
  adultery 52–3, 62n4, 86, 119,
    121–2
  bigamy 78, 90n8, 91n12
  divorce 53, 89–90
  incest 29–30
  premarital intercourse 53, 120,
    121, 122, 128n83
  social 52–3, 54, 55, 61, 62n4,
    86, 89–90, 120–2, 126n66,
    126n65, 128n83
Perry 110
pets 16
Phelps 37, 49n73
Philadelphus [F. Pott] 49n67,
  49n71
Phillimore 45n19
Philo 161, 162
philosophers 7, 11, 146, 174, 191,
  193, 199, 200, 206n11, 206n12,
  215, 218n35
Piers *see* Cloncurry
Plutarch 161, 166
Pocock 186, 193, 199
political platforms 5, 18–19,
  39–40, 87, 109, 138–9, 140,
  142, 143, 146–7, 148–9, 191,
  192, 194, 205–6, 211–12

rich and poor 51, 83, 87,
  148–9, 206
polygamy 35, 36, 38
Pondo 185n97
poor 31–2, 84, 93n34, 114, 139,
  148–9
population 88, 97n76, 105–6
  married 88, 105–6, 160n79
Powell, E. 217n13
preferential marriage 174, 180
premarital sexual intercourse 53,
  117, 120–2, 126n64, 128n83
  see also extra-marital sexual
    relations, sexual inter-
    course
primitive societies 6, 169, 177,
  169–80, 187–90
primogeniture 75n11
procreation 1, 119, 120–1, 129,
  132, 191
prohibited degrees 2, 21–30,
  35–44, 141–2, 191, 197, 204
  affinity 26–8, 36–44, 51n98
  changes 2, 21–30, 40–4
  Church of England 26, 27,
    41–2, 47n35, 50n92,
    51n104, 157n29
  Commission 1940 7n9, 41,
    188–9
  Commission 1984 41–2,
    51n104, 157n29
  consanguinity 27, 36, 43,
    49n69
  dispensations 21, 28
  Henry VIII 21, 23, 28
  incest 29–30, 42–4
  jurisdiction 27–9, 42
    common law courts 27
    ecclesiastical courts 27,
      28–9, 42, 45n9A
  legislation
    Henry VIII's Statutes 21,
      23–8
    Lord Lyndhurst's Act 1835
      28, 30, 46n26
    Deceased Wife's Sister's
      Marriage Act 1907
      21–3, 30, 40,
      142–3

prohibited degrees—*cont.*
  Deceased Brother's
    Widow's Marriage Act
    1921 40, 143
  Marriage (Prohibited
    Degrees of Relation-
    ship) Act 1931 40−1,
    143
  Marriage Enabling Act
    1960 41, 143
  Punishment of Incest Act
    1908 42−4, 51n106,
    142, 192
  Leviticus 23, 24, 26−7, 35−8,
    166, 168
    literal 27, 35
    parity of reason 26−7,
    35−6, 166, 168
  Parker's Table 25−30
  private Acts 41, 46n22
  Roman Catholic 21, 22, 27,28
  Royal Commission 1848 31,
    32, 42−3
  Scotland 31, 39
  voidability 29−30, 42−3,
    46n22, 46n26
  see also deceased wife's sister,
    degree reckoning, incest,
    prohibitions of sexual
    unions between relatives,
    marriage, relationship
prohibitions of sexual unions
  between relatives 21−44,
  137−47, 161−80, 186−90
  theories about 137−47,
    161−80, 187−90
    Alliance 162, 166−9, 174,
      175, 179−80, 187, 188,
      189−90
    biological 137−47, 164
    Chastity 162−3, 167−9,
      175, 188
    empirical testing 161, 168,
      177−80, 185n97
    evolutionary 169−74,
      186−7
    expert 161−80
    household 77, 162−9,
      178−9

popular 137−58
  Rivalry 33, 163−4, 165,
    167−9, 174, 175, 187,
    188, 190
  Social roles 33−4, 162,
    164−6, 167−9, 174, 175,
    179n80, 185n99, 187,
    188
  Westermarck 164, 177−8
promiscuity 163, 181n14
  see also extra marital sexual
    relations
property 3, 18, 75n11
  divorce 154
  entailed estates 67, 71, 75n11,
    121, 213
  inheritance 17, 34, 67, 75n11,
    121, 208, 213
  death duties 34, 75n11
  intestacy 34, 75n11
  will 75n11, 213
  married women's 108−13,
    151−4
Protestant 78, 79, 153
Provision for Dispensation &c
  Act 1536 23, 26, 27, 45n4
Prussia 90
public 3, 56−7,59, 62n12
public mourning 3, 56−7, 59,
  62n12
public opinion 31, 95n52
public penance 29, 42
Punishment of Incest Act 1908 3,
  42−4, 51n106, 138−47,
  157n21, 192

Queen Caroline 83, 95n53
Quine 7, 8n11, 159n47, 200,
  206n11, 206n12

R. v Chadwick 1847 27, 45n11
R. v Clarence 119−20
R. v Hall 83, 92n25, 95n51
R. v Harrald 113, 124n48
R. v Sherwood & Ray 1837 29,
  45n18
R. v St. Giles-in-the-Field 1847
  27, 45n11

Radcliffe-Brown 161, 165−6,
    172−3, 174, 186, 189
rank 69−73
rape 74, 119−20, 125n56, 127n74
rationality 6−7, 12, 36, 39−40,
    137, 146−7 190−2, 193, 194,
    202, 204−5
  acts 190−2, 194, 202
  assertions 191−2
  beliefs 137, 146−7, 192−3
  see also actions, assertions,
    beliefs
Reformation 13, 27, 30, 77−8, 145
relationship 1−3, 12, 37−40, 41,
    64−9, 198, 204, 208
  absence of 3, 12, 16−17,
    66−7, 188, 198, 204
  adoptive 143, 144, 156n3,
    157n30, 173, 208, 210
  affinal 12, 17, 27−8, 36−8, 39,
    40−4, 51n98, 56, 64−6,
    142, 144−5, 156n3, 173,
    188, 198
    in-law 12, 17, 41−2, 64−6,
      71, 72, 74n2, 165
    step- 12, 17, 41−2, 64−6,
      142, 144−5, 157n29, 165
    see also affinity
  ancestor 12, 13
  ascendant 13, 65, 68
  blood/consanguineous 11, 12,
    17, 27, 36, 43, 49n69, 64,
    188, 198
    full blood 13, 138
    half blood 13, 65, 138
    illegitimate 13, 27, 29,
      46n22, 59, 67, 121, 145,
      208
    legitimate 13, 59, 67, 138,
      145
  claiming 60−1
  cognatic 2, 4, 7n8, 188−90,
    195n17, 204
  collateral 13, 67, 68
  decline 40, 53
  degrees 13−15
  descendant 12, 13, 68
  direct line 12, 41, 67−8, 143,
    178
    disclaiming 61
    distance 13−15, 64, 198
      natural 13
    unilinear 4, 7n8,11, 169, 170,
      173, 179, 182n39, 188, 189,
      204
      matrilineal 4, 7n8, 11,
        182n39, 188
      patrilineal 4, 7n8, 11,
        182n39, 188
    see also degree reckoning,
      cousins, incest, kinship
      terminology, prohibited
      degrees
*Report of the Committee
  of Inquiry into Human
  Fertilisation and Embryology
  see* Warnock Report
Representation of the People
  Act 1918 113, 125n49,
  152
Representation of the People
  (Equal Franchise) Act 1928
  113, 125n49A
reproduction 120, 207−16,
    217n2−3, 217n11,
    217n13
  conception 120, 207
  new techniques 207−14,
    217n3
  surrogacy 207−14, 217n13
  therapy 212−14
  Warnock report 216−17
  see also conception, genetic
    theory, heredity,
    maternity, paternity,
    sexual intercourse,
    surrogacy
Rich, Lady 90n8
rich and poor 19, 83, 109, 148,
  206
Richardson 70, 73
ridicule 114, 126n65, 151
Rivalry theory 33, 163−4, 165,
    167−9, 174, 175, 187, 188,
    190
Roman Catholic 14, 22, 27, 28,
    77−8
Romans 15, 19n1, 66, 73, 181n32

Roos, Lord 78−9
Rosebery 29, 46n2, 52, 61n2, 82, 83, 84, 94n42, 95n52
Rover 124n50
Royal Commission on Divorce & Matrimonial Causes 1912−13 88, 97n76, 99, 103−6, 127n66A, 148−9
Royal Commission on Marriage and Divorce 1956 88, 97n76, 99, 104−6, 148, 150−1
rules 197, 201
    breaches 201
    see also customs
Russell, Lord John 49n69
Russia 2, 66, 75n1

St. Augustine 161, 166, 167−8, 179, 181n29, 181n31−2
Salkeld 45n17
Scarisbrick 23, 28
Schneider 20n13
science 5, 6, 7n9, 146
Scotland 2, 3, 5, 7n1, 19, 31, 39, 78, 83, 85, 97n76, 111, 139, 153, 156n8, 158n31, 205, 206
    deceased wife's sister 31, 39
    divorce 2, 78, 85
    incest 3, 139, 156n8, 158n31
Scottish Law Commission 1981 158n31
Selbourne 113
Seligman, B.Z. 173
servants 4, 56−7, 61n2, 70, 82
sexual intercourse 115, 117, 118−21, 127n73A, 145, 207−14
    extra-marital 117
    see also extra marital sexual relations
    marriage 115, 118−22, 127n73A
    replacement of 207−14, 217n3
Sexual Offences (Amendment) Act 1976 125n56
Shakespeare 29, 45n20
Shanley 92n25, 99, 107, 123n1
Shaw 57

Shaw Lefevre 109, 123n14
Shorter 7n3
sibling 68, 188, 208, 214
similarity *see* classification
Simpson 47n36
Simpson, Mrs 73
sisters 16, 17, 31, 33, 64−8, 164, 168, 210, 213
    half- 43, 65
    in-law 23, 31−6, 64−7
    step- 65, 66
Small & Small (Marriage Enabling Act) 1982 41, 51n100
social anthropology 1, 2, 4, 11−13, 43, 137, 143, 157n30, 161, 162, 164, 166, 186−94, 197−206
social class 69−72, 78−81, 85, 87−8, 93n34, 95−6n60, 126n64, 127n73
    divorce 78−81, 85, 100−1
    marriage 69−72
social penalties 52−3, 54, 55, 61, 86−7, 116−18, 120−2, 126n66, 128n83
Social roles theory 33−4, 162, 164−6, 167−9, 174, 175, 179n80, 185n99, 187, 188
Social Trends 88, 97n76, 104, 106
sociologists 43
Somerville College 124n44
sons 17, 67, 68, 158n45, 165, 188, 197
    in-law 17
sororate 161, 180n2, 213
sources 3, 31, 47n34, 54, 81, 92n22, 97n76, 98
Sovereign 52, 56−7, 59, 62n12, 67, 72−3, 201
    consort 52
Spencer, Lady Diana (18C) 95−6n60
Spencer, Lady Diana (20C) 117
Starcke 172
step-relative 12, 17, 41−2, 64−6, 142, 144−5, 157n29, 165
    see also relationship

Stone, L. 2, 99, 120−1, 122, 126n63A, 127n73, 127n81, 174, 184n78
Stone, O.M. 124n38A, 125n57
structuralism 18, 186−7, 193−4, 197−206, 206n15
  concepts 181
  models 18, 187, 193
succession 17, 67, 75n11, 121
  throne 67, 75n11, 121
surnames 18, 67, 188
surrogacy 207−16
  Baby Cotton 207, 209, 211, 217n2
  money 209−16, 217n3, 218n20
  Surrogacy Arrangements Act 1985 210, 217n13
  Warnock report 207−16
Surrogacy Arrangements Act 1985 210, 217n13
Swabey & Tristram 45n15
Swazi 185n97
symmetrical cross cousin 176, 184n91

Talbot 94n47, 95n55
Tayleur 92−3n27
Taylor, C. 191
Taylor, J. 161, 164−5
Teush (Mrs) 92n20
Thackeray 59, 60, 65−6
The Marriage Act 1835 28−9, 30, 46n26
The Qualification of Women Act 1918 113, 125n49B
The Sex Disqualification (Removal) Act 1919 113, 125n49B
Theft Act 1968 111
theologians 3, 137, 174, 188
theories 1, 137, 149−55, 161−80
  expert 137, 141, 149−55, 161−80
  false 1, 137, 149−55, 161−80
  popular 137−40, 149−55
  see also explanation
Thonga 185n97
Thrupp 38, 50n81, 50n84

Tikopia 178, 185n97
Tolstoy 66, 75n9
totemism 170−1, 173, 204
transitive relation 204
tribes 169−70
Trobriands 1, 12, 127n81, 178, 185n97, 191
Trollope 60, 93n34, 127n73
  Barchester Towers 1858 93n34, 127n73
  Doctor Thorne 1858 93n34
  Framley Parsonage 1861 55, 58−9, 93n34
  Can You forgive Her? 1864 126n63A, 60, 62n4, 62n9
  Miss Mackenzie 1864 93n34
  The Small House at Allington 1864 72, 118, 126n65−6
  The Claverings 1867 52−3, 126n65−6
  The Last Chronicle of Barset 1867 72, 93n34, 114
  Phineas Finn 1869 126n65
  The Vicar of Bullhampton 1870 74n5, 122, 128n83
  Ralph the Heir 1871 71
  The Prime Minister 1875 60, 61, 70, 72, 109
  The Eustace Diamonds 1876 39, 56, 60−1, 108
  Is he Popenjoy? 1878 70, 113, 114−15
  John Caldigate 1879 74n4, 197
  The Duke's Children 1880 56, 70, 71, 72, 117
  Ayala's Angel 1881 72, 76n29
Tswana 178, 185n97
Turner 166, 182n33
Turton (Mrs) 29, 46n22, 92n20, 95n49
Tylor 166, 169, 174

uncles 15, 35, 60, 64−6, 68, 93n34, 144, 166
  & nieces 15, 35, 60, 93n34, 144, 157n30, 157n31
unilinear 4, 7n8, 11, 169, 170, 173, 179, 182n39, 188, 189, 204

United States 2, 20n13, 90, 139
unity of husband and wife 16−18,
    39, 64−5, 107, 115, 122, 198,
    205
    see also husband and wife,
        marriage, one flesh
unlawful sexual intercourse 44,
    51n110, 125n56, 144−5
    see also extra-marital sexual
        relations
useful purpose 6, 187−93, 204
    see also explanation, function,
        functionalism
utilitarianism 215−16

Vaughan 45n10
Venda 185n97
verbal enquiry 200
verdict at law 79, 84, 91n16
    see also criminal conversation,
        divorce

Waldy 95n55
Warnock 209−10, 218n35
Warnock Report 207−18
Watson 19n1, 50n87, 159n75
Webster B.N. 156n3
Webster 1851 82, 94n46
wedding 116−17, 120, 129−34,
    200, 201, 204
    bride 116, 121, 125n59
    bridegroom 116, 125n59
    day 125n59
    dress 121
    guests 201
    night 117
    presents 116
    ring 130−1
    service 116, 119, 120, 129−34
    trousseau 116
Wellesley 94n41
Westermarck 164, 173, 174, 177
    Westermarck's theory 164,
        177−8
White 174, 175−6
Who Was Who 156n13
widows 60−1, 62n9, 63n30, 108,
    122, 165

mourning 62n9
weeds 61, 62n9, 63n30
remarriage 62n10A, 122
Wilde 60
will 75n11, 213
Wing v Taylor 28, 45n15
witchcraft 193
Wolfram 7n2, 8n11, 20n10,
    20n12, 51n99, 51n106, 92n25,
    92n34, 92n58−60, 156n11
    158n30, 159n47, 178−80,
    180n4, 184n91, 185n96−101,
    191−2, 195n17, 206n11−12,
    217n13
women 46n22, 73−4, 79, 86−7,
    107−15, 149−54, 152, 154
    divorce 28, 46n22, 79, 86−7,
        91n17, 92n18, 97n75
    education 113, 114, 124n43,
        124n44, 72
    emancipation 111, 125n48B,
        149−54, 192, 194
        definition 153, 159n73
    equality 18, 73−4, 86−7, 151,
        214
    legislation 107, 108−10, 113,
        124n71
    marriage settlements 108−9,
        111
    married 73−4, 107−14,
        125n55
    movements 109−11, 112−13,
        151
    property *see* married women's
        property
    rights 109−15, 152
    suffrage 110, 113, 125n49A,
        152
Wood 47n36
Woolsey 91n8
Wordsworth 48n56, 49n68
world wars 41, 57, 89, 151, 152
Wootten, Baroness 41

Xosa 185n97

Zulu 185n97

—